A Beautiful Sickness

T0325238

Books by Thomas Hauser

Non-Fiction
Missing
The Trial of Patrolman Thomas Shea
For Our Children (with Frank Macchiarola)
The Family Legal Companion
The Black Lights: Inside the World of Professional Boxing
Final Warning: The Legacy of Chernobyl (with Dr. Robert Gale)
Muhammad Ali: His Life and Times
Muhammad Ali: Memories
Arnold Palmer: A Personal Journey
Confronting America's Moral Crisis (with Frank Macchiarola)
Muhammad Ali: In Perspective
Healing: A Journal of Tolerance and Understanding
Muhammad Ali and Company
Miscellaneous
With This Ring (with Frank Macchiarola)
A Beautiful Sickness

Fiction
Ashworth & Palmer
Agatha's Friends
The Beethoven Conspiracy
Hanneman's War
The Fantasy
Dear Hannah
The Hawthorne Group
Mark Twain Remembers
Finding The Princess

For Children
Martin Bear & Friends

Theatre
The Four Chords

A Beautiful Sickness

Reflections on the Sweet Science

Thomas Hauser

The University of Arkansas Press
Fayetteville
2001

Designer: John Coghlan

⊛ The paper used in this publication meets the minimum requirements
of the American National Standard for Permanence of Paper for Printed
Library Materials Z39.48-1984.

Library of Congress Cataloging-in-Publication Data

Hauser, Thomas.
    A beautiful sickness : reflections on the sweet science / Thomas
Hauser.
      p. cm.
    ISBN 1-55728-718-X (pbk. : alk. paper)
    1. Boxing—United States. 2. Boxers (Sports)—United
States—Anecdotes. I. Title.
    GV1125 .H287 2001
    796.83'0973—dc21

                                                    2001004445

For Mollie

Don Elbaum is a boxing guy. A lot of people in the sport call him a character. Others call him worse. "Don't call me a character," says Elbaum. "I hate that word. 'Worse' I can live with."

Without people like Don Elbaum, there would be no professional boxing.

"I love it," says Elbaum. "I've given my life to boxing. It's the reason I've been broke, in jail, lived out of crummy motel rooms. You name it, and boxing has done it to me. But if I had my life to live over again, I'd do it all the same way. Boxing is in my blood. It's a beautiful sickness."

Contents

Round 4: Issues and Answers

Round 5: Curiosities

Author's Note

Four years ago, all of the boxing articles I'd authored up until that time were published in *Muhammad Ali & Company,* which will be reissued by The University of Arkansas Press in 2002. *A Beautiful Sickness* contains the articles I've written since then about the sweet science. Special thanks are due to Houseofboxing.com, HBO Boxing, and *Boxing Digest* under whose aegis all but three of the articles in this book first appeared.

Round 1
Muhammad Ali

When I began writing for Houseofboxing.com in April 2000, my first
column was about one of my favorite subjects: Muhammad Ali.

The Sanitization of Muhammad Ali

Later this year, Sony Pictures is scheduled to begin principal pho-
tography on a feature film about Muhammad Ali.

Ali is an important figure in world history. In the 1960s, he stood as
a beacon of hope, not only for black Americans, but also for oppressed
people around the globe. Every time he looked in the mirror and
preened, "I'm so pretty," he was saying "black is beautiful" before it
became fashionable to do so. When he refused induction into the United
States Army during the height of the war in Vietnam, he stood up, not
just to the United States government, but to armies around the world in
support of the proposition that war is wrong.

But—and this is a big "but"—one of the reasons Ali caused as much
turmoil as he did was because there was an ugly edge to what he was saying. Part of his impact lay in the fact that he was pushing beyond, and in
some cases against, the prevailing integrationist norm. And sadly, most of
the recent tributes to Ali have failed to offer an honest exposition of his
past.

An ABC made-for-television movie about Ali entitled *King of the
World* that was broadcast earlier this year is a case in point. The film pur-
ported to follow young Cassius Clay from early in his professional career
through his 1964 defeat of Sonny Liston to capture the heavyweight
championship of the world.

There were several problems with the movie. First, the screenplay was
awful. In addition to the usual distortions of fact that were deemed necessary "for dramatic purposes," the story line was hopelessly convoluted.
The movie also suffered from the hard reality that no one but Muhammad
Ali can play Ali.

But the biggest problem with the film was that it sanitized Ali. In an
effort to create a simple conflict between good and evil (with Ali being

good), it ignored the fact that, during what might have been the most important fourteen years of his life, Ali adhered to the teachings of the Nation of Islam—a doctrine that Arthur Ashe later condemned as "a racist ideology; a sort of American apartheid."

Watching the movie, the uninformed viewer was left with the impression that Nation of Islam doctrine was, and still is, Islam as practiced by more than one billion people around the world today. ABC depicted only that portion of Nation of Islam doctrine that taught black pride, black self-awareness, and self-love. The movie showed a strong loving bond between Ali and Malcolm X. It gave no hint that, when Malcolm later broke with the Nation of Islam to pursue orthodox Islamic beliefs, Ali abandoned his former mentor.

The Nation of Islam taught Ali that white people were devils who had been genetically created by an evil scientist with a big head named Mr. Yacub. It taught Ali that there was a wheel-shaped Mother of Planes one-half mile wide manned by black men in the sky, and that, on Allah's chosen day of retribution, fifteen hundred planes from the Mother of Planes would drop deadly explosives destroying all but the righteous on earth. Neither of these views are part of traditional Islamic thought or find justification in the Qur'an. Indeed, while the concepts of Heaven and Hell are central to traditional Islamic thought, the National of Islam rejected both. For much of the period from 1961 to 1975, Muhammad Ali was the Nation of Islam's most visible and vocal spokesman in America.

Unfortunately, when it comes to Ali, this sort of revisionism has become common. It began in 1977, when Ali himself starred in a feature film about his life entitled The Greatest. The Greatest was fictionalized and mediocre. Frank Deford summed it up when he wrote, "Of all our sports heroes, Ali needs least to be sanitized. But The Greatest is just a big vapid valentine. It took a dive. A genuine film about this unique man and his times must wait until Ali can no longer indulge himself as star and censor."

Yet even when Ali has relinquished control, the celluloid results have been questionable. In 1997, the Academy Award for "best documentary feature" went to When We Were Kings—a film about Muhammad Ali recapturing the heavyweight championship of the world from George

Foreman in Zaire. Much about *When We Were Kings* was laudable. But in 1974, when Ali and Foreman did battle, Ali still adhered to the teachings of the Nation of Islam. Did the film show that? No. Rather, in an effort to create a clear distinction between "the good Negro" (Ali) and "the bad Negro" (Foreman), a lot of footage of Ali extolling the virtues of Louis Farrakhan was left on the cutting-room floor.

Now comes Sony Pictures, with Will Smith reportedly set to play the role of Ali. One hopes that this movie will be more honest than its predecessors.

Ali's views on religion have changed considerably since he was young. In 1984, he publicly repudiated the separatist doctrine of Nation of Islam spokesman Louis Farrakhan, declaring, "What he teaches is not at all what we believe in. He represents the time of our struggle in the dark and a time of confusion in us, and we don't want to be associated with that at all." Later, Ali acknowledged, "When I was young, I followed a teaching that disrespected other people and said that white people were 'devils.' I was wrong. Color doesn't make a man a devil. It's the heart and soul and mind that count."

Not everyone has been pleased with Ali's transformation. Football great Jim Brown, who was intricately involved with Ali's early career, later opined, "The Ali that America ended up loving was not the Ali I loved most. I didn't feel the same about him anymore, because the warrior I loved was gone. He became part of the establishment. And I suppose, in a sense, there's nothing wrong with that because, if you can make all people feel good, maybe that's greater than being a fighter for black people. But I didn't like it."

Still, it's ironic that the same media forces that savaged Ali earlier in his life now seem determined to sanitize him. And it's also sad because, in the end, it's important that memories of the young Muhammad Ali be honestly preserved. Oftentimes, great men are considered great, not only because of what they achieve, but also because of the road they travel to reach their final destination. Sanitizing Muhammad Ali and rounding off the rough edges of his journey is a disservice both to history and to Ali himself.

As the year 2000 progressed, members of Congress from both sides of the aisle were effusive in praising Ali. Much of that praise was genuine, but at times it seemed a bit hypocritical. Again, I ventured into the past.

Muhammad Ali and Congress Remembered

At long last, Congress has enacted the Muhammad Ali Boxing Reform Act. As a cure for what ails boxing, the proposed legislation leaves a lot to be desired. Still, it's a step in the right direction. Meanwhile, Senator Jim Bunning of Kentucky is sponsoring legislation that would authorize President Clinton to award Ali with a Congressional Gold Medal (the highest civilian honor that Congress can bestow upon an individual). Thus, it's worth remembering what an earlier generation of congressmen had to say about Muhammad Ali at the height of the war in Vietnam.

On February 17, 1966, Ali was reclassified 1-A by his draft board and uttered the immortal words, "I ain't got no quarrel with them Vietcong." One month later, Congressman Frank Clark of Pennsylvania rose in Congress and called upon the American public to boycott Ali's upcoming bout against George Chuvalo:

> The heavyweight champion of the world turns my stomach. I am not a superpatriot. But I feel that each man, if he really is a man, owes to his country a willingness to protect it and serve it in time of need. From this standpoint, the heavyweight champion has been a complete and total disgrace. I urge the citizens of the nation as a whole to boycott any of his performances. To leave these theater seats empty would be the finest tribute possible to that boy whose hearse may pass by the open doors of the theater on Main Street USA.

In 1967, Ali refused induction into the United States Army at which point he was stripped of his title and denied a license to box in all fifty states. That same year, he was indicted, tried, convicted, and sentenced to five years in prison. Then, in October 1969 while the appeal of his conviction was pending, ABC announced plans to have Ali serve as a TV commentator for an upcoming amateur boxing competition between the United States and Soviet Union. Congressman Fletcher Thompson of Georgia objected:

> I take the floor today to protest the network that has announced it will use Cassius Clay as a commentator for these contests. I consider this an affront to loyal Americans everywhere, although it will obviously receive much applause in some of the hippie circles. Maybe the American Broadcasting System feels that it needs to appeal more to the hippies and yippies of America than to loyal Americans.

In December 1969, there were reports that Governor Claude Kirk of Florida would grant Ali a license to fight Joe Frazier in Tampa. Congressman Robert Michel of Illinois took to the podium of the United States House of Representatives to protest:

> Clay has been stripped of his heavyweight title for dodging the draft. And I consider it an insult to patriotic Americans everywhere to permit his reentry into the respected ranks of boxing. It should be recalled that Mr. Clay gave as one of his excuses for not wanting to be drafted that he is in reality a minister and that even boxing is antagonistic to his religion. But apparently, he is willing to fight anyone but the Vietcong.

Ultimately, the authorities in Florida refused to give Ali a license to box. Then, in September 1970, it was announced that Ali would fight Jerry Quarry in Georgia. Once again, Congressman Michel had his say:

> I read with disgust today the article in the *Washington Post* concerning the upcoming fight of this country's most famous draft dodger, Cassius Clay. The article said that Mr. Clay was out of shape, overweight, and winded. No doubt, this comes from his desperate and concerted efforts to stay out of the military service while thousands of patriotic young men are fighting and dying in Vietnam. Apparently, Mr. Clay feels himself entitled to the full protection of the law, yet does not feel he has to sacrifice anything to preserve the institutions that protect him. Cassius Clay cannot hold a candle to the average American boy who is willing to defend his country in perilous times.

Ali fought Jerry Quarry in Atlanta on October 26, 1970. Then a federal district court decision paved the way for him to fight Oscar Bonavena on December 7 (the anniversary of Pearl Harbor) in New York. And after that, he signed to fight Joe Frazier at Madison Square Garden. Each fighter was to receive the previously unheard-of sum of $2,500,000. That outraged Congressman John Rarick of Louisiana, who spoke to his colleagues as follows:

> Veterans who have fought our nation's wars feel that any man unwilling to fight for his country is unworthy of making a profit or receiving public acclaim in it. Cassius Clay is a convicted draft dodger sentenced to a five-year prison term which he is not serving. What right has he to claim the privilege of appearing in a boxing match to be nationally televised? The Clay affair approaches a crisis in national indignation.

On March 8, 1971, Ali lost a hard-fought fifteen-round decision to Joe Frazier. Meanwhile, he remained free on bail while the United States Supreme Court considered the appeal of his criminal conviction. This was too much for Congressman George Andrews of Alabama, who spoke to his brethren and compared Ali to Lieutenant William Calley, who had been convicted of murder in the massacre of twenty-two South Vietnamese civilians at Mylai:

> Last night, I was sickened and sad when I heard about that poor little fellow who went down to Fort Benning. He had barely graduated from high school. He volunteered and offered his life for his country. He was taught to kill. He was sent to Vietnam. And he wound up back at Fort Benning, where he was indicted and convicted for murder in the first degree for carrying out orders. I also thought about another young man about his age; one Cassius Clay, alias Muhammad Ali, who several years ago defied the United States government, thumbed his nose at the flag, and is still walking the streets making millions of dollars fighting for pay, not for his country. That is an unequal distribution of justice.

On June 28, 1971, fifty months to the day after Ali had refused induction, the United States Supreme Court unanimously reversed his conviction, and all criminal charges pending against him were dismissed. The next day, Congressman William Nichols of Alabama expressed his outrage:

The United States Supreme Court has given another black eye to the United States Armed Forces. The decision overturning the draft evasion conviction of Cassius Clay is a stinging rebuke to the 240,000 Americans still serving in Vietnam and the 50,000 Americans who lost their lives there. I wish the members of the Supreme Court would assist me when I try to explain to a father why his son must serve in Vietnam or when I attempt to console a widow or the parents of a young man who has died in a war that Cassius Clay was exempted from.

Not to be outdone, Congressman Joe Waggonner of Louisiana echoed his fellow lawmaker's expression of contempt:

The United States Supreme Court has issued the edict that Cassius Clay does not have to be inducted because he does not believe in war. No draft-age young man believes in a war that he will have to fight, nor does any parent of a draft-age son believe in a war that their own flesh and blood will have to fight and possibly give his life in so doing. But our people have always heeded the call of their country when asked, not because they love war, but because their country has asked them to do so. And I feel strongly about this. If Cassius Clay does not have to be drafted because of question-able religious beliefs or punished for refusing induction simply because he is black or because he is a prizefighter—and I can see no other real justifi-cation for the Court's action—then all other young men who wish it should also be allowed a draft exemption. Cassius Clay is a phony. He knows it, the Supreme Court knows it, and everyone else knows it.

Times change.

As a general rule, I choose my own column topics. But a Japanese publication, Sports Graphic, specifically asked that I write about Muhammad Ali's quest for redemption after each of his first three ring defeats.

The Hardest Thing to Do in Boxing

Sugar Ray Robinson once said that the hardest thing for a fighter to do is to come back and beat a man who has beaten him badly before. Joe Louis did it once. After being knocked out by Max Schmeling in the twelfth round of their 1936 bout, the "Brown Bomber" came back two years later to destroy Schmeling in one round

Muhammad Ali did it three times.

Ali's quest for redemption in the ring had its origins in two defeats that would have broken the spirit of a lesser man. The first of those defeats came in the only bout truly named the "Fight of the Century." Muhammad Ali versus Joe Frazier on March 8, 1971, was for the heavyweight championship of the world. Both men were undefeated. Each had a legitimate claim to the heavyweight crown. But the night belonged to Frazier. He beat Ali up, knocked Ali down, and won an unanimous fifteen-round decision. After that loss, Ali won his next ten bouts. Then, two years later, his comeback was derailed when Ken Norton pounded out a twelve-round decision and, in the process broke, Ali's jaw.

The loss to Norton marked the end of the road as far as many of Ali's fans were concerned. It seemed as though he would never win his title back again. But as Michael Katz later observed, "Ali was the embodiment of the human spirit. You just couldn't keep him down. A lot of fighters are broken by defeat. They fly so high that, when they're shot down, it destroys them. But losing never destroyed Ali. Each time he lost, he learned from defeat and came back stronger to win."

Thus it was that Muhammad Ali returned to conquer Joe Frazier and Ken Norton, not once but twice each. And at the end of his career, after losing to Leon Spinks, he came back to defeat Spinks and capture the heavyweight championship of the world for an unprecedented third time.

What motivated Ali? How was he able to achieve redemption in situations where so many other great athletes have failed?

Part of the answer lies in the fact that Ali had marvelous physical gifts and was a great competitor. But perhaps more important, Ali had something larger than himself to flow into. An athlete's state of mind is important. And that's particularly true in boxing, where determination and the willingness to accept pain are as important as physical skills. When Ali stepped into the ring, he believed he was fighting for millions of people around the world. Their hearts were with him. If he lost, they would lose, too. He drew strength from that belief and from the prayers of those who loved him. Like Evander Holyfield against Mike Tyson, Ali believed that he was fighting for God.

The rematches against Joe Frazier, Ken Norton, and Leon Spinks posed daunting challenges. After all, God may, or may not, take sides in sports contests. But Ali was a man who loved to challenge and be challenged. At age twenty-five, he had stood up to the United States government and refused induction into the United States Army during the height of the war in Vietnam. He had been stripped of his title, exiled from boxing, criminally tried, and convicted—and come back to prevail. No man who risks all in standing up to the most powerful government in the world will be intimidated by the sight of a solitary opponent in the ring.

"I believed in myself," Ali said recently. "And I believed that, if I did everything to the best of my ability, God would do whatever else was necessary to help me achieve my goals."

That was path the Muhammad Ali followed to redemption in the ring. And it is the path he has followed throughout his life.

In choosing an Athlete of the Century, I tried to set aside my personal fondness for Muhammad Ali and be as objective as possible.

The Athlete of the Century

As 1999 moves toward its long-awaited close, there have been numerous attempts to designate the Athlete of the Century. Whoever is accorded the honor will doubtless also be recognized as Athlete of the Millenium. The consensus list for number one has boiled down to three finalists—Babe Ruth, Muhammad Ali, and Michael Jordan. There's no right or wrong answer, just points of view.

It's hard to imagine anyone being better in a sport than Michael Jordan was in basketball. His exploits are still fresh in the mind, so suffice it to say that the Chicago Bulls won six world championships during his reign and Jordan was named the series' Most Valuable Player on all six occasions. He led the NBA in scoring ten times, has the highest career scoring average in league history, and was one of the best defensive players ever.

Babe Ruth had an unparalleled genius for the peculiarities of baseball. In 1919, the American League record for home runs in a season was twelve. Ruth hit 29 homers that year, and 54 the year after. In 1927, the year Ruth hit 60 home runs, no other *team* in the American League had as many. Indeed, in all of major league baseball, there were only 922 home runs hit that year. In other words, Babe Ruth hit 6.5 percent of all the home runs hit in the entire season.

Ruth's lifetime batting average was .342. Two-thirds of a century after his career ended, he stands second in RBIs, second in runs scored, and second in home runs. And these marks were established despite the fact that Ruth was a pitcher during the first five years of his career. In 1916, at age twenty-one, he pitched nine shutouts en route to a 23 and 12 record and led the league with an earned run average of 1.75. From 1915 through 1919, he won 94 games, lost only 46, and compiled an earned-run average of 2.28. In other words, if Mark McGwire pitched 29-2/3 consecutive scoreless innings in the World Series (which Ruth once did, a record that stood for forty-three years), you'd have a phenomenon approaching The Babe. And one thing more. Ruth was a winner. He was with the Boston Red Sox for five full seasons, and they won the World Series in three of them. Then he was traded to the Yankees, who had never won a World Series, and the Yankee dynasty began.

As for Ali, a strong argument can be made that he was the greatest fighter of all time. His lifetime record of 56 wins and 5 losses has been matched by others. But no heavyweight ever had the inquisitors that Ali had—George Foreman, Sonny Liston twice, and Joe Frazier three times. Ali in his prime was the most beautiful fighting machine ever assembled. Pound-for-pound, Sugar Ray Robinson might have been better. But that's like saying, if Jerry West had been six-foot-six, he would have been just as good as Jordan. You are what you are.

Ali fought the way Michael Jordan played basketball. Michael Jordan played basketball the way Ali fought. Unfortunately, Jordan didn't play baseball the way Ruth did. But then again, I doubt that Ruth would have been much of a basketball player. However, The Babe was known to punch out people rather effectively as a young man.

Thus, looking at Michael Jordan, Babe Ruth, and Muhammad Ali from a purely athletic point of view, it's Jordan (three points for first place), Ruth (two points for second place), and Ali (one point for third place) in that order.

But is pure athletic ability the standard? If pure athleticism is the only test, men like Jim Thorpe, Jim Brown, and Carl Lewis should also be finalists in the competition for Athlete of the Century. The fact that they aren't stands testament to the view that something more than achievement on the playing field must be measured: that social impact is also relevant. That's a bit like saying maybe Ronald Reagan should be considered the greatest actor of the twentieth century because of his impact on society. But here goes.

Ruth, Ali, and Jordan reflected the eras in which they were at their respective athletic peaks. Ruth personified the "Roaring Twenties." Ali was at the heart of the social and political turmoil of the 1960s. And Michael Jordan speaks to the "Nineties" with its booming stock market, heightened commercialism, and athletes as computer-action-game heroes.

Jordan hasn't changed society. Not yet, anyway. Babe Ruth brought sports into the mainstream of American culture and earned adulation unmatched in his time. Nor was The Babe's impact confined to the United States. During World War II, long after his playing days were over, Japanese soldiers sought to insult their American counterparts by shouting "to hell with Babe Ruth" at Guadalcanal. Meanwhile, Ali (to use one of his favorite phrases) "shook up the world" and served as an inspiration and beacon of hope, not just in the United States, but for oppressed people around the globe.

One can argue that Jack Johnson, Joe Louis, and Jackie Robinson all had a greater societal impact than Ali. Arthur Ashe once opined, "Within the United States, Jack Johnson had a larger impact than Ali because he was the first. Nothing that any African-American had done up until that time had the same impact as Jack Johnson's fight against James Jeffries."

Joe Louis's hold on the American psyche was so great that the last words spoken by a young man choking to death in the gas chamber were, "Save me, Joe Louis." When the Brown Bomber knocked out Max Schmeling at Yankee Stadium in 1938 in a bout that was considered an allegory of good versus evil, it was the first time that most people had heard a black man referred to simply as "The American."

Meanwhile, Jackie Robinson opened doors for an entire generation of Americans. If there had never been a Jackie Robinson, baseball would have become integrated; and eventually, other sports would have followed. But that's like saying, if there had been no Michelangelo, someone else would have painted the ceiling of the Sistine Chapel.

Still, Ali's reach, more than that of any of his competitors, was worldwide. So for impact on society, it's Ali (three points), Ruth (two points), and Jordan (one point). That means there's a 4-4-4 tie, and we go to tie-breakers.

Babe Ruth seemed larger than life. So do Muhammad Ali and Michael Jordan. Ruth and Ali had much-publicized personal weaknesses. Jordan has flaws, although they're less well known. All three men have been idolized. Ali has been loved. It would be presumptuous to choose among them as human beings.

So where do we go from here?

Sixty-four years after Babe Ruth hit his last home run, a half-century after his death, men like Mark McGwire still compete against him. Without Ruth ever having been on *SportsCenter* or HBO, he is still in the hearts of most sports fans. Ali might enjoy that type of recognition fifty years from now. It's less likely that Michael Jordan will.

That brings us down to Babe Ruth and Muhammad Ali.

And the envelope please . . .

The time I spent with Muhammad Ali has provided me with a treasure trove of memories to write about.

Muhammad Ali at Notre Dame: A Night to Remember

Notre Dame versus Michigan, 1990. The first game of the season for two of college football's most fabled institutions. Notre Dame was the top-ranked team in the country. Michigan was rated as high as number two, depending on which poll you followed. The game had been sold out for months and was the hottest ticket in the nation.

Meanwhile, Howard Bingham and I were tired. Howard is Muhammad Ali's best, truest, most loyal friend. I was Ali's biographer. It was the day before the game, and we'd been reading aloud for five days. More specifically, we'd been reading the manuscript for *Muhammad Ali: His Life and Times*—all one thousand pages—with Muhammad and his wife Lonnie. I'd just finished the first draft of the book and wanted to make sure it was factually accurate. Also, I knew that reading it aloud would be the best way to elicit further thoughts from Muhammad.

Howard and I are sports fans. And since Notre Dame is only a twenty-minute drive from the Ali's home, we thought it would be fun to go to the game. Ali doesn't care a whole lot about football. But his presence opens doors; he likes big events; and he's a sweetheart when it comes to doing things for friends. Thus, my call to the Notre Dame Athletic Department: "Would it be possible for Muhammad Ali to buy three tickets for tomorrow night's game?"

There was a long pause on the other end of the line. "Let me call you back," the woman said. Five minutes later, the telephone rang. "How do we know the tickets are really for Mr. Ali?"

"That's easy," I told her. "He'll pick them up in person."

"All right, come by the athletic department today before five o'clock."

A BEAUTIFUL SICKNESS

"Do you want Muhammad to bring his driver's license for identification?"

"That's not necessary. I think we'll recognize him."

Shortly before noon, we drove to Notre Dame to pick up the tickets. The athletic department wanted to give them to us, but we insisted on paying, a small gesture given their open-market value. Then we went home, read *Muhammad Ali: His Life and Times* for another five hours, read some more on Saturday, and drove back to Notre Dame.

The game was scheduled for 8:00 P.M. Central Standard Time. We arrived around six o'clock. The weather was perfect, and the scene surrounding the stadium was quintessential big-time college football. Tens of thousands of fans had set up grills and were barbecueing everything from hamburgers to shrimp. Many of them didn't even have tickets to the game. They just wanted to be near the action, and their reaction to Muhammad was as expected. As we walked around, we heard a lot of "Omigod! It's Muhammad Ali." And Muhammad has certain opportunities that aren't available to the rest of us. For example, he can walk around a tailgate party until he finds something that looks particularly good to eat, and what he invariably hears is, "Muhammad Ali! Please join us."

In other words, we ate quite well thanks to the generosity of strangers. Then we went inside the stadium to our seats, which happened to be on the fifty yard line. That was nice for us and, I suspect, also good for Notre Dame recruiting since the folks around us were suitably impressed by Ali's presence.

Muhammad sat between Howard and myself. Notre Dame was coached by Lou Holtz. Its brightest star was Raghib Ismail, who was joined in the backfield by Rick Mirer, Tony Brooks, Ricky Watters, and Rodney Culverhouse. Michigan was in its first year under new head coach Gary Moeller, who had the unenviable task of succeeding Bo Schembechler. But his job was made easier by the presence of Elvis Grbac, Jarrod Bunch, Jon Vaughn, and Greg Skrepenak.

It was a great game. Notre Dame surged to a 14-3 lead, and it seemed as though everyone on earth was singing, "Cheer, cheer for old Notre Dame." Then Michigan began to roll and scored three unanswered touchdowns, whereupon "Hail to the victors valiant" was very much in vogue.

Meanwhile, as the game progressed, I began to talk with an elderly woman sitting to my left. She was Ellen Stonebreaker, grandmother of the Notre Dame co-captain and middle linebacker, Mike Stonebreaker. If I had to guess, I'd say she was about eighty. She was charming. And when Notre Dame was on defense, her eyes never left the field. Even Ali noticed the intensity with which she was watching. "Look at that old lady," he told me. "She's like a hawk."

Notre Dame won. Down ten points going into the fourth quarter, they rallied for two late touchdowns capped by an eighteen-yard scoring pass from Mirer to Adrian Jarrell with 1:40 left to play. But one moment in particular stands out in my mind.

It came in the second half. Ellen Stonebreaker had been sneaking glances at Muhammad for some time. Finally she said to me, "You know something, that boxer is a good looking fellow."

"Tell her I don't fool around with white women," Muhammad advised me. Which I duly reported to Mrs. Stonebreaker, who seemed more bemused than disappointed. However, she did have one request.

"I haven't done this since I was a young girl," she acknowledged. "But could you get me that fellow's autograph."

I asked how she'd like her name written. She said she'd prefer it if Muhammad used her maiden name. She spelled it for him. He wrote it out, drew a little heart, and signed "Love, Muhammad Ali."

Then he kissed her.

It was just another day for Muhammad, one that I'm sure he's long since forgotten. But as is often the case, whenever and wherever he travels, it was a memorable night for everyone around him.

Round 2
The Fights

Boxing is the only major sport in which the schedule is a story unto itself.
And sometimes, even fights that are scheduled don't happen. Such was
the case with George Foreman versus Larry Holmes.

Foreman–Holmes:
The Countdown Begins

Six months is a long lead time for the marketing of a fight. But the
hoopla for George Foreman versus Larry Holmes has begun. The
"Birthday Bash" won't be held until January 23, 1999 (thirteen days after
George's fiftieth birthday). But on a steamy mid-July morning in New
York, the combatants met the media at the Palace Hotel to make it
official.

The pre-fight promotion will be fun. Foreman and Holmes are legitimate Hall of Famers and great pitchmen when they set their mind to it.
Everything is on track for a strong crossover event. "The question is, will
it be a great fight?" It would have been if they'd fought twenty years ago.
Who would have won if they'd met when they were young? My guess
is Larry. The guys George had trouble with back then were guys who
could move and had a good jab. But it would have been a toss-up then,
and it is now.

As for how good the fight will be, both men are past their prime.
Both have become "safety first" fighters. And both have been slow and
sluggish in recent outings. Holmes's last true glory in the ring came in
1992, when he decisioned Ray Mercer. Meanwhile, Foreman has been
competitive since then against the likes of Shannon Briggs, Lou Savarese,
and (let's not forget) Michael Moorer. George's style is different than what
it was when he was young. He's a unique physical phenomenon and has
adjusted with age to maximize his skills. Larry's style is the same as it
always was. He's just not as good as he used to be. Holmes's hope lies in
the fact that Foreman is one of the few fighters out there who's slower
than he is at this stage in his career. If Larry were to put himself in the
hands of a good physical trainer and keep busy for twelve rounds against

George, he'd win. But he won't train any differently for this fight than in the past, which means he'll get tired early against Big George.

Still, it's possible that this will be a great fight. When Muhammad Ali and Joe Frazier met for the third time, they were in decline as fighters. Yet the downward curve of their respective careers coincided perfectly and the "Thrilla in Manila" resulted. Like Ali and Frazier, George Foreman and Larry Holmes have championship heart. And despite what anyone says about their impending bout being "only for the money," both men have extraordinary pride. They're fighting for their place in history vis-à-vis each other—and for something more.

Larry wants what George has now. It's not the title. It's more ephemeral and more precious than that. When Larry Holmes was heavyweight champion, he suffered first in Ali's shadow. Then he endured the Gerry Cooney phenomenon. And when he lost his title to Michael Spinks after an extraordinary seven-year reign, not many people seemed to care. George Foreman suffered through a similar reign as champion in the 1970s, when he didn't seem to be having much fun. But in his reincarnation as a fistic Santa Claus, George has basked in glory and good cheer. Now, Larry feels it's his turn to be loved.

George Foreman versus Larry Holmes. It might not mean much to most people, but it means a lot to Larry and George. One of them will lose, which is too bad. But the man who wins will deserve it. Both have had long and distinguished careers. Boxing owes them.

In mid-2000, I penned an introductory note for a photo essay on Cedric Kushner's monthly fight cards in Manhattan.

Styles Make Fights

Each month, Cedric Kushner promotes a Heavyweight Explosion fight card in Manhattan. The incongruous site for this happening is the Hammerstein Ballroom, a turn-of-the century opera house opened in 1906 by Oscar Hammerstein (grandfather of the famed composer). Over time, these events have become as much about glamour as boxing. It's boys night out as scantily-clad women recruited from local strip clubs dance on platforms between bouts, while others serve as round-card girls between rounds. With each passing month, more and more men and women come to the fights to be seen, and they dress accordingly. In sum, the scene resembles 42nd Street the way 42nd Street was before Disney. Indeed, at times, it seems as though the fights are merely a backdrop for the real action, as loud music pulsates through the room at decibel levels sufficient to cause as much brain damage as the fighters' punches. Meanwhile, Cedric Kushner watches over it all the way a day trader watches stock quotes flash by on a computer monitor.

Roy Jones Jr. is an artist in the ring. Even when he's not at his best, it's a privilege to sit in the press section at ringside and watch him work.

Roy Jones Jr. and the Pensacola Invasion

On July 18, 1998, Roy Jones Jr. came into town like a good sheriff to clean up the mess that Don King Productions had left behind.

"D-Day" had been a disaster for New York boxing and Madison Square Garden. The June 6 fight card featuring Evander Holyfield was torn apart by hepatitis-B (Henry Akinwande and Ray Mercer), a second-trimester pregnancy (Maria Nieves-Garcia), and enough other problems (weak ticket sales and slow pay-per-view orders) that, by June 6, nothing was left but the bad aftertaste of the card's cancellation. Thus, it was left to Jones to resurrect New York boxing at Madison Square Garden's first fight card of the year.

The featured undercard bout shaped up as a good one—Kevin Kelley versus Derrick "Smoke" Gainer. Kelley has fought on HBO more often than any fighter of 135 pounds or less, and deservedly so. He's a warrior. But he's thirty years old, and an "old thirty" at that because of the wars he's been through. One of those wars was against Gainer. In their 1996 bout, Kelley's left eye was swollen shut. He'd been sent to the canvas and was being beaten to a pulp, when a cinematic left hand put Gainer down for the count. Since then, Kelley had gone to war five more times (including a fourth-round stoppage at the hands of Prince Naseem Hamed), while Gainer had gotten stronger. The word on the streets was that Kelley didn't want the fight, and the confidence he usually radiates before a bout was absent this time.

Both men fought cautiously in their rematch, as evidenced by the meager number of punches landed—102 for Gainer and 80 for Kelley. Kevin moved forward for most of the night, but he wasn't really the aggressor. Meanwhile, Gainer fought a solid disciplined fight. His hands were fast; he was quick on his feet. Kelley had trouble catching up to him and getting inside his jab. And when he did, Gainer outpunched him, scoring a flash knockdown in the first round and one that hurt considerably more in the seventh. From then on, the best Kevin's fans could hope for was that he would finish on his feet (he did) and not get hurt (he didn't). Score a unanimous decision for Derrick "Smoke" Gainer.

Then came the main event: Roy Jones Jr. versus Lou Del Valle. Jones happens to be the WBC light-heavyweight champion, but in this day and age, title belts are superfluous. Witness Del Valle's claim to the WBA's 175-pound throne despite never having beaten a world-class foe. For a while, Jones seemed to be playing with his opponent. More than a minute passed before he threw his first punch of the night. In round two, he turned southpaw and engaged in other fun and games. But Del Valle had come to fight; and to his credit, he fought the fight of his life. For twelve rounds, he took blow after blow to the body, ignored an ugly gash over his left eye from an accidental head butt, and displayed admirable courage in absorbing hellacious punishment. In round eight, he even had the audacity to knock Jones down; the first time in Roy's professional career that he'd tasted the canvas. In the end though, Del Valle simply didn't have the tools to compete with Jones. He was outpunched 483 to 286, outlanded 233 to 113, and won only one round. Lou himself put things in perspective after the bout, paying tribute to Jones with the acknowledgment, "He's a great fighter; I'm a good fighter." That was the difference between them.

As Jones's critics will be quick to point out, the knockdown proved that Roy Jones Jr. isn't Superman. Others will continue to complain that he's a "reluctant warrior." Still, in recent years, Jones has dominated the likes of James Toney, Bernard Hopkins, Thomas Tate, Tony Thornton, Merqui Sosa, Bryant Brannon, Mike McCallum, Montell Griffin (the second time around) and Virgil Hill. Do any of his victims have legitimate Hall of Fame credentials? Maybe not. But put his conquests together, and you have an impressive body of work.

Ask fifty fighters today, "Pound-for-pound, who's the best fighter in the world right now?" Forty-nine of them will answer "Roy Jones Jr." One hopes that Jones will complete the task of unifying the 175-pound title and then move on to bigger and better things to confirm his greatness.

The first opportunity I had to write about Shane Mosley came when I saw him at Madison Square Garden against Eduardo Morales.

A New "Sugar" Is Crowned

Every now and then, a fighter comes along who's just better than the rest. There are inklings of it in flashes of young brilliance and the way he finishes off opponents in four-round preliminary bouts. Then he moves on to tougher foes and pretty much dominates them, too. When such a fighter grows into greatness, it's exciting to behold. And it happened at Madison Square Garden on September 22, 1998, when "Sugar" Shane Mosley defend his IBF lightweight championship by knocking out Eduardo Morales at 2:06 of the fifth round.

Mosley is a three-time national amateur champion, with an amateur record of 250 wins against 10 losses. He won the IBF title from Phillip Holiday in August 1997 and has successfully defended it five times en route to a professional record of 29 wins and no losses with 27 knockouts.

Great athletes look different from the rest of the field in the way they go about their work, and Mosley has moved into that class. Morales was a credible opponent. He was undefeated coming into the bout, and had a fast left hook with good power. When hit, he fired back, but he was no match for Mosley. Mosley knocked him down in round three with a counter left that drove the challenger into the ropes, followed by two hooks to the body. He decked him again in round five with a barrage of punches, and was pummeling him mercilessly when referee Arthur Mercante Jr. stopped the contest. At bout's end, Mosley had landed 84 of 111 power punches and been hit by a meager 21 blows.

Anyone who uses the moniker "Sugar" had better be good. Correct that. Better than good—great. And Mosley is. He bears an uncanny facial resemblance to Sugar Ray Robinson and was born in 1971 (precisely fifty years after the original "Sugar Ray"). But more to the point, Mosley has moved into that realm where his bouts are now part competition and part performing art.

Mosley is a complete fighter. He's fast, well-schooled, and punches with power. On those occasions when he suffers a defensive lapse, he takes his punishment well. Outside of Roy Jones, no one active in the sweet science today has more pure physical talent. And pound-for-pound, Mosley deserves to be ranked in the top five, possibly as high as number two, behind Jones. All he needs is the opponents to test him.

Shane Mosley has the right to use the name. A new "Sugar" has been crowned.

Watching Roy Jones Jr. and Shane Mosley on the same fight card was the equivalent going to a concert where the Rolling Stones opened for the Beatles.

"Pound-for-Pound" and "Sugar" Shane

For fight fans on November 14, 1998, the bingo hall at Foxwoods Casino was the place to be. First up, Shane Mosley successfully defended his IBF lightweight title with a ninth-round stoppage of Jesse James Leija. Then Roy Jones Jr. stopped Otis Grant to retain his WBC light-heavyweight crown. But the belts were extraneous. Indeed, Jones's WBA championship wasn't even on the line. What mattered was that one has to go back a long way to find a night when two better fighters were on the same card. There were no mariachi bands, no smoke machines, no Hector Camacho costumes, no Naseem Hamed dances, no Angel Manfredy masks. Just boxing at its best.

Leija came into the ring for his fight with the words "No Fear" emblazoned on his trunks, and he fought that way. He's a tough customer; but unfortunately for him, so is Mosley. Over time, "Sugar" Shane broke him down with a mix of body shots and constant pounding of the skull, landing 249 punches to Leija's 109. Round six was the most exciting of the fight. Mosley decked Leija and battered him pretty effectively, taking several shots himself in the process. In round eight, a right hand over the top caught Leija on the ear, put him down again, and hurt him badly. In round nine, Leija visited the canvas for a third time, and, between rounds, the bout was stopped.

In sum, during the course of the night, Mosley dominated a world-class fighter from beginning to end and didn't lose a round. The only negative for him in his performance was that, three years ago, Leija fought Oscar De La Hoya at the same 135-pound weight and was stopped in round two. Thus, in today's pound-for-pound rankings, the "Golden Boy" deserves a slight edge over "Sugar" Shane.

As for Roy Jones, he has a problem—the absence of a defining fight. Since he fought James Toney in 1994, the available competition (with the exception of the Montell Griffin blip on Jones's radar screen) simply hasn't been good enough, and Otis Grant was no exception.

Grant seemed to know what he was in for. And he acknowledged as much before the bout with comments like, "It's rare that an athlete gets the opportunity to compete against the best in his sport . . . It's the opportunity of a lifetime, and I can't afford to let it pass me by . . . If I can stay in there and fight well for twelve rounds, that's a victory in itself . . . I can't do much worse than the other thirty-eight guys he fought."

As for the fight itself, there's a cruel beauty in the way Jones goes about his work. Grant is a finesse fighter, but finesse is just one of the many weapons in Roy Jones Jr.'s arsenal. He fought a cautious measured patient fight, mostly as a counterpuncher. But there was always the feeling that, at any moment, he could explode. And at times, he did.

Jones staggered Grant in round four and had him holding on like they were partners at a slow-dance, high-school makeout party. In round six, he put Grant down. Otis fought valiantly, knowing he was overmatched. But Jones kept pressing the issue, landing 173 blows (145 of them power punches) to Grant's 66. After a hard right put Grant down again in the tenth round, his corner threw in the towel. Like Mosley, Jones won every round.

As for what comes next, the most talked-about opponent for Jones in the light-heavyweight division is WBO champion Dariusz Michalczewski. But Jones doesn't want to go to Germany, and Michalczewski seems content to keep his title and make money by fighting lesser competition at home. Jones versus IBF titleholder Reggie Johnson would also give Roy the possibility of a third 175-pound belt. But Jones has just fought two southpaws in a row, so that title-unification bout is temporarily on hold.

Meanwhile, one of the oddities about Roy Jones Jr.'s career is that, for all his accomplishments, he still doesn't have a nickname. He just fights better than anyone else in the world right now. So until further notice, "Pound-for-Pound" will do nicely. And having said that, one can observe that the memory of Sugar Ray Robinson was well-served on November 14, when "Pound-for Pound" and "Sugar" appeared on the same card.

For years, Lennox Lewis and Shannon Briggs were regarded as fighters who hadn't lived up to their potential. Then Lewis started getting better and the two men met.

Lennox Lewis versus Shannon Briggs

It was a good fight, although in truth, it was a fight that shouldn't have been made at all. Shannon Briggs was there by virtue of a twelve-round decision over George Foreman that was questionable at best. And while some commentators referred to Lewis-Briggs as the "Battle of the Dreadlocks," "Crime Pays" might have been a better slogan.

Both fighters came out hard in the first round—Lewis because he thought he could blow Briggs away, and Briggs because he seemed to want to get things over with in a hurry, one way or the other. Late in the round, a left hook caught Lennox off balance, and he stumbled backward into the ropes. It could have been scored a knockdown because only the ropes kept him from going down. Then Briggs "swarmed." Unable to regain the initiative, Lewis covered up; Briggs caught him with a right hand on the back of the head. And this time, Lewis wobbled.

Two minutes into round two, Briggs backed Lewis into the ropes with another left hook—maybe his best punch of the night—and "swarmed" again. After that round, HBO's Jim Lampley expressed the surprise felt by many when he opined, "Lewis looks like anything but a world-beater; and Briggs looks like anything but a stiff." Even Lewis seemed a bit surprised. Indeed, after the fight, he observed, "Shannon had a little game in him." Or phrased differently, Briggs was fighting with heart. And Lennox seemed to have gone in overconfident without the nervous edge a fighter needs to protect himself.

Also, Lewis appeared to be in less than top condition, since he seemed more tired after two rounds with Briggs than after ten rounds with Ray Mercer. However, Shannon was just as tired. And once Briggs got tired, two things happened that were very bad for him. One, he lost the edge in hand speed that had enabled him to land early in the fight. And two, he began to stand still at the end of Lewis's punches.

By round three, the only time Briggs was moving his head was to shake it "no" to show that he wasn't being hurt each time Lewis landed his thunderous overhand right. In round four, Shannon took a ferocious beating and went down twice. In round five, after Briggs hit the canvas twice more, referee Frank Cappucino stopped it.

The fight reaffirmed that, while Lewis might be the best of the heavyweights at present, he's certainly beatable. This is a guy who got knocked out by Oliver McCall. And then, in the rematch, he couldn't put McCall down, even though the "Atomic Bull" dissolved into tears and refused to throw punches, necessitating a disqualification. Lewis was losing to Frank Bruno, when one punch turned that fight around. And he had his hands full against Ray Mercer. Keep Lennox off balance with side-to-side movement; counter over his left hand; go inside, because he doesn't fight particularly well inside; and you have yourself a fight. Also, because Lewis throws a lot of overhand rights, he's susceptible to someone with fast hands and a good left hook. People should remember that if Lennox ever signs to fight Mike Tyson.

Meanwhile, as far Briggs is concerned, Shannon said before the bout that he was ready to fight. And it was more than false bravado. He really tried to win. If Shannon had fought George Foreman the way he fought Lennox Lewis, he would have legitimately won that fight. But at the end of the day, Briggs hadn't done his homework before facing Lewis. Instead, he came into the ring like a marvelously gifted doctoral candidate with a high IQ who hasn't attended classes or done his homework properly during the preceding years and is now being called upon to defend his doctoral thesis.

Thus, Larry Merchant spoke for many when he said after the bout, "Briggs was not equipped and not ready to fight someone of Lennox Lewis's caliber tonight. If they [his management team] had paid more attention to teaching him how to be a fighter and getting him to where he could handle a shot at the title instead of putting so much effort into marketing, maybe he would have turned out to be a good fighter. But basically he didn't belong in the ring with Lewis if the point of it was to win the championship. It's not unusual for a guy to come out and make a fight of it for a few rounds. But to win, you've got to put in the work, and I don't think they've put in the work. Frankly, I think they're more into marketing than fighting. They tried to make a sting, a con job. And at the end of the day, they settled for a nice payday instead of bringing Briggs along patiently, where maybe one day he would have made a hundred times more."

In sum, Lewis-Briggs might have been Shannon Briggs's finest hour. He showed true skills and he fought with heart. But fighters whose finest hours are in defeat rarely go far in boxing. It's now up to Briggs to determine how far he goes from here.

By mid-1999, when he was the key participant in a fight doubleheader at Madison Square Garden, Michael Grant was appearing on a lot of radar screens as a potential challenger for the heavyweight title.

The Next Generation

It was billed as "The Next Generation." A face-off at Madison Square Garden between four heavyweights with a combined record of 133 wins, 5 losses, and 110 knockouts. But a closer look raised some doubts. Michael Grant, Lou Savarese, Jeremy Williams, and Hasim Rahman might have had 133 victories between them. But none of those victories had come against a legitimate top-ten opponent. Against the top ten, these guys were 0 and 4. Then Rahman pulled out of his bout against Williams, and Maurice Harris stepped into the breach. The card was recaptioned "Fight for the Future," but the story line remained unchanged.

Harris against Williams was a fast-paced bout between two men who would probably be more comfortable fighting at 195 pounds. But since cruiserweight translates into loserweight in terms of box office appeal, they've forged ahead in the heavyweight division.

Williams is an exciting fighter when things go well for him. However, when things go poorly, either he gets very cautious (as he did against Larry Donald—L12) or he gets knocked out (see Henry Akinwande—KO by 3). Harris started fighting professionally at age seventeen and split his first twenty bouts. But now he's being groomed; and lately, he's looked reasonably good.

Williams came out aggressively, as he usually does, and pressed the action until Harris hurt him with a chopping right hand midway through the second round. That set the pattern for the fight. Williams would advance, walk through Harris's jab, and fire to the head and body. Then Maurice would whack him with a right hand, and Jeremy would spend the rest of the round trying to survive. The high point for Harris came in round four, when a hard right stopped Williams in his tracks and put him on a rather wobbly bicycle. The image that came to mind was of a young child whose parents have just taken the training wheels off his bike and are hoping their child won't go down with a crash. Williams didn't crash; but he never really got back into the fight either and lost a unanimous decision.

After the bout, Harris said he failed to knock out his opponent because he'd taken the bout on short notice and thus wasn't in the best of shape and also that he'd hurt his hand somewhere in the middle rounds. But the truth is, Maurice Harris lacks fire. It cost him against Larry Holmes, when he lost an ill-considered decision by not pushing the action aggressively enough in the middle rounds. And it kept him from inflicting more damage on Williams. Maurice has the peculiar habit of starting each round standing in the middle of the ring with his hands on his hips. In some ways, that's a metaphor for his fighting style.

As for Michael Grant versus Lou Savarese, Savarese got beaten up, badly.

Grant has prodigious physical gifts and an aura of confidence about him. He's six-foot-six (maybe six-seven) and weighs 256 pounds without an ounce of superfluous fat on him. He has been brought along slowly in deference to his limited amateur background. But now, largely by default, he has moved into the upper echelons of boxing's heavyweight division and is being billed as the heir apparent to the heavyweight throne.

Savarese is one of the nicest guys in boxing. But at age thirty-three, he's no longer "the next generation." And except for two guys named Buster (Mathis and Douglas), Lou's record is devoid of victories over recognizable opponents. Maybe if Grant had changed his name to "Buster," Lou would have had a chance.

In truth, the bout was over almost as soon as it began. Savarese is a large man; six-feet-five-inches tall, 240 pounds. But in the ring with Grant, he seemed small by comparison. Fifteen seconds into the bout, the two men clinched, and Grant shook Savarese like a rag doll. Thereafter, Michael moved methodically forward. Occasionally, he got hit flush, but he didn't go anywhere when that happened. Over time, he wore Savarese down, muscling him around the ring, leaning, tugging, and punching. All totaled, he landed 274 blows to Lou's 99. Savarese fought courageously. But by bout's end, his face was a bloody mess. He was knocked down twice, both times in the last round. The judges were generous in giving him two rounds.

Thus, the story of the night was the continuing emergence of Michael Grant. Great physical gifts don't necessarily translate into a great fighter. Grant himself acknowledged as much after the bout when he said, "I've still got some work to do. There's more to being a fighter than being strong." And Donald Turner, Grant's trainer, echoed his charge, grading his performance on a scale of one to ten as "an eight."

Still, there's a growing sense among the boxing elite that today's heavyweights would be well-advised to fight Michael Grant before he fully learns his trade. "In ten fights," says Lou DiBella of HBO Sports, "this kid could be illegal."

Maybe so. Still, whether Michael Grant is the next great heavyweight or the next Primo Carnera remains to be seen.

*The end of 1999 saw a flurry of fights and considerable action outside
the ring as well. I tried to put it all in perspective.*

Has the Landscape Changed?

The last year of the millennium ended well for boxing. Some say that
the sweet science has been on the ropes lately. But boxing always seems
to be on the ropes, and somehow it always manages to endure. Thus it
was fitting that late 1999 saw a remarkable ten-week period during which
eight of the top ten fighters on most "pound-for-pound" lists were in
action. And that's not counting the heavyweights—Lennox Lewis,
Evander Holyfield, Mike Tyson, Michael Grant, and Andrew Golota.

The festivities began on September 11, when Floyd Mayweather
pummeled Carlos Gerena for seven rounds before Gerena was unable to
answer the bell for round eight. After the bout, Mayweather turned down
an HBO offer of $12.5 million for six fights over three years, calling the
offer "slave wages." Pretty Boy has been spending a lot of time lately with
Mike Tyson and Don King, although not as a threesome. He would do
well to seek financial advice elsewhere.

Next, on September 18, Oscar De La Hoya and Felix Trinidad did
battle in their long-awaited "Fight of the Millennium." It was a great
matchup, but great matchups don't necessarily make for great fights. De
La Hoya should have won. He outlanded Felix 263 to 166, but lost where
it counted most: on the judges' scorecards. And because of the way he
fought (cautiously at first and running for the last three rounds), he lost
both public sympathy and the right to complain. The general feeling was,
hey, Oscar has won some close ones, and now he's lost a close one. Or
phrased differently, to get the decision in a major bout, you should come
to fight. De La Hoya acted as though he were campaigning for the Nobel
Peace Prize, and the judges were unimpressed by the idea that boxing is
"the manly art of self-defense."

One week later, stepping up in weight, Shane Mosley stopped
Wilfredo Rivera in round ten of their welterweight contest. Rivera might

take a great punch, but he doesn't have one. Seven days after that, Ricardo Lopez pounded out a clear-cut decision over Will Grigsby. Lopez is a fine fighter, but he dominates a small universe without any true inquisitors. After the bout, he announced his retirement, but he'll be back.

October 22 saw a doubleheader in Detroit. First, Wayne McCullough hit Erik Morales hard and often with his best shots. But while McCullough might have iron in his chin, he's got pillows for fists. Thus, the unanimous decision for Morales. On the same card, Naseem Hamed fought Cesar Soto after a protracted ring entrance that was so predictable and tiresome as to make Larry Merchant long for the mariachi bands of Bob Arum. It was a boring fight. Hamed mugged for the cameras and showed off some professional wrestling tactics (most notably a fifth-round body slam of his opponent) en route to a unanimous decision. What he didn't do was fight like a champion. Hamed's luster has dimmed noticeably since his 1997 arrival in the United States. There's an old axiom in boxing: to wit, if a fighter isn't getting better, he's getting worse. Hamed isn't getting better. Hamed-Morales would be a defining fight for both men.

The last of the top ten "pound-for-pound" fighters in action was Mark Johnson. "Too Sharp" was taking care of business against Raul Juarez on November 19, when a low blow felled Juarez in round four. The general view was that the challenger could have gotten up. But as Juarez noted afterward, the general viewers hadn't gotten whacked in the testicles. Regardless, Raul stayed on the canvas, and the bout was declared "no contest."

Meanwhile, as autumn leaves turned, the heavyweights took center stage. On October 23, Mike Tyson was in the ring against Orlin Norris. Iron Mike was paid $8.7 million for the bout, and the machinery was in place for a broad-based "Mike Tyson is back" campaign. All that was needed, and expected, was a spectacular knockout. But at this point, sending Mike Tyson into the ring is like sending the Titanic out to sea for a second voyage along the same route with the same captain. There might be a spectacular ocean crossing, but you're flirting with disaster.

Against Norris, Tyson showed better timing than he had against Frans Botha. And he still hits harder than anyone else in the business. But as far as personality is concerned, the "New Tyson" is like the "New Nixon."

In other words, he ain't changing. Tyson at his peak was a virtual force of nature who obliterated all opponents. But against Norris, he looked like a man in search of a free shot that would make the fight easier. With eleven seconds left in round one, Iron Mike was warned by referee Richard Steele for throwing a forearm and elbow on the break. Then, clearly after the bell, he decked Norris with an uppercut, also on the break. End of bout. No contest. The fight was Tyson's fiftieth as a pro. Once upon a time, people thought that number fifty for Iron Mike would be the bout that broke Rocky Marciano's record. But then again, once upon a time when Mike Tyson fought, people turned on their television sets to see a scintillating ring performance. Now, the motivation is morbid curiosity.

As for Lennox Lewis versus Evander Holyfield, their November 13 championship bout shaped up as a big-money curiosity rather than compelling drama, and it was faithful to those lowered expectations. Lewis fought essentially the same fight the second time around as he had the first, although he jabbed less. Holyfield was better that before, but not by much. There were a few good rounds. But for long stretches of time, Holyfield did nothing while moving forward, and Lewis did nothing while moving backward. It says a lot that the dominant emotion after the fight was relief that the judges had gotten it right in scoring the contest for Lewis.

But as Shakespeare wrote, "All's well that ends well." And the busiest ten weeks boxing has seen in a long time ended with a good fight. Michael Grant versus Andrew Golota was a war of attrition. Two-thirds of the way through round one, both men threw right hands and Grant went down in a heap. He visited the canvas again just before the bell and seemed shaky through round two as well. Indeed, with Golota pressing the action, Grant didn't win a round until the fifth; and after nine rounds, he was behind on the judges' scorecards by five points. But trouble was brewing in Golota's corner. Following round eight, trainer Roger Bloodworth told Golota, "It's all mental now." After round nine, Bloodworth added, "Now, it's all a head game." That was all Golota needed to hear. In round ten, a good right hand followed by a barrage of punches put him down. Golota was up at the count of three. Referee Randy Neumann asked if he wanted to continue. And Golota quit.

In a way, the fight was reminiscent of Golota's second bout against

Riddick Bowe. In that fight, Golota got off fast. Then he faltered and wanted to quit but the referee wouldn't let him, so he went low. That cost him points, but it also turned the tide in his favor. He was beating Bowe up badly until he began to tire, got frustrated, went low again, and was disqualified. Against Grant, when the going got tough, instead of going low, Golota said *no mas*. "I wouldn't have stopped the fight if he hadn't wanted me to," referee Randy Neumann explained afterward. "But this is boxing. You can't conduct a psychiatric evaluation in the middle of a round."

As for what comes next in the heavyweight division, Lennox Lewis and Michael Grant seem to be pointing toward one another. Grant-Golota was the kind of fight that was supposed to bring out the best in Grant. And it did, to the extent that he showed enormous heart and physical strength. He took a beating and came back to win. But the bout also exposed Grant's limitations. His boxing skills need considerable honing, and the one thing you can't rush in boxing is experience.

Also, there are "mandatory" challengers for Lewis to face. And Lennox talks often and fondly about fighting Mike Tyson. Tyson is now central to the dreams of a lot of heavyweights. Beating him means public acclaim and big money. Thus a thought for Lennox Lewis and all the others who want to fight Iron Mike: Be careful about what you wish for. You might get it. Lennox Lewis carries his hands low and takes a long time to deliver his right. Tyson, for all his flaws, still has fast hands and hits a lot harder than Oliver McCall.

Meanwhile, for all the action of a busy ten weeks, the balance of power in boxing remains largely unchanged. The Muhammad Ali Boxing Reform Act was stalled in Congress as the 1999 legislative session ended, and its provisions have been sufficiently gutted by the House of Representatives so that its impact upon passage will be limited. Despite the indictment of Bob Lee and several other IBF officials, the world sanctioning bodies appear to be doing business as usual. And the other powers that be in boxing are continuing to play musical chairs and follow the leader.

HBO remains the most powerful entity in the sport and the closest thing that boxing has to a moral authority at the present time. De La Hoya lost and HBO has problems with both Mayweather and David

Reid, neither of who seems willing to fight a top opponent for reasonable dollars. But six of the eight "pound-per-pound" fighters in action during boxing's fall festival fought on HBO. Roy Jones Jr. is under contract to HBO. And four of the five big-name heavyweights in action (including Lewis and Grant, who are tied to exclusive contracts) fought on HBO. Lest anyone forget, the heavyweight division is where the big money and power in boxing traditionally reside. That leaves Showtime treading water with Mike Tyson.

As for the promoters—Don King won big with Trinidad, but lost when Evander Holyfield lost his belts to Lewis. Bob Arum lost with De La Hoya, won with Morales, and may lose Mayweather to King. Main Events still has Andrew Golota and co-promotional rights to Lennox Lewis. But it no longer has promotional rights to Michael Grant who, like Naseem Hamed, is a free agent. Panix Promotions is Lewis's primary promoter, and America Presents has Tyson.

Perhaps the most intriguing promotional figure is Cedric Kushner, who is becoming a force in the heavyweight division. From 1995 through 1999, Kushner promoted roughly seventy Heavyweight Explosion cards. Those cards produced a few industrial-quality diamonds and a lot of sludge. But the bottom line is that Kushner now has exclusive long-term promotional rights to Kirk Johnson, Ike Ibeabuche, Hasim Rahman, and Oleg Maskayev; fifty-fifty promotional deals on Derrick Jefferson, Zelko Mavrovic, Chris Byrd, and Shannon Briggs; and long-term contracts with three dozen more heavyweights. It's ironic that, for all the heavyweights Kushner has promoted, his most glittering gems are Shane Mosley and Mark Johnson. Cedric has never had a fighter like Mosley to work with before, and it will be interesting to see if he can raise both the fighter and himself to mega-bucks stardom.

Meanwhile, it should be noted that, at the same time boxing's ten-week mega-fight extravaganza was going on, there was a disturbing undercurrent. More and more often, the sport is turning to vaudeville; and oftentimes, the public can't tell the difference.

The undercard of Felix Trinidad versus Oscar De La Hoya was an opportunity to showcase some marvelous fighters. But instead, Bob Arum gave us Butterbean and Mia St. John (two carnival acts) in blatant mismatches. Then, on the second weekend in October, the lead stories were

Loi Chow versus Margaret MacGregor and Laila Ali versus April Fowler. Those bouts proved respectively that (1) a man who has no physical gifts and no boxing skills whatsoever can lose to a woman and (2) a woman who has no physical gifts and no boxing skills whatsoever can lose to a woman. After that came Lewis-Holyfield with an embarrassingly bad undercard. HBO puts up most the money for these mega-fights. And to give fair value to its customers (the buying public that shells out $49.95 for a TVKO bout), it should insist on contract clauses that guarantee quality control for big-fight undercards. Otherwise, the public will lose whatever ability it has to distinguish between good fights and nonsense. And that would be very sad because some exciting things lie ahead for boxing in the year 2000.

When Michael Grant challenged Lennox Lewis for the heavyweight crown, I was privileged to spend the entire day with Michael, including the hours in his locker room leading up to the fight.

The Heir Apparent

The 1960s gave birth to a new breed of athlete: men like Muhammad Ali and Jim Brown, who were big, well-coordinated, and fast. Now, at the start of a new century, athletes have retained their speed and coordination and are even bigger than in the past.

On February 8, a month into the new millennium, Michael Grant stepped before the assembled media at Madison Square Garden at a press conference called to announce his April 29 battle against Lennox Lewis for the heavyweight championship of the world. Grant is 27 years old, stands 6-feet-7-inches tall, and weighs 250 pounds. Some observers call him the best pure athlete ever to come into boxing. Virtually everyone in the sport has marveled at his strength, coordination, and stamina. He has been viewed by many as a prototype athlete for the new millennium and the "Heir Apparent" to the heavyweight throne.

But on February 8, there were also questions regarding Grant's skills. He had turned pro in 1994 with only twelve amateur bouts to his credit, and was a "project" insofar as boxing was concerned. Thus, while he was praised by some, he was derided by others. Indeed, one week prior to the press conference, Michael had sat with his trainer, Donald Turner, in the living room of Turner's home and complained, "D, they're dissing me. They don't take me seriously as a fighter, and they don't even treat me right as a person. Events are scheduled. I get there on time, and then I'm treated like a stand-by. I arrange my schedule; I stop whatever I'm doing so I don't keep other people waiting; and then when I get there, they make me wait for an hour."

Turner had listen patiently and replied, "That's because you're walking around thinking this fight is about you, and it isn't. Anytime there's a fight for the heavyweight championship of the world, it's about boxing. And you haven't made your imprint on boxing yet."

At the press conference, there were the usual introductory speeches. Turner and advisors Craig Hamilton and Jim Thomas spoke for the Grant team. Promoter Panos Eliades, manager Frank Maloney, and trainer Emanuel Steward represented Lewis. In the middle of the speeches, Turner pumped his fists spontaneously into the air. Joy and anticipation were etched on his face.

There was an interesting energy in the air. Most of the boxing intelligentsia had entered the room thinking Lewis would win. But now, there was a growing sense that maybe Michael Grant's time had come, that Holyfield-Lewis had been about boxing's past and Lewis-Grant would be about boxing's future. Michael Katz, the dean of American boxing writers, had been skeptical about Grant for most of his pro career. Now Katz opined, "One way or the other, one of them won't be standing at the end. I think Grant will win." Lou DiBella of HBO was also present. On his way out of the Garden, with excitement and some surprise in his voice, DiBella said simply, "I think we're in for a changing of the guard."

The Next Great Heavyweight . . . The Heir Apparent . . . Expectations for Michael Grant were running high. But if the burden was enormous, so were the potential rewards. The heavyweight crown is the most coveted prize in sports. Its holder can trace his lineage to Jack Johnson, Jack Dempsey, Joe Louis, Rocky Marciano, Muhammad Ali, and their brethren.

Thus, it was that Michael Grant awoke in his room at the Grand Hyatt Hotel in Manhattan at 6:00 A.M. on the morning of April 29. For two hours, he lay in bed listening to gospel music. Then he ordered breakfast—fruit salad, scrambled egg whites, and ham. At ten o'clock, Donald Turner came to the room and the two men talked for twenty minutes. That was followed by a light snack.

At 12:30, Grant went down to the hotel lobby and sat in a large cushioned chair surrounded by friends for an hour. "There have been other fights where I was more relaxed than this one," he acknowledged. "But this is okay. I'm cool with it. I know this is for the heavyweight championship of the world; but I'm focusing on the fight; not the belt."

This was the first time in his career that Grant had found himself an underdog in one of his fights. Lennox Lewis had been installed as a solid five to two favorite. The prevailing view was that Lewis's boxing skills gave him an edge. Also, Grant might be stronger, but Lennox was believed to be the harder puncher and he seemed to have an edge in hand speed as well.

Grant's edge was his stamina. In the past, Michael had worn his opponents down. And in the past, Lennox had shown stamina problems. The bottom line was, the longer the fight went, the better Michael's chances. Or phrased differently, the early rounds were expected to belong to Lewis and the late rounds to Grant. The outcome would hinge on what happened early; and if that wasn't dispositive, on how early it got late.

Thus, the objective of the Lewis camp was that there not be any late rounds. Emanuel Steward's plan was for Lennox to jump on Michael. But Craig Hamilton had a different view. Standing in the hotel lobby, Hamilton observed, "When you're in the center of the ring looking at Michael and the referee is giving final instructions, Michael can look very imposing. Lennox could be forgiven for asking himself at that moment, 'Do I really want to jump on this guy? Maybe I should just use my superior boxing skills.' Still," Hamilton continued, "there are times when Michael invites disaster. He backs up. He lowers his hands. He waits. He knows he shouldn't do any of those things. But he's won thirty-one fights in a row fighting that way, and I'm afraid there will be times when he does it again tonight."

"It won't be easy," Donald Turner added. "Lennox has plenty of guts. He's not that good when he's backing up. Most fighters aren't. But he's very good coming forward. Michael has to fight a hungry fight. If Michael lays back, Lennox controls the fight and outboxes him. Michael has to back Lennox up and make it an action fight to win. He has to impose his will. Get off first. Initiate everything. Dictate the rhythm of the fight. If Michael does what he's capable of doing, he doesn't have to worry about what Lennox is doing. We know about Lennox. This fight is about Michael. I try to distance myself from the emotional part of it. I have to stay objective and level-headed, be a stabilizing force for Michael and keep him in the real world. But Michael is adamant in believing he'll win this fight, and I believe with him. If Michael loses, I'll be the most surprised guy in the joint."

At two o'clock, Grant went out for a walk. An hour later, Turner, Hamilton, Jim Thomas, and associate trainer Bobby Miles walked over to Madison Square Garden to arrange for last-minute ticket requests and check out the condition of the ring. Meanwhile, Michael returned to the hotel, had a three o'clock snack, took a nap, and spent the rest of the afternoon in his suite with his wife and a few friends. At 7:00 P.M., he ate his final pre-fight meal. Like every fighter who ever fought for the heavyweight championship of the world, he had dreams.

"I like Lennox," Michael had said earlier. "I think he's a gentleman. He's not an open person; he's very private. But if we were neighbors, there'd be a connection. We'd be in each other's homes from time to time. Still," Grant continued, "I know what I have to do when we fight. This is a wonderful opportunity for me, and it's about more than money and personal glory. Making other people happy is what makes me happiest, and there's a lot I can do if I'm heavyweight champion. People are starting to learn about me, and I want to learn about them, too, the writers, the TV people, the fans, so we can be on the same page. I'm not just a piece of meat. Get to know me, and I'll get to know you. When I'm champion, I'll just say what's in my heart. I hope people will recognize the goodness in me. Not my position, but who I am. I won't change. My character won't change. But when I win the title, my life will."

At 8:30 P.M., wearing a dark-blue jogging suit and gray peak cap, Grant left his hotel with Don Turner, Jim Thomas, and Bobby Miles. Fifteen minutes later, their limousine arrived at Madison Square Garden. Their assigned dressing room was twenty by twenty-four feet with scuffed gray linoleum underfoot and white cinderblock walls. A blue rubdown table stood in one corner of the room. Nine lilac-colored folding chairs were scattered about. A TV monitor graced the wall by the door.

Michael crossed the room to the rubdown table and seated himself in an upright position with his legs dangling over the side. Then he lowered his head in contemplation. Following his lead, everyone else in the room remained silent.

"The most nervous I ever was before a fight was before my first amateur fight," Michael Grant once said. "I remember being in the locker room, banging the back of my head against my locker, saying, 'I can't believe I'm doing this.'"

He looked nervous now.

At 8:52 P.M., an inspector from the New York State Athletic Commission entered the room and gave a pair of plastic gloves to each of Grant's cornermen. A NYSAC physician who had come in with the inspector took Michael's blood pressure.

At 8:58, Grant lay down on the rubdown table with a half-dozen towels beneath his head and closed his eyes. Two minutes later, another commission operative came in and asked for a urine sample. Michael got up, went into the adjacent lavatory, provided a sample, and returned to the rubdown table where, once again, he lay down and closed his eyes. The table was a foot too short. Michael's feet and then some dangled over the end.

The TVKO monitor on the wall heralded the start of the evening's live telecast. As several members of the Grant team watched, Wladimir Klitschko knocked out David Bostice in two rounds. Next up, Arturo Gatti KO'd Eric Jakubowski, also in two. Michael slept, or pretended to sleep, through it all.

At 9:43, the monitor showed Lennox Lewis arriving at Madison Square Garden. Three minutes later, someone from TVKO came into the room and asked if it would be possible to wake Michael for an interview. The answer was "no."

At ten o'clock, an hour after Michael lay down and closed his eyes, Donald Turner roused him gently. At 10:05, Keyshawn Johnson entered the room and approached Grant. "You came this far," the NFL star exhorted. "You're gonna get it done, definitely."

Paul Ingle versus Junior Jones, the next-to-last fight of the evening, came onto the TV monitor.

At 10:15, Donald Turner began taping Michael's hands. Fifteen minutes later, he was done and a commission inspector initialed the wraps.

At 10:30, Grant and Turner left the dressing room and walked to a nearby freight-loading area, where Michael jumped rope for three minutes. Four times, he missed a beat and the rope slid off his shoe against the floor. Then he returned to the dressing room and began a series of stretching exercises.

The number of people inside had grown to twelve, but the room was strangely silent. There was no aura of confidence and no crackle of electricity to signify that this was a fight for the heavyweight championship of the world. The atmosphere seemed more suited to an eight-round preliminary bout. And more significantly, the positive energy so abundant at the February kick-off press conference was gone.

As Grant began to loosen up, for the first time since he'd entered the room, his face seemed to transform into the face of a fighter. His eyes grew more focused, angry, and intense.

Then the look receded.

Paul Ingle KO'd Junior Jones in the eleventh round.

At 10:50, the stretching exercises ended. Michael put on his protective cup and trunks and gloved up. Cutman Joe Souza applied Vaseline to his face. At eleven o'clock, referee Arthur Mercante Jr., who would preside over the title fight, came into the room and offered final pre-fight instructions. Mercante was brief and to the point. Two minutes later, he was gone.

For the first time, gospel music from a portable CD player sounded. Still, the room seemed strangely unalive.

At 11:02, Bobby Miles put on a pair of handpads. For the next six minutes, Grant hit the pads under Donald Turner's watchful eye with Miles shouting instructions: "Jab, hook the body . . . Jab, hook the body, follow with a right."

When the two men were done, Michael began to pace in a circle around the room. Now it was just a matter of time.

But something was missing.

Bobby Miles put the handpads on again, and Grant pounded them for another two minutes. It was 11:15 P.M.

"Three minutes," a voice from doorway sounded.

Everyone in the room joined hands in a circle, readying for prayer.

"Be sincere, please," Michael implored them.

They prayed together. Then Michael turned for a silent moment of his own. "I always shed a tear before a fight," Michael Grant had once said. Now he appeared to be shedding many of them.

The room still didn't feel right.

There would be no violent transfer of power tonight.

After Michael Grant was defeated by Lennox Lewis, he began planning a comeback.

The Long Road Back

The last time Michael Grant entered the ring, he was regarded by many as the "Heir Apparent" to the heavyweight throne. The date was April 29, 2000. Grant's record stood at thirty-one wins and no losses. He was one of the most physically gifted athletes ever to come into boxing and an imposing physical force. Lennox Lewis knocked him down four times en route to a second-round stoppage. Grant showed enormous courage in getting up again and again but, in truth, he was annihilated.

In the aftermath of his loss to Lewis, Grant's stock fell like a bad dot-com company. Emotionally, it was hard for him to deal with the defeat. He was also frustrated by the slow healing of a torn cartilage in his knee, which had been damaged during the fight. At times, he thought about quitting boxing. He even considered offers from a handful of NFL teams (including the Seattle Seahawks, San Francisco 49ers, Philadelphia Eagles, and Dallas Cowboys) that invited him to attend training camp.

Also, there was a trainer controversy. Grant has been trained for his entire professional career by Donald Turner. Now there were whispers . . . "Donald Turner isn't a very good trainer. He only succeeds with fighters who already know their trade . . . Donald Turner didn't teach anything to Larry Holmes or Evander Holyfield. He only monitored them."

And Lewis's trainer, Emanuel Steward, added fuel to the fire when he said, "I thought it would go pretty much the way it went. The biggest asset we had was Don Turner. Don had no respect for Lennox, and that surprised me. Don thought Lennox had won all his fights because of his size and strength and, now that Don had a guy who was bigger and stronger than Lennox, Lennox would crumble. He brainwashed Michael. Michael really believed that all he had to do was be aggressive and Lennox would fold. And yes, Michael is a big man, but he doesn't use his height well. Plus Don Turner never gave Michael a realistic back-up plan, which meant that, by the time the fight came and Michael started having doubts, it was too late to change."

There were those who came to Turner's defense. "It wasn't the strategy," said Bobby Miles, who served under Turner as associate trainer for the Lewis fight but is no longer in the Grant camp. "My feeling is that stage fright set in. Some guys think they're ready to take center stage before they really are. Whatever his skill level, Michael wasn't ready emotionally for Lennox. By the time he went down the aisle and up into the ring, he had an expression on his face like he wasn't there. And then, he didn't fight. Once the bell rang, he should have moved, jabbed, given himself time to get his legs under him. But instead, he attacked, except it wasn't really an attack. His heart wasn't in it. If I'm assaulting you, I'm going to throw the first punch and keep punching. But against Lennox, Michael ran out, attacked, and jumped back."

And Turner himself said in response, "Emanuel has always had a hard-on for me. I'm not going to talk bad about Emanuel, but I will tell you that he doesn't know what he's talking about. He doesn't know what went on in Michael's camp and what I said and did and strategized with Michael. On the afternoon of the fight, I tried to talk with Michael about what it meant to fight for the title, and he didn't want to talk with me. On his worst day, I'd never seen him like that. To be honest with you, it's still something of a mystery to me. We had a game plan; Michael just didn't use it. The fighter doesn't always do what you want. So Emanuel is entitled to his opinion, and why don't you ask Emanuel what the strategy was the night Tommy Hearns got knocked out by Marvin Hagler."

Whatever the truth, several months of indecision followed. And Turner had to sit quietly by while reports surfaced that Grant was reaching out to Teddy Atlas, Roy Jones Sr., Jesse Reid, even Emanuel Steward.

"Michael disappeared for a few months," Turner acknowledges. "I heard all the rumors. Then, finally, he called and said he wanted me with him for the duration of his career and this had just been about someone to assist me. And I was honest with him. I told him how things were between me and Evander when Evander lost to Michael Moorer and Riddick Bowe; and, no matter what, Evander and I always kept talking. I told Michael that he wanted to be the boss, but he was incapable of being the boss until he took more responsibility for his actions. And I told him that, in order be heavyweight champion of the world, he'd have to accept his defeat and learn from it. I also told him, 'I can't surmise everything that went on in your mind the night you fought Lennox Lewis, but I do know that you didn't have your mind on your job.'"

Michael Grant is now primed to enter the ring again. On January 13, he will do battle in Tunica, Mississippi, against Cuban expatriate Eliecer Castillo. The fight will be televised on *Boxing After Dark* in conjunction with a bout between Vernon Forrest and Raul Frank for the IBF welterweight title.

Tunica is only a thousand miles from Madison Square Garden, where Grant lost to Lewis. But in boxing terms, it's light years away. Likewise, Grant's purse will be a small fraction of the $3,500,000 he earned when he challenged for the heavyweight crown. "That's to be expected," says Bobby Miles. "When you lose the way Michael lost to Lennox, particularly in a title fight, you go to the end of the line."

Initially, Grant was to have begun his comeback on November 30 against Sedreck Fields at a Heavyweight Explosion card in New York. "Fields is perfect for Michael," Grant's advisor Craig Hamilton had said when that fight was signed. "He doesn't punch too hard, and he's there to be hit." Then Corrie Sanders was designated as Grant's opponent for January 13, and the Grant camp wanted more time to prepare for the South African's southpaw style. Castillo was substituted after Sanders broke his leg while training for the bout. Hamilton denied turning down Danell Nicholson and Lance Whitaker (both of whom later became unavailable) as HBO opponents. But he did acknowledge, "Michael has to have some anxiety after what happened to him against Lennox. Down the road, he'll be one way or another. But right now, we have to get guys in front of him who he can handle and get his confidence back."

And again, the naysayers are whispering, "From a technical standpoint, Grant is a terrible fighter. He beats people physically, not with any level of skill . . . If Grant were six-foot-three, 230 pounds, instead of six-foot-seven and 260, he'd be a .500 fighter . . . Forget about Michael Grant. He has no desire."

Donald Turner remains optimistic. "Michael still has everything it takes to become heavyweight champion of the world," Turner says of his charge. "He can beat anybody if he trains properly and takes what he's learned into the ring with him. It won't be easy. Even doing everything right, it will be a long process. But I'd say, in five or six fights, Michael will be ready to fight for the title again."

However, Bobby Miles sounds a cautionary note. "The problem," says Miles, "is that Michael doesn't really like boxing. It's just not something he likes to do; and he still thinks like an athlete, not a fighter. In most sports, there's a code of sportsmanship and gentlemanly conduct. In boxing, you have that too. But the truth is, if you're a fighter, you have to approach each fight like a gladiator in the Roman Coliseum. You have to be mean. You're fighting for survival. Tyson, Duran, guys like that, they understand. All great fighters do. Ray Leonard might have smiled and said nice things, but in the ring he was a mean son-of-a-bitch. Right now, Michael just isn't mean enough."

And that leaves one person to be heard from: Michael Grant himself.

"I'll be honest with you," Grant says, looking back over the past eight months. "Against Lennox, I was out of control. I was overwhelmed. I didn't fight. I watched the tape a few times right after the fight, but none of it made sense to me. I tried to make things less painful by telling myself, 'No one got hurt; it didn't end my career; I made a lot of money.' But all I was doing was trying to escape, and there was no peace for me. I needed time to heal. And then I realized I'd been robbing myself. I hadn't been doing what I needed to do to be as good as I can be. I'd come such a long way in such a short period of time in boxing that I'd been satisfied with the way things were instead of doing everything I could do to be the best that I can be. I thought I could get by on being an awesome physical force, and I was wrong. Lennox was well-schooled and I wasn't. That was the difference. I was a guy with great physical tools and heart and will but no education of the game. And I blame myself. I was the one who didn't do certain things in training. I was the one who was in the ring fighting. April 29th made me raise my eyebrows and say, 'Okay, now I know what I have to do to become heavyweight champion of the world.' And that's given me more of a passion to learn. I have no excuses for what happened against Lennox. Now I'm going to take my time and do things right. Someday, I still expect to hear the words, 'And the new heavyweight champion of the world . . .'"

Will it come to pass?

"Michael is talking all the right things now," says Craig Hamilton. "He seems more dedicated in the gym. He's looking to the future. It's still possible that, someday, Michael will be The Man. But I can't tell you whether it will happen or not. And whatever happens, it's not up to Don Turner or Bobby Miles or Jim Thomas or me. We can help but, at the end of the day, it will be up to Michael."

Lennox Lewis and Emanuel Steward

At the end of a week in which American democracy became as chaotic as professional boxing, two foreign nationals fought on American soil for the heavyweight championship of the world. When they did, in the eyes of many, the third man in the ring wasn't referee Joe Cortez. It was Emanuel Steward.

Steward was born on July 7, 1944. A national Golden Gloves winner, he has worked as an electrician, an insurance salesman, and a cosmetics distributor. Along the way, he began training fighters and turned the Kronk Gym in Detroit from a neighborhood recreational center into one of the most famous gyms in the world. Over the years, he has worked with twenty-five world champions. He has been named Manager of the Year twice and Trainer of the Year three times by the Boxing Writers Association of America. Those are "legendary" credentials.

Steward was in Oliver McCall's corner on the night of September 24, 1994, when McCall defeated Lennox Lewis to capture the WBC heavyweight crown. He began working with Lewis before the deposed champion's next fight (a fifth-round knockout of Lionel Butler) and has been with him ever since. Lewis-Tua was their fourteenth fistic collaboration.

"There's a special bond between a fighter and his trainer," Steward says in describing his job. "Often, they're the closest two people in camp. Look at the young men who become fighters. Many of them never had a father at home when they were growing up. Or if the father was there, he wasn't a positive influence. So when the relationship between a fighter and his trainer is right, oftentimes the trainer becomes a father figure and the fighter's best friend. The two men develop similar thought patterns and become spiritually synchronized with one another. Now with Lennox, things are a little different. Lennox isn't looking for a father figure. He's his own man. In a lot of ways, he's made it through life on his own. Lennox was separated from his mother when he was young. And when they were finally reunited, he saw that his mother was looked down upon and treated badly by a lot of people. That hurt Lennox and made him very wary of people. It's one of the reasons he's so conscious of loyalty. Tommy Hearns was different. Tommy was loyal, but if someone turned his back on him after a defeat, Tommy would shrug and say, 'That's human nature; people want to run with a winner.' Lennox isn't like that. Lennox demands loyalty from the people around him. There's also a tough street side to him, but most people never see it. And he's very sensitive, very intense, and more competitive than most people imagine.

"In terms of working together," Steward continues, "Lennox and I caught on to each other's thought patterns very quickly. We work exceptionally well together. The first week at camp, we plan a mental strategy for the fight. For example, when Lennox fought Holyfield, I knew it was important to never let Evander get his rhythm. So we developed a strategy where Lennox's jab was the key. He should never stand still and just block Evander's punches because, even if he blocked them, that would allow Evander to get his rhythm. It had to be jab, jab, jab. And we do that together. Lennox watches tapes of his opponent before a fight, and I value his input. You know, you can't dominate your fighter in training. You have to listen to him and work on what he wants to do, too. But it's not just about throwing the jab or an uppercut. Sometimes it's about finding the spiritual key that turns a fighter on. When Buster Douglas fought Mike Tyson, he fought well over his head because he was motivated by his mother's death. I had an amateur fighter once—a young man named Rodney Trusel—who was motivated because he wanted to outshine his older brother. Every fighter is different. You have to get into the mindset of your fighter, and that's particularly true with Lennox, who has a mind of his own. For example, against Ray Mercer, Lennox started backing against the ropes, blocking punches, and firing back. He'd done it in training, and he was doing it in the fight. That wasn't what I wanted, but there are times when you have to work off what your fighter is doing. Don't spend the fight arguing with him because, if you do, you'll win the argument and lose the decision. So what I did to motivate Lennox was, after the eighth round, I said to him, 'Remember, I told you once, that someday you'd be in a fight where your natural talent and skills aren't enough; that you'd just have to go out and outfight the other guy to win. Well, that time is now.' And Lennox responded. He went out and plain outfought Ray Mercer the rest of the way to win."

Lewis, for his part, remembers the Mercer fight well and says, "I believe in myself because I've been through tough fights. Razor Ruddock was tough in the beginning, but Mercer was easily the hardest fight I've been in."

As for Lennox Lewis versus David Tua, prior to the bout, one could have made a pretty good argument in favor of the Samoan. The durability factor; the relative ability of both men to take punishment in general and the big punch in particular; the fact that Tua had never been badly hurt, never been on the canvas, and never been cut as a pro. Moreover, Tua is only twenty-seven years old and had seemed not to wear down during his fights, whereas Lewis is thirty-five and there were questions regarding his stamina.

Still, Steward was confident before the bout, declaring, "People say that David Tua has never been hurt. That sounds good, but the truth is, Tua seldom gets hit clean because he keeps his chin tucked down very nicely and picks off punches with his shoulders. And Tua has never been hit by anyone as big and strong as Lennox, so I don't know how good a punch David Tua really takes. But we'll find out. The fight Lennox and I looked at a lot in training camp was Tua against Hasim Rahman. That fight showed how to beat Tua and also what can happen if you get careless against him. But most of all, it showed Tua's vulnerability against a taller opponent. And believe me, not only is Lennox a big man, he uses his height. The key to this fight will be to keep Tua preoccupied with Lennox's jab and then smash him with right hands. Tua's only hope is to get inside, but that will be very difficult for him. Lennox has been working on hand speed for this fight. And he's been working a lot to build up his arm strength. He wants to be able to control Tua inside with his arms. Tua will force the fight and force Lennox into some explosive situations. But David Tua is stepping out of his league. If he thinks he's prepared to fight Lennox, he's mistaken."

Steward was right. Lewis-Tua was like Tua-Rahman, but without Tua landing a big left hook. Lewis looked good in round one, throwing a stinging jab and occasional right hands. Then he put the right in moth-balls and went almost exclusively with his jab, controlling the fight like a cat toying with a mouse. The crowd had come in anticipation of a slugfest, and more than a few onlookers began booing with the realization that they were watching a tactical fight. But, hey, it's called "boxing."

"I was conserving energy," Lewis explained later. "Everyone was talk-ing about how dangerous Tua is late, so I wanted to make sure I had some-thing left at the end. Also, even if I land a hundred punches, all he needs is two good ones. That's what Tua was looking for all night, one or two good punches; so I wanted to be careful. I'm a more confident fighter now that I've unified the title, and that makes me a better fighter. But I said 'confident,' not 'foolish.' A fighter should never think he's invincible. The first fight against Oliver McCall taught me that."

Also, it's worth noting that the lack of excitement was more Tua's fault than Lewis's. Lewis was winning, and Tua was losing. Thus, it was incumbent upon the challenger to change the pace of the fight, and he never did. Instead, Tua kept coming forward without really forcing the action and waited for Lewis to make a mistake. In fact, from round nine on, Tua looked as though he had stopped trying to win altogether and was simply going through the motions. By the end of the evening, the champion had landed 300 punches to 110 for the challenger, and the decision was no longer in doubt. Emanuel Steward was correct in observ-ing, "Lennox shut him down completely. He made David Tua look like a sparring partner."

As for what comes next, Lewis says he'd prefer to fight less often in 2001 than in the past. "Four fights in twelve months put me in front of the public," he acknowledges. "But I'd like to slow down a bit now and not have more than two fights next year."

The most frequently mentioned opponent for Lewis is, of course, Mike Tyson. The champion appears to want the fight. "Beating Tyson would add to my legacy," he says. But in the next breath, he voices doubt that the bout will happen, noting, "Riddick Bowe called me names and then joined the Marines. Maybe Tyson will join the Marines."

Meanwhile, boxing fans can count on one hand the number of world-class fighters who have gotten better in their mid-thirties. But that's what seems to be happening with Lennox Lewis. Lewis himself agrees with that evaluation and gives much of the credit to Steward. "I've worked hard to improve my technical skills," he says, "and a lot of what's happened is due to Manny. The first thing he corrected in me was never having my head go past my front knee, and I've been getting better and better ever since. But even now, there's things I see other boxers do in the ring that I want to be able to do, so I'm still improving."

Steward responds with equal praise, declaring, "Lennox is a perfectionist. He has fast hands and explosive power, which is a devastating combination. He can box and he can punch. He's still learning and, once he catches on to something, he's got it. He's physically big, and we're not talking big and clumsy. He's fast and well-coordinated. The old perception of Lennox as a big old clumsy boy with dreadlocks is gone now. And Lennox is more relaxed in the ring these days than ever before. He was always confident, but his belief in himself has grown and he's more comfortable with his skills. And another thing: Lennox wants to be great. He talks with me about that a lot now. It's not just about winning fights. He wants to be recognized in history as a great heavyweight champion. That's one of the reasons he wants to fight Mike Tyson. If you think about it, the only two major heavyweights of Lennox's era that he hasn't fought are Bowe and Tyson. And neither guy wanted to fight him. In fact, both guys gave up their WBC championship belt rather than get into the ring with Lennox. Lennox wants Tyson badly so he can show the world how much better he is than Tyson."

Meanwhile, let's give Lennox Lewis credit. In a little less than a year, he has fought Evander Holyfield, Michael Grant, Frans Botha, and David Tua. He has become boxing's dominant heavyweight. No nickname, no frills. Just Lennox Lewis: Heavyweight Champion of the World.

The Greatest Olympic Boxing Team of All Time

The first Olympic gold medalist to win a professional world championship in boxing was Fidel La Barba of the United States, who won gold at 112 pounds in Paris in 1924 and, three years later, captured the flyweight championship of the world. Still, it would be a long time before the Olympics became a conventional path to professional stardom. Indeed, of all the Olympic gold medalists through 1972, only eleven went on to become champions as pros. Six of those names are familiar to boxing fans: Muhammad Ali, Joe Frazier, George Foreman, Floyd Patterson, Nino Benvenuti, and Pascal Perez. The others, in addition to La Barba, were Willie Smith, Frankie Genaro, Jackie Fields, and Mate Parlov.

Then, in 1976, the landscape changed. A group of brash young Americans led by Ray Leonard and Howard Davis went up to Montreal and captured five gold medals. But more important, they captured the imagination of the American public and went on to win five professional championships. The 1980 Moscow Olympics were marked by an American boycott because of the Soviet invasion of Afghanistan. But in 1984 at Los Angeles, the United States won nine gold medals in boxing, and six team members later earned world titles as pros.

It's now accepted logic that an Olympic gold medal is the ideal launching pad for a career in professional boxing. But the question lingers: Which team was better—1976 or 1984?

Let's start by taking a look at the 1976 roster:

106 pounds	Leo Curtis
112	Leo Randolph
119	Charles Mooney
125	Davey Armstrong
132	Howard Davis

139	Ray Leonard
147	Clint Jackson
156	Charles Walker
165	Michael Spinks
178	Leon Spinks
Heavyweight	John Tate

Of these eleven fighters, five won gold medals—Leo Randolph, Howard Davis, Ray Leonard, Michael Spinks, and Leon Spinks. Charles Mooney won a silver medal, and John Tate brought home a bronze.

Fast-forward to 1984. The United States Olympic boxing team consisted of

106	Paul Gonzales
112	Steve McCrory
119	Robert Shannon
125	Meldrick Taylor
132	Pernell Whitaker
139	Jerry Page
147	Mark Breland
156	Frank Tate
165	Virgil Hill
178	Evander Holyfield
201	Henry Tillman
Superheavyweight	Tyrell Biggs

Of these twelve fighters, nine won gold medals—Paul Gonzales, Steve McCrory, Meldrick Taylor, Pernell Whitaker, Jerry Page, Mark Breland, Frank Tate, Henry Tillman, and Tyrell Biggs. Virgil Hill won a silver medal, and Evander Holyfield took home a bronze.

At first glance, the numbers might seem to dictate that the 1984 team was better. But wait a minute! In 1984, the Soviet Union and thirteen other Communist bloc countries stayed home in retaliation for the 1980 United States boycott of the Moscow Olympics. That meant there were no Soviets, no Cubans, no East Germans, no Poles, and no North Koreans for our fighters to contend with. And that made all the difference in the world.

To prove the point, let's return to 1976 and look at the American fighters who lost. Leo Curtis was defeated in the first round by a Pole. Charles Mooney lost in the finals to gold medalist Yong-Jo Gu of North

Korea. Davey Armstrong lost a 3-2 decision to gold medalist Angel Herrera of Cuba. Charles Walker lost a 3-2 decision to gold medalist Jerzy Rybicki of Poland. And John Tate was stopped in the semi-finals by gold medalist Teofilo Stevenson of Cuba. The only American who lost to a non-Communist-bloc fighter was Clint Jackson; and he lost to the eventual silver medalist, Pedro Gamarro of Venezuela.

Moreover, if you look at the men the American fighters beat in 1976 to win their gold medals, their triumphs seem even more impressive. Leo Randolph decisioned Ramon Duvalon of Cuba in the final round. Howard Davis won a unanimous decision over Simion Cutov of Rumania. Ray Leonard did the same against Andres Aldama of Cuba. Michael Spinks stopped Rufat Riskiev of the Soviet Union. And Leon Spinks KO'd Sixto Soria of Cuba.

With that in mind, Teddy Atlas (who will be NBC's boxing commentator at the upcoming Olympics) says, "Let's be honest about this. You're not going to find many, if any, amateur teams better than the 1976 Americans. The 1984 American team had some great fighters, but whatever they won was diluted. If the Soviets and Cubans and other Communist countries had been in Los Angeles, the United States would have won maybe two gold medals."

So as an amateur squad, the nod goes to 1976. But what about the records of the two teams as pros?

As noted earlier, five members of the 1976 United States Olympic team won professional championships as opposed to six members from the 1984 squad. But world titles are no longer the marker of greatness that they once were. After all, Mark Breland won his belts by beating Harold Volbrecht and Seung-Soon Lee on American soil, while Howard Davis came up just short against James Watt and Edwin Rosario on their home turf. And while one member of the 1984 team (Evander Holyfield) became superb heavyweight champion, three entries from the class of 1976 (Leon Spinks, Michael Spinks, and John Tate) once claimed all or part of the heavyweight crown.

Direct matchups? The only time members of the 1976 and 1984 teams squared off against one another as professionals came in 1986, when Howard Davis and Meldrick Taylor fought to a ten-round draw.

So let's take things to the next level. Two members of the 1976 United

States Olympic boxing team went on to become truly great professional fighters—Ray Leonard and Michael Spinks. Two members of the 1984 United States Olympic boxing team went on to become truly great professional fighters—Pernell Whitaker and Evander Holyfield.

Three members of the 1976 team went on to become genuine world-class pros—Howard Davis, Leon Spinks, and John Tate. Three members of the 1984 team went on to become genuine world-class pros—Virgil Hill, Meldrick Taylor, and Mark Breland.

Two members of the 1976 team had solid professional careers—Leo Randolph and Clint Jackson. Four members of the 1984 team had solid professional careers—Paul Gonzales, Steve McCrory, Frank Tate, and Tyrell Biggs.

That makes things close. But as a professional unit, let's give the nod by the thinnest of margins to 1984.

So which team qualifies as "The Greatest Olympic Team of All Time"?

"That's a tough one," says Howard Davis, who won the Val Barker award as the outstanding boxer at the 1976 Olympic Games. "If you throw everything into the mix—amateur and pro—I'd say we were pretty much even."

Mark Breland (America's flagship boxer at the 1984 games) concurs. In fact, matching the two teams against one another division-by-division as amateurs, Breland comes out dead even.

For the record, the two matchups that intrigue Breland the most are Howard Davis against Pernell Whitaker and Leon Spinks against Evander Holyfield. "Pernell was slick, but Howard was so fast," says Breland. "I think that, as amateurs, Howard would have beaten him."

And Spinks against Holyfield?

"Evander was tough and Leon was tough," Breland answers. "But I think Evander was a smarter fighter and would have won."

So call it even. It's one of those rare occasions when a draw is satisfying in boxing. And let's raise a glass to all the young men—past, present, and future—who pursue Olympic gold.

Round 3
Non-Combatants

Don Elbaum is . . . Well, Don Elbaum is Don Elbaum.

Don Elbaum

The year was 1965. Sugar Ray Robinson was nearing the end of a glorious career, and wanted one more crack at the world middleweight championship. Thus, his trainer, George Gainsford, called Don Elbaum.

"Ray needs to reestablish his credentials before he gets another title shot," Gainsford pressed. "Who in the top ten do you think he can beat?"

Elbaum suggested Joey Archer, with the winner to fight then-champion Joey Giardello. But first, he wanted to build Robinson up with a few easy wins.

"Anyway," Elbaum recalls, "We had Ray fight Peter Schmidt in Johnstown, Pennsylvania, on October 1, 1965, which was almost twenty-five years to the day from his first professional fight. And to get some publicity, I looked around for the two most battered boxing gloves I could find. Then we had a dinner in Ray's honor. There was a twenty-fifth anniversary cake. The media was all there. And the highlight of the evening was when I got up and said, 'Ray, don't ask me how I got these; but twenty-five years ago, you made your professional debut at Madison Square Garden, and these are the gloves you wore in that fight.' Ray's eyes actually teared up," Elbaum continues. "He was genuinely moved by the moment. He took the gloves and cradled them in his arms like he was holding a newborn babe."

Then someone suggested that Robinson put the gloves on for a photo op. That's when the world discovered that Don Elbaum had given Sugar Ray Robinson two left gloves.

Don Elbaum is a boxing guy. He was born circa 1940 and grew up in Erie, Pennsylvania. When Elbaum was nine, his uncle took him to a fight. "I was mesmerized by it," he recalls. "And ever since then, all I've wanted out of life is to be in boxing."

Elbaum started boxing at age thirteen, and compiled a 40-10

amateur record. "I had a great chin and I was a good boxer, but I couldn't break an egg," he remembers. During his amateur career, he scored three knockouts. "The first, when my opponent threw up between rounds and couldn't continue. The second, when an opponent who was pounding the crap out of me broke his hand on my head and couldn't continue. And the third, when I cut a guy and they stopped the fight."

Meanwhile, Elbaum's father was taking him to professional bouts in Buffalo, Cleveland, and Pittsburgh on a regular basis. By age fifteen, he was matchmaking for established promoters. At age eighteen, he promoted his first fight.

Don Elbaum has now been in professional boxing for four decades. And along the way, he has developed a reputation for being something of a character. Indeed, legend has it that he once went to the Olympic boxing finals and complained because there weren't any round-card girls.

Be that as it may, Elbaum has promoted or co-promoted more than one thousand shows, including 196 over a five-year period at the Tropicana. He has been the matchmaker for at least ten thousand bouts. Almost as a sidelight, between 1960 and 1971, he had ten pro fights of his own, compiling a 6-3-1 record with no knockouts either way. Four of those bouts were on cards that he himself promoted and were necessitated by the fact that a fighter fell out at the last minute and no other substitute was available.

Don Elbaum introduced Don King to boxing and served as a cutman for Ron Stander. He has been the manager or "advisor" for countless fighters, the most accomplished of whom have been Aaron Pryor, Tony Tubbs, Simon Brown, and Maurice Blocker.

"I enjoy building fighters," Elbaum says about his role as an advisor. Listen to him wax eloquent about latest projects:

"Chris Mills: an Irish light-heavyweight from Scranton, 12 and 0 with ten knockouts . . . Dale Crowe: a cruiserweight from Cincinnati, southpaw, 12 and 0 with eight knockouts . . . Tom Chute: another cruiserweight, white, from Niagara Falls. I found him at a toughman contest. He's only three and three, but he can punch . . . Chi Woo: five wins in six fights, a great welterweight prospect. He's one of only three full-blooded-Chinese professional fighters in the world that I know of, and his father used to be lieutenant governor of Delaware . . . Kenny Ellis; a 21-1-1 junior-middleweight. Take my word for it, this kid can fight."

The list goes on. Elbaum is currently "advising" John Bizzarro and Lou Bizzarro Jr. (the sons of Lou Bizzarro Sr., who Elbaum matched against Roberto Duran in Erie, Pennsylvania, twenty-two years ago). Duran knocked out Bizzarro Sr., but it took him fourteen rounds to do it because Elbaum had arranged for a thirty-foot ring. And Elbaum has a soft spot in his heart for Rocky Phillips, a 20-3 white heavyweight from Dayton, Ohio, whose most notable bout was against Michael Dokes in 1997. "Dokes weighed in at 284 pounds," Elbaum recalls, "but that was embarrassing, so we announced him at 282. Rocky broke his jaw and stopped him in two. I was in seventh heaven for about a day. Then I learned that Rocky had worked part-time as a bodyguard for a gentleman who had come back from Texas with a suitcase full of drugs and that there was a problem."

Rocky was recently released from prison after serving a one-year sentence, and Elbaum is looking forward to his return to boxing.

Elbaum's most promising current project is David Telesco, who he has been advising since February 1993. Telesco is a light-heavyweight from Port Chester, New York, with a 20 and 2 record and 17 knockouts. Like Phillips, Telesco has served time in prison for drug-related offenses, three years to be precise. But since his release from incarceration in late 1996, he has been undefeated in nine bouts, including a fourth-round stoppage of former middleweight champion Frank Tate this past October. Telesco is a party animal who lives a fast life, is undisciplined, and is not the easiest guy in the world to get along with. But Elbaum touts him as "the most exciting light-heavyweight in the world today," and observes, "There's a time bomb in there. I just hope it goes off when David is in the ring with Roy Jones." And indeed, Telesco has been mentioned recently as a 1999 opponent for Jones, assuming he receives permission from his parole officer to leave Westchester County.

So that's Don Elbaum. Still in the trenches, still full of hope. He *knows* that someday he'll be at a toughman contest in Kentucky or Pennsylvania or Missouri or Ohio. He'll see some monster heavyweight with more natural talent than any fighter ever, who needs an advisor to help him out. Don, of course, will step into the breach, and the two of them will make history together.

Meanwhile, about those gloves that Elbaum once gave Sugar Ray Robinson. "Russell Peltz has offered me five thousand dollars for them," Elbaum said recently. "I've got to find those gloves, or two gloves that look like them."

Johnny Bos is another of the behind-the-scenes personalities who are the mainstay of professional boxing.

The Wizard of Bos

Go to a club fight. Look around the arena. You might see a large man with shaggy dirty-blond hair, six-feet-three-inches tall, 255 pounds (down from a previous high of 300), who bears a faint resemblance to Hulk Hogan. Engage him in conversation. If the man knows more about boxing than anyone you've ever encountered, there's a chance it's Johnny Bos.

Johnny Bos fits between the cracks of what everybody else does in boxing. He's part matchmaker, part manager, part booking agent, and so forth. "I manage the managers," is how he describes what he does. Bos even had one amateur fight, which he won on a decision in 1971. But he doesn't remember it very well because he was drunk at the time.

So what do boxing people think of Johnny Bos?

Michael Katz (noted curmudgeon and boxing writer extraordinaire) sums up for his brethren, when he says, "Johnny Bos is one of the best minds in boxing. There are very few guys around who know and love the game as much as he does. And he cares about the fighters. The only complaint I have is that he should be in a position of influence and authority instead of doing what he does today. I wouldn't mind it if Johnny Bos ran the sport."

"The Wizard of Bos" was born in Brooklyn on Valentine's Day in 1952. His father was a shipyard worker, who later worked as a doorman in the building where Barney Ross lived.

"My father was a big fight fan," Bos says. "As far back as I can remember, I'd be sitting on his lap, watching the *Friday Night Fights* on television. That's where my interest in boxing came from."

Bos was kicked out of Fort Hamilton High School when he was in tenth grade. "I was bored all the time, so I never paid attention in class," he acknowledges. "Nowadays, they'd probably call it 'attention deficit disorder.' And I was a frequent truant and an alcoholic."

After leaving school, Bos worked as a stockboy at Ohrbach's department store. Then, at age eighteen, he began an eight-year stint as a mail handler on the graveyard shift for the United States Postal Service. "Meanwhile, I was hanging around boxing," he remembers. "I'd go to the gyms, Jack Dempsey's restaurant, any place there were fighters. And I was writing for *Flash*. That started when I was fifteen. Bruce Trampler, Don Majeski, and I used to stand outside Madison Square Garden on fight nights and sell copies of *Flash*."

In 1978, Bos left the post office to concentrate on boxing. "Managers and promoters had been calling me for years, asking questions about this fighter and that opponent, and I'd tell them everything I knew for free. Finally, I said to myself, 'Don't be a jerk. Everybody else in boxing gets paid for what they do. So should I.'"

Bos's first paying gig was as matchmaker for a January 1978 Tiffany Promotions card on Long Island. "Ronnie Harris was scheduled to fight Angel Ortiz in the main event," he says. "And the day of the show, there was a terrible snowstorm. Ronnie had trouble getting to the arena, and didn't arrive until fifteen minutes before his fight." One of the other matches Bos made that night was Austin Johnson against a novice heavyweight named Gerry Cooney.

"And then, it was like, all of a sudden, I was hot," Bos remembers. "Mike Jones and Dennis Rappaport began paying me to choose opponents for Cooney, Harris, and all their other fighters. Mickey Duff hired me for John Mugabe, Cornelius Boza-Edwards, Lloyd Honeygan, and Frank Bruno. I was the matchmaker for Main Events in the 1980's, when they had their greatest years. Evander Holyfield, Mark Breland, Pernell Whitaker, Meldrick Taylor, Tyrell Biggs, Rocky Lockridge, I was there for all those guys. Bill Cayton and Jim Jacobs hired me for Mike Tyson. I was doing everything for everyone—making matches, choosing opponents, recommending sparring partners. I even stopped drinking. I remember the date: November 17, 1986. My life was good; but I was an alcoholic. The way I was drinking, it wouldn't have been long before I was dead. And I decided I'd rather live than die."

"The best time of my life came in 1992," Bos continues. "In the course of six weeks, I had four guys fight for world championships, and three of them won. Joey Gamache knocked out Chil-Sung Chun to win the WBA lightweight title. Tracy Harris Patterson knocked out Thierry Jacob in a WBC superbantamweight bout. And Tyrone Booze, who was a 30-to-1 underdog, stopped Derek Angol to win the WBO cruiserweight championship."

That was the peak.

"But then," Bos remembers, "everything fell apart. I wish I was as good a businessman as I am a matchmaker, but I'm not. I was never a 'let's have a written contract' kind of guy. I always did business on a handshake. So the first thing that happened was, after Tracy won the title, I got screwed by Floyd Patterson. All he said to me was, now that Tracy was champion, he didn't need me anymore. That was seven years of hard work down the drain. Then Michael Bentt, Darrin Allen, and some of the other promising fighters I was working with walked. My father died. And two months after that, my little brother died of AIDS. You take blows like that, and you lose your confidence. And to make matters worse, I'd moved to Florida, which was a mistake because it took me out of the mainstream. And in boxing, like every other business, guys are more likely to screw you if they don't see you face-to-face."

By 1995, Bos was, to use his own words, "reduced to being a fringe guy in boxing. I was still a fan; I'll always be a fan. But I wasn't much of a factor in the business anymore. Then I decided to give it one more shot. I came back to New York, started doing my thing again; and you know the rest."

Johnny Bos is now back. At present, he's advising dozens of managers, promoters, and fighters: foremost among them, heavyweight prospect Kirk Johnson. He fields between fifty and a hundred telephone calls a day, goes to the gyms, and watches endless hours of boxing on tape each week. That's good for "The Wizard of Bos." And it's also good for boxing. For as Michael Katz once said, "Without guys like Johnny Bos, there is no boxing."

Donald Turner is more than an accessory to fighters. His story merits telling on its own.

Donald Turner

Donald Turner was born on May 7, 1939, the second oldest of six children. He grew up in Cincinnati. "I have no idea what my father did," he would say years later. "We were on welfare and lived in the projects about four blocks from Ezzard Charles. In Cincinnati, boxing was a thing with most young guys. Boxing or basketball or track. I chose boxing because, when I was growing up, Ezzard Charles was one of the greatest fighters in the world."

Turner started boxing at age twelve, and compiled a 4 and 2 amateur record with no knockouts. He married at seventeen (the marriage ended in divorce five years later), and turned pro on November 18, 1959, losing a six-round decision to Kitten Hayward. Overall, he fought as a middleweight and light-heavyweight for ten years, en route to a 20-10-1 record with no knockouts. He was stopped twice, once by Roger Rouse and once by Giulio Rinaldi. What was his biggest win as a fighter? "I didn't have one," he acknowledges. "But if I had to choose, I'd say it was a decision over Ike White on the undercard of the first fight between Dick Tiger and Joey Giardello."

In 1969, Turner retired from ring combat and began training fighters. He's been doing it ever since. Among the fighters of note he has worked with are Mike McCallum, Aaron Pryor, and John David Jackson. And then there's his "Big Three"—Larry Holmes, Evander Holyfield, and Michael Grant.

Turner was with Holmes from 1991 through his 1997 victory over Maurice Harris, a stretch that included title bouts against Ray Mercer, Evander Holyfield, and Oliver McCall. After Holmes came Holyfield. Evander and Turner have been together now for two fights each against Mike Tyson, Lennox Lewis, and Michael Moorer, and single bouts against Vaughn Bean, Bobby Czyz, Ray Mercer, and Riddick Bowe.

"If I had my choice, out of all the fighters in the world today," says Turner, "if I could train only one, it would be Evander. He's the most disciplined, hardest working fighter I've ever known; a real joy. No one in history has done what Evander has done at his age. Joe Louis couldn't do it. Ali couldn't do it. I always knew Evander was courageous. I always knew Evander was hard-working. But I never knew how smart Evander was as a fighter until he fought Tyson. Tyson was the best fighter in the world at what he did well. He was an awesome offensive fighter. But I grew up in the projects, so I knew that the bully isn't necessarily the bravest guy in the world or the toughest. And against Tyson, Evander went out and did everything right."

And then, of course, there's Michael Grant. Turner has been Grant's trainer for his entire professional career. Their relationship began with a telephone call from Richard Steele, whose wife was Grant's first manager. "Richard wanted to know if I'd work with Mike," Turner remembers. "So I told him to send Mike to me for a week and I'd evaluate him. And I told Richard that, if Mike was really six-foot-seven, I knew he couldn't fight. But after two days with Mike, I called my wife and said, 'Baby, we hit the jackpot.' And I told Richard, 'Not only is this is a future world champion; he has the potential to be better than all of them.'"

These are good times now for Donald Turner. He lives in Norristown, Pennsylvania, with his second wife to whom he's been married for thirty-seven years. There's one discordant note. Their son, age thirty-five, has been incarcerated since 1991 for murder. "You can write about it," says Turner. "My life is an open book; there's no secrets. The whole government knows about it. It's on the public record."

Meanwhile, at long last, there is a growing feeling both in and out of boxing that Donald Turner has become a top-tier trainer.

What are the keys to his success?

"First of all," says Turner, "you've got to have a good fighter. The trainer helps the fighter, but it's a two-way street. The better the fighter, the better the trainer. And you have to keep an open mind. There's no one set way of fighting. The way a fighter gets results is the way he should fight. After a trainer has been at it a while, he picks up certain techniques and habits. But you can't impose those on your fighter, because all fighters are different. Who was better than Joe Louis at doing what he did?

Who was better than Sugar Ray Robinson or Willie Pep at doing what they did? So you have to take a little bit from here and a little bit from there and see what your fighter does naturally."

"I learned the basics from some very disciplined trainers," Turner continues. "Fighters today don't have the teachers that fighters had in the past. They have conditioners and made-for-television trainers. But I was lucky. Bobby McQuillan, Charlie Goldman, Sid Bell, and Al Smith all trained me at different times. Lee Black was a big influence on me. What I'm trying to do now is pass on what I learned from them to my guys."

In terms of Donald Turner's legacy, the most important of his guys is Michael Grant. Turner professes not to care how he's remembered in boxing history. "I'd be a different person if stuff like that crossed my mind," he says. But there's no doubt that, if Grant becomes great, Turner's name will be inextricably linked with that of his student.

So is Michael Grant on track to meet expectations?

"If Mike trained like Joe Louis, Rocky Marciano, or Evander Holyfield," Turner says wistfully, "he'd be better than all of them. But the way boxing is today, most fighters only train when they're preparing for a fight, so Mike's learning process hasn't been what it could be. The fighters of today don't compare with the fighters of yesterday," Turner continues. "The conditioning might be better. They pop a few vitamins and lift a few weights. But technically, as a group, their skill level isn't as good. Joe Louis was the best fighter ever. Joe Louis would destroy these guys today. Rocky Marciano, every fight, he was getting the crap knocked out of him; and then, all of a sudden, the other guy was out. Evander is special. Evander is a throwback to Louis and Marciano. The fight I'd love to see is Rocky Marciano against Evander Holyfield. I'd give the scalpers whatever they wanted for a ticket to that one. But getting back to Mike, I know he could train harder, but I haven't pressed him about it. Mike would train more if I asked him to, but I know he wouldn't give me what the old pros used to give in the gym. That's not personal to Mike. Most of today's fighters and most of today's athletes and most of today's young people travel the road of least resistance. So Mike does most things at eighty percent because, in the past, eighty percent has been good enough for him to keep winning."

Maybe so. But training at eighty percent for Andrew Golota, Grant came perilously close to falling short. And on top of that, this is boxing, where careers can be short-circuited by what goes on outside the ring as well as in it. Ratings are rigged. Bad decisions are common. Fighters are stolen from trainers and managers.

"I know there's a lot of bad people in boxing," Turner acknowledges in closing. "Boxing is like society, and the American public is basically bad people. When I was a kid growing up, I never dreamed that this society would come to what it has today. I know that there's always people out there who will try to steal Mike from me, and try to steal from both of us when we stay together. And those people should know what kind of person I am. I live an honorable life. When I'm wrong, I admit it and apologize for what I did. But I'll get in your face if I think you're wrong. And I'll come at you with a baseball bat if you try to take what's mine."

While at HBO, Lou DiBella was one of boxing's good guys and also one of the most powerful men in the sport. Then, in mid-2000, he left the corporate world and set sail on his own.

Lou DiBella: (1)Promoter, (2)Manager, (3)Advisor, (4)None of the Above

When Lou DiBella left HBO earlier this year, his future was very much in doubt. It still is.

DiBella joined HBO in 1989 after a four-year stint as an attorney on Wall Street. He rose quickly through the ranks and was the driving force behind HBO's *Boxing After Dark,* as well as an integral member of the team that elevated *World Championship Boxing* to an industry-wide standard.

While at HBO, DiBella also developed a reputation as a white knight within the boxing community. He loved boxing, and that passion was evident whether he was sitting at ringside or testifying before one of the many legislative tribunals that are perpetually investigating the sweet science. "I felt a fiduciary duty to the sport when I was a TV executive," he acknowledges. "With the checkbook I had at HBO, in addition to my corporate responsibilities, I felt an obligation to be a force for reform. I put a lot of pressure on myself in a way that most TV executives don't."

For a while, DiBella was considered the heir apparent to Seth Abraham as president of Time Warner Sports. Then, earlier this year, things soured and DiBella left the cable giant to form a company of his own. According to industry sources, as part of his severance package, HBO earmarked certain funds for DiBella Entertainment to pay bonuses to sign Olympic fighters. It also gave DiBella twelve to fifteen TV dates on *World Championship Boxing, Boxing After Dark,* and *KO Nation* over a three-year period. DiBella can program these dates, provided his matchups meet HBO's standards. HBO has a right of first negotiation and last refusal with regard to bouts in which fighters contractually bound to DiBella participate. The first of these dates was the September 9 card featuring Winky Wright against Bronco McKart and Clifford Etienne versus Cliff Couser. The second will be a *Boxing After Dark* show on December 1 featuring Bernard Hopkins against Antwun Echols and Marco Antonio Barrera versus Jesus Salud. Number three will be Paul Spadafora versus Billy Irwin and Winky Wright against Keith Mullings on December 16 on *KO Nation*. The fourth card is slated for January 27, when DiBella hopes to showcase five United States Olympians making their pro debuts at Madison Square Garden.

DiBella has already signed Olympian Ricardo Williams for a reported $1,400,000 bonus, and hopes to have four more Olympians—Jermaine Taylor, Clarence Vinson, Michael Bennett, and Jose Navarro—in the fold shortly. HBO hopes that this crop of Olympians will comprise its "next generation" of fighters in the manner of Fernando Vargas, David Reid, and Floyd Mayweather Jr.

Also, DiBella and Madison Square Garden are currently negotiating what Seth Abraham (who has since moved to the Garden) calls "a creative multi-dimensional deal" that would make additional funds for signing fighters available to DiBella. The deal contemplates DiBella's clients fighting at Madison Square Garden and Radio City Music Hall, with some of their bouts televised on MSG Network.

All of this raises a question. How does one characterize what Lou DiBella is doing? His standard form contract calls for him to provide "matchmaking, distribution, and marketing services" for fighters. But is he a promoter? A manager? An advisor?

DiBella prefers to eschew labels and says, "Call me what you will. I'm not a lawyer. I gave up that profession a long time ago. I'm not a manager. It won't be my job to set up the training camp and arrange for sparring partners or travel. And I'm not a promoter. I'll have a fiduciary duty to my fighters, and a promoter doesn't. What I am doing is controlling the flow of money. I'll be the fighter's business representative. That involves matchmaking, advising, negotiating, and providing television dates whenever I can. What I want to do is control the bouts on a fighter's behalf from an administrative point of view.

"The laws governing boxing are antiquated," DiBella continues. "They were written at a time when the promoter was the one who put up the money and the manager really negotiated with him. Managers and promoters should bring something separate and distinct to the table. But too often in boxing today, managers and promoters simply double-dip on the fighter. A lot of the time, all the manager does is take a third of a fighter's purse and hand the fighter off like a football to a promoter, who's the manager's business partner. It's no secret how things work. Promoters no longer take risks. The money today emanates from television, site fees, and sponsorships. All a promoter is these days is a license and a line producer. Look at Lewis-Tua. The real promoters of that fight were TVKO and Mandalay Bay, and everyone knows it. I want to change the paradigm. I'll work for the fighter and I'll hire the promoter, who will be responsible for promoting each fight in accordance with the laws of the state in which the fight is held. The promoter will control the legal administration of the show. But the promoter will not make the major economic decisions governing TV and site. I'll negotiate the site fee and close the TV deal. In most instances, the promoter will negotiate sponsorships. In other words, the promoter will work for the fighter."

And then DiBella sounds the watchword of his faith: "A fighter should never make less money than the promoter or anyone else involved with a fight."

Under DiBella's standard form contract, he and his fighter will split net revenue. That is, revenue after the deduction of expenses such as sanctioning fees, licensing fees, attorney's fees, travel, insurance, and undercard costs. The split will vary, but DiBella says he'll never take more than thirty percent of net revenue to the fighter's 70 percent. DiBella will pay the promoter out of his end. The fighter will pay his manager, trainer, and attorney. DiBella Entertainment will also have the right to serve as a nonexclusive representative for the fighter on merchandise deals, the proceeds from which will be split eighty-twenty in the fighter's favor. DiBella's form contract also calls for him to own the copyright on each fight, and HBO has agreed to that with regard to the fifteen shows that DiBella will be involved with as part of his severance package.

DiBella's September 9 *KO Nation* card was promoted by Mike Accri, who will also be the promoter of record on December 16. Banner Promotions will handle the chore on December 1, and Cedric Kushner is expected to get the nod at Madison Square Garden on January 27.

A BEAUTIFUL SICKNESS

"I have no desire to amass a giant stable of fighters," DiBella says, elaborating on his goals. "I want a small group of fighters who are television viable. What I'm suggesting doesn't work unless the fighter is a champion, an Olympian, or has some other type of following. Will the formula work for an unknown four-round fighter? Of course not. But up until now, virtually all fighters have been treated unfairly. I think I can help some of them. I'll work with fighters on an exclusive long-term basis or fight by fight. Whatever the deal, I'll stick by my belief that a fighter is entitled to know all of the economics of every event in which he participates; and that includes knowing what everybody else is making. I'll never lie to a fighter. And I'll never dictate to a fighter who he must fight."

DiBella's intentions are honorable. He's offering fighters his competence, his knowledge, his integrity, and HBO exposure. He's bringing an alternative way of doing business to the table, and that could be very good for fighters.

But then there's the matter of reality. DiBella is currently advising Bernard Hopkins and Winky Wright. Suppose Hopkins wants to fight Felix Trinidad? There's no way that Don King will promote that fight for a piece of DiBella's thirty percent. Ditto for Bob Arum should Wright fight Oscar De La Hoya. So what would DiBella do then? "I'd have to bring the offer back to the fighter," he admits. "And maybe then the promoter would make more than the fighter."

Also, while the issue for fighters contemplating the use of DiBella's services might be simple—"What will it cost to use those services and what will the fighter gain in return?"—there's another set of issues for the industry at large: (1) How will DiBella and his designated promoter split their thirty percent; and (2) How much of the fighter's seventy percent will go to his lawyer, trainer, and manager?

In essence, DiBella is saying to fighters, "Let's pay the manager less. Let's pay the promoter a lot less. You and I will split the savings."

That's not calculated to make promoters and managers happy. And rubbing salt into the wound, DiBella goes so far as to opine, "If a quality fighter has a good lawyer, he doesn't need a manager. And he certainly doesn't need a manager who takes one-third of his purse."

Those who benefit from the status quo in boxing generally fight with one another until a larger threat to their common interest is perceived.

Then they become allies. Lou DiBella is threatening the status quo in boxing, and it's not unreasonable to suggest that there will be a concerted effort to ensure that he fails. "People didn't do to him at HBO what they'll do to him now," says Shelly Finkel. Already, the sniping has begun.

"Lou is doing for Lou, not for the fighters . . . If Don King or Bob Arum were doing this, people would scream bloody murder . . . Lou is a promoter looking for a co-promoter who will take short money . . . Lou is a manager looking to avoid the nuts-and-bolts burdens of the job . . . This is no different from what Mike Trainer did for Ray Leonard, except Lou is charging a percentage instead of a smaller hourly fee . . . There's an inherent conflict of interest here. Lou has a deal with HBO for certain TV dates and certain numbers. Under those circumstance, how can he aggressively represent his fighters and explore all options? . . . The real commodity Lou has is television dates. Without those dates. Lou DiBella is nothing. Wait and see what happens to Lou and his fighters when his dates run out."

DiBella knows what he's in for. Somewhat ruefully, he acknowledges, "A lot of people told me that, when I left my lofty perch at HBO, I'd see how nasty and dirty this business really is. They were right. The truth is, boxing is a miserable business, and there's a part of me that wonders if I wouldn't be happier if I redirected away from it. But there's also part of me that loves the sport and loves the fighters and thinks I can make money and have a positive impact on boxing at the same time.

"I'm trying to make a point," DiBella continues. "I'm trying to rattle the cage and do things differently. I can't turn boxing upside down overnight. But it's as important to me now to shake this business up as it is to make money. Yes, I want to be monetarily successful, but not at the expense of who I am. I'm forty years old. I'm going to stay in boxing for three years [the length of his guaranteed TV dates] because it's my family's financial future. But I won't let this business destroy me. So if it isn't working for me after three years, I'll get out.

"Also," DiBella says in closing, "I have to say, I'm disappointed with the way some of my personal relationships have changed. When I was at HBO, I tried to treat everyone fairly and with respect, and I think I left HBO with as many positive relationships as anyone in the business. But I've learned since then that your business friends are just that. It's business. I was worth a lot more to people when I was at HBO than I am now. And when my role changed from being the biggest buyer in the world to a potential competitor, a lot of people started treating me differently. Can I handle it? Yes. Am I surprised? No. There's only one thing I'm not sure I could handle. It would kill me if I do everything the right way and then I start having problems with the fighters themselves."

Meanwhile, paying his own bills is a new experience for Lou DiBella. And what once made sense to him from one side of the negotiating table doesn't necessarily make as much sense to him now.

Is it harder to be a good guy now that it's his money on the line rather than HBO's?

"That's a good question," says DiBella. "And the answer is 'yes.'"

Dan Goossen is the driving force behind America Presents, which is vying to become a major promotional entity in boxing.

Dan Goossen and America Presents

November 11 was a bad night for Dan Goossen. Goossen is president of America Presents, which has a five-year promotional contract with David Tua. "It's virtually impossible to make money in boxing without having a major pay-per-view fighter," Goossen had said earlier in the week. "The license fees you get from Fox SportNet and ESPN2 won't do it. We've invested a lot of time and money in this business. If David wins, we'll be in position to turn things around."

Tua didn't win. And to make matters worse, Lawrence Clay-Bey and Ben Tackie—also America Presents fighters—lost on the undercard. That means Dan Goossen will have to struggle a while longer.

Goossen was born in California in 1949. He's one of ten children: eight boys and two girls. Their father was a Los Angeles cop, who later became a private detective. "I grew up in a good Catholic family," Goossen remembers. "I got married at eighteen, and had the responsibility of being a father at age twenty, so my business life started young. I sold clothes. I sold shoes. At twenty-three, I went to Pierce Junior College in California and played some basketball. Then I went back to work as a salesman. I made a lot of money in the 1970s selling pens and pencils over the telephone."

At the same time, Goossen was getting interested in boxing. "Randy Shields (a California welterweight) was a family friend," he explains. "I used to go to all his fights and hang out at the gym with Randy and his father. In 1979, I went with Randy to Chicago for a fight against Pipino Cuevas. My brother Joe was there too to work Randy's corner. One night in Chicago, Joe and I went to a club called Dingbats for a drink. It was a black club and the bouncer gave us a hard time, but eventually he let us in. Anyway, the bouncer's name was Lawrence Tearaud. We hit it off. He did some security work for Randy that week, and then he asked me if

I'd manage him. He had this idea that he could be an actor or a personality or something. I said okay, and got him entered in an NBC television special, *The World's Toughest Bouncer,* which he won. After that, through sheer persistence, I got him an audition for *Rocky III.* Lawrence, as you might have figured out by now, later became known as Mr. T. He got the role of Clubber Lang, and then he dumped me. I sued, we settled, and that was the start of my representing people."

After Mr. T left the fold, Goossen was faced with the question of what to do for a living. He loved boxing. And he was either romantic or foolish, or both. Thus, in 1982, he started Ten Goose Boxing (named for the ten Goossen children). "It costs hundreds of millions of dollars to own a Major League Baseball franchise," he explains, "but you can become a boxing promoter by paying a hundred-dollar license fee. Our first gym was the backyard of my brother Greg's house. We had a speed-bag and heavy-bag hanging from a tree. One of the ring posts was on top of what had once been home plate for our family whiffle-ball games. Every morning, I'd sweep leaves out of the ring."

Ten Goose trained and managed fighters. After receiving a waiver from the California State Athletic Commission that allowed it to simultaneously promote and manage, it began promoting shows at the Country Club in Los Angeles. "The first major fighter we signed was Michael Nunn," Goossen remembers. "We brought Michael to 37 and 0 and the middleweight championship, and then he left us for Bob Arum. We developed Gabriel and Rafael Ruelas, and Gabriel broke his elbow. We were promoting Terry Norris, and Don King came in and stole him. And to emphasis the cruelty of boxing, our office and gym were destroyed in an earthquake."

At that point, Goossen tossed in the towel and went to work for Bob Arum. "We had an understanding that I was the heir apparent at Top Rank," he recalls. "At least, that was my understanding. But after a year-and-a-half, I learned that Arum's step-son had been designated to take over the business, so I left."

Then, hoping to stay in boxing, Goossen reached out to Mat Tinley, who had previously sold international television rights for Ten Goose. In 1996, the two men formed America Presents, receiving significant financial backing from Tinley's uncle. America Presents today has fifteen employees. Goossen is president and Tinley is CEO, although Goossen pretty much runs the boxing end of the business. And lest anyone think Goossen has forgotten his roots, three of his brothers (Joe, Larry, and Pat) train America Presents fighters; brother Mike is the attorney for America Presents; and brother-in-law Tom is the matchmaker for America Presents. Among the roughly thirty fighters that the company has under promotional contract are Tua, Clay-Bey, Tackie, Michael Nunn (again), David Reid, Joel Casamayor, Lance Whitaker, Hector Camacho Jr., Diosbelys Hurtado, Alex Trujillo, Enrique Sanchez, and Robbie Peden.

And then, of course, there's Mike Tyson. America Presents is Tyson's promoter of record, and the relationship has been a rocky one. Iron Mike may, or may not, have punched Goossen in a parking lot earlier this year. "That story started with Arum," Goossen says when asked about it. "If I had something to say on the subject, I'd say it."

However, what Goossen does say is, "Signing Mike Tyson was the worst deal I ever made. I've had to become somewhat indifferent to Mike's conduct in order to survive emotionally. And financially, it hasn't been a very good deal for America Presents either. The original contract was for three fights. We'll end up doing six. We get a fixed sum for each fight. The problem is, we're Mike's promoter of record, but basically all we are is a salaried name entity. The deal doesn't allow us to be promoters. We're not part of the decision-making process. There are a lot of things I'd do differently if America Presents was really his promoter but, in truth, we're not. We're not as involved as most people think we are."

Warming to his subject, Goossen continues: "There's nothing worse than being a passenger in a car and getting lost when you know that, if you were driving, you'd get to your destination. I don't like being relegated to the role of hanging up banners at press conferences. But the way the deal is structured, we aren't the ones who are directing the athlete. We know that Tyson's ship isn't heading in the right direction. We made our statement when Mike fought in England and we didn't accompany him. I wouldn't have been standing behind my own values if I'd gone to England. Look, I would have loved the opportunity to really promote Mike Tyson. Unfortunately, we never got it. It turned out to be a bad deal for America Presents. We haven't been able to maximize Mike's income or our own. But the only one I blame for this is myself. The experience has taught me a lot. There's one fight left on our contract and, under the present conditions, we won't renew it."

As for the future, the two biggest promoters in boxing (Don King and Bob Arum) are pushing seventy, and Goossen figures to be around for a while. "We're very good at building up fighters," he says. "David Tua is an example of that. David was a tremendous heavyweight for a long time, but no one except boxing insiders knew or cared. We could have sat back and simply waited for his mandatory challenge to take effect. But instead, we went out and truly promoted him. We took risks and added value to the fighter. In less than a year, we put David's name on the lips of a lot of people, which meant that he was paid more for fighting Lennox Lewis than would have been the case without us. And if he'd won, he would have been worth far more than if we'd never gotten involved."

Meanwhile, Dan Goossen is building a pretty good reputation for himself. He's not a saint, but he's not much of a sinner either. He's a salesman, but he's not a liar. When asked about him, a lot of people who dislike promoters furrow their brow in thought and answer, "I can't think of anything particularly bad to say. I've never had a problem with him."

One person who did have a problem with Goossen was Seth Abraham. Earlier this year, when Abraham was president of HBO Sports, the two men met in New York. "A number of things were building," Abraham remembers. "Tyson, Tua, David Reid. It was a series of events that led to a steamy situation. So when Dan came into my office for a meeting, I refused to shake his hand. Instead, I said something like, 'Let's just do our business and not pretend.'"

Goossen responded with words to the effect of, "If you won't shake my hand, we have no business to discuss." Abraham said he'd decide whether or not to shake hands after the meeting, and Goossen told him that the meeting was over.

"For whatever reason, it seemed important to me at the time," Abraham says, bringing closure to the moment. "In retrospect, I was wrong. Dan and I have shaken hands several times and had several productive discussions since then. The public doesn't care who you're squabbling with. It just wants to see good fights. You have to remind yourself of that if your job is to bring fights to the public. And you also have to remind yourself not to take things personally if you're in the business of boxing."

Meanwhile, life is pretty good for Dan Goossen at the moment. He's the father of two grown children and two young ones from a successful second marriage. He likes his job, and he's happy with where he is in life. "I don't have to be best friends with my fighters," Goossen says in closing. "But I want to have more than a business relationship with them. I want them to know that I care about them as people, and I certainly don't want the relationship to be adversarial like it is between some fighters and their promoters." To which Houseofboxing's Michael Katz adds, "The Goossens understand their fighters and seem care about them. Also, it's worth remembering that there are ten Goossens and they stick together. So if you mess with one, you get all of them."

Over the past two decades, numerous executives have tried to restore Madison Square Garden's status as the "Mecca of Boxing." Kevin Wynne is the latest to try.

Kevin Wynne and the New York Renaissance

On the evening of February 26, 2000, Kevin Wynne (vice president, MSG Sports Properties) sat in his seat at Madison Square Garden and surveyed the late-arriving crowd. Wynne oversees college and high school basketball, track and field, and other special Garden athletic events; but his primary responsibilities involve boxing. He manages the fights from early contract negotiations through the bouts themselves. That involves more than sitting in his office waiting for the telephone to ring. Wynne travels around the country, actively selling his venue to managers, promoters, TV executives, and fighters. His message is simple: "Madison Square Garden is a place where a fighter can jump-start his career or revive his career if he's been thrown off course by a bump in the road."

Now Wynne was presiding over the return of Oscar De La Hoya and Arturo Gatti to Madison Square Garden. The two warriors had last fought in the main arena on December 15, 1995, when Gatti pounded out a twelve-round decision over Tracy Harris Patterson and De La Hoya pulverized Jesse James Leija in two rounds. Since then, Oscar had fought twelve times, earning an estimated $90 million in ring purses. Meanwhile, Gatti had endured more wars than he cared to remember, including returns from the brink of extinction against Wilson Rodriguez and Gabriel Ruelas and losses to Angel Manfredy and, twice, to Ivan Robinson. Indeed, there was a theory that Arturo couldn't be stopped on cuts anymore because he was all out of blood.

Gatti's return to the Garden came against Joey Gamache. Thanks to some questionable maneuvering by officials from the New York State Athletic Commission, Arturo entered the ring at 161 pounds, fifteen pounds heavier than his foe. Joey's fight plan was to survive early and then go to work. But a hard right hand midway through round one put him down and took him completely out of the fight. KO2.

De La Hoya's opponent was Derrell Coley, who talked a good fight beforehand but failed to deliver when it counted. The high-point for Coley came in round four, when he landed a solid right and unloaded a barrage of punches on Oscar. But Oscar unloaded back, and Derrell hardly looked like the number-one contender he was supposed to be. He spent most of the evening on his bike while Oscar tracked him down, beat him up, and eventually knocked him out with a vicious hook to the body in round seven.

Wynne had hoped for more competitive fights, but the fact that the bouts happened at all was an important part of his development plan.

Kevin Wynne was born in Washington, D.C., in 1964. After graduating from law school, he spent five years as an attorney in Baltimore, specializing in tax and business transactions. In the early 1990s, he represented trainer Emanuel Steward in several matters. "I didn't know much about the fight business," Wynne acknowledges. "At the time, I wouldn't even have labeled myself a fan. But Emanuel flew me to my first live fight (the May 1993 bout between Gerald McClellan and Julian Jackson). The scene interested me, and I decided I wanted to get involved in sports law."

In late 1993, Wynne moved to Detroit to work fulltime with Steward. The next few years were spent observing and learning. Then he went to work for IMG, where he was involved in tax planning for some of the world's wealthiest athletes. That was about the time IMG got involved with marketing for Evander Holyfield and Muhammad Ali, and the marketing giant was also considering a direct involvement with boxing itself. Thus, in mid-1998, Wynne was dispatched to Madison Square Garden to meet with Bill Jemas (then executive vice president of MSG Properties) to see if there was a synergy that could lead to a joint venture between the two companies. That meeting led to a job offer to Wynne to leave IMG and spearhead MSG's return to bigtime boxing.

Wynne found Madison Square Garden boxing in a state of decline. And it wasn't just the Garden. It was all of New York. Once upon a time, the city had been the boxing capital of the world. Fight clubs had flourished at venues like Sunnyside Gardens and St. Nicholas Arena. Indeed,

Joe Louis had defended his championship in New York City a total of seventeen times.

But times change. Madison Square Garden hadn't hosted a block-buster fight since Ali-Frazier I. The small clubs were gone. Boxing at Yankee Stadium was a thing of the past. The last regularly scheduled fight cards in Manhattan had ended in 1993.

Fast-forward to the year 2000. Cedric Kushner is now promoting monthly Heavyweight Explosion shows at the Hammerstein Ballroom a block north of the Garden. The New York media is homing in on boxing. And MSG boxing is alive again. Felix Trinidad versus Pernell Whitaker, Holyfield-Lewis I, Roy Jones versus David Telesco at (MSG corporate kin) Radio City Music Hall. And the next big one—Lennox Lewis versus Michael Grant on April 29 for the undisputed heavyweight championship of the world.

"We've made some very good matchups over the past year," Wynne acknowledges. "The fights themselves haven't always been memorable, but we're on the right track and we're looking to go further. Holyfield-Lewis I was particularly important to us because it proved internally and to people on the outside that, even in the current era, the Garden can host big fights."

MSG hasn't been particularly successful with summer fights, so Wynne doesn't expect anything for a while after Lewis-Grant. "Basically, we're looking at the fall of 2000 for our next show," he says. "We'd like to do two more big fights toward the end of the year. Then, realistically, what we're looking at is two or three big fights a year in the main arena and a few more at smaller venues like Radio City Music Hall or The Theatre. Dave Checketts [president and CEO of MSG] is committed to reestablishing the Garden as the premier venue in boxing, so the corporate commitment is there."

Also—and this is significant to the business side of boxing—the Garden is once again considering the possibility of promoting its own fights. At present, it simply rents out the arena or buys rights to the live gate from promoters. But as Wynne notes, "In the current boxing climate, promoters don't have to sell tickets for big fights like they did in the old days. The sites and TV networks do most of the work. That means we're already the driving force behind marketing the big Garden fights, but we don't share in some of the revenue streams that promoters typically share in. If we decide to go in that direction, fighters of the caliber and character of, say, Roy Jones Jr. would be of great interest to us."

Madison Square Garden will always be relevant to boxing. But will it ever be dominant again?

"Time will tell," Wynne answers.

Jim Thomas is another behind-the-scenes player who has considerable influence in boxing by virtue of the fighters he represents.

Jim Thomas

More and more often in recent years, a forty-eight-year-old man with a clean-shaven head has been at Evander Holyfield's press conferences. If he wasn't standing at Holyfield's side, he might go entirely unnoticed. With his quiet laid-back public persona, he could pass for everyman. The look is deceiving.

Jim Thomas grew up in Allentown, Pennsylvania, amidst what he describes as "humble economic origins." "I remember standing on a milk crate at age ten, washing dishes in my grandfather's Pennsylvania Dutch diner," he says with a smile. "I was on line to become a busboy and someday a short-order cook. Then I scored well on a scholastic aptitude test and was admitted to an Opportunity School for Gifted Children run by the local public school system."

That put Thomas on a superstar track from which he has never wavered. A gifted athlete, he was the starting tailback and cornerback on his high school team in the competitive East Penn football league. He was also a championship wrestler, and received scholarship offers from William and Mary, Princeton, Pennsylvania, Cornell, Trinity College, and the University of Virginia. He chose William and Mary, in part because he wanted to play football for its head coach, Marv Levy. Then, before Thomas arrived on campus, Levy left and was succeeded by another future coaching legend: Lou Holtz.

"After one season, I didn't want to play for Holtz anymore," Thomas recalls. "I was in school on an academic scholarship that didn't cover training table and books. The difference between what I was getting and what the other football players were getting was only a few hundred dollars. But given my family's financial situation, that was a lot of money. I'd had a good freshman year, so I went to Holtz and asked for his help. He told me, 'Son, you're already here. We need your books and training table to bring in someone else.' That offended me, so as a matter of principle, I quit."

Several months later, Thomas hurt his shoulder wrestling and was forced to abandon that sport as well. Next, he took up karate and won the Eastern collegiate black-belt championship. Eventually, he journeyed to Japan, where he compiled a 63-0 record in karate competition mixed in with some kick-boxing. Then he returned to William and Mary to study law and graduated second in his class after serving as editor-in-chief of the school law review. From there, he went to Atlanta and joined the fledgling law firm of Long and Aldridge. Twenty-three years later, Long Aldridge and Norman has 195 attorneys and Jim Thomas is co-chairman of its litigation department.

Thomas dabbled in sports during his early years in Atlanta, performing occasional legal chores for Falcon's quarterback Steve Bartkowski, golfer Jan Stephenson, and the Professional Karate Association. Then, in 1990, his life changed radically. Evander Holyfield had just won the heavyweight championship from Buster Douglas, and former Atlanta mayor Andrew Young advised Holyfield to get a top-notch law firm to represent him. Holyfield chose Long and Aldridge; and suddenly, Jim Thomas was at the heart of professional boxing.

"The first order of business," Thomas remembers, "was litigation against Don King and Mike Tyson. The WBC had ruled that the winner of Holyfield-Douglas would be required to make a mandatory defense against Tyson. But Evander had been Buster's mandatory; and Evander wanted to fight George Foreman for twenty million dollars."

King and Tyson sought an injunction; the injunction was denied; and Holyfield won a twelve-round decision over Foreman. Thereafter, Thomas stayed busy litigating on Evander's behalf against adversaries like Riddick Bowe and Rock Newman. He even wound up in court against Foreman, who claimed an oral contract for a Holyfield-Foreman rematch. And his firm restructured Evander's contracts with Shelly Finkel and Main Events.

Meanwhile, Holyfield was doing his thing in the ring—struggling against Bert Cooper, Ray Mercer, and Bobby Czyz; going the distance with Larry Holmes and Alex Stewart; and losing three of four bouts to Riddick Bowe and Michael Moorer.

All of that was prelude to Holyfield-Tyson. "Evander always wanted to fight Tyson," Thomas recalls. "He was very confident about that matchup."

But first, there were the negotiations. "We were in Toronto," Thomas remembers, "Evander and myself, Don King and his lawyers, plus Jay Larkin and Roy Langbord from Showtime. Almost as soon as the negotiations began, Evander told me he wanted to go home. I asked why, and he said it was clear that Don wasn't going to be fair about the money. There was roughly $42,000,000 on the table. Evander was willing to split it two-to-one in Tyson's favor, but Don was holding at three-to-one. So I took Evander aside and told him, 'Look, we have very little leverage here. I thought you understood that.' Evander said he understood, but he still wanted to go home. So I said, 'Okay, we'll go. But let me ask you one thing. Do you truly think you can beat Tyson?' That hurt Evander. He looked at me—I could see the surprise in his eyes—and he told me, 'I thought that, out of all the people in the world, you were the one who knew.' 'I do know,' I told him. 'I just want to make sure that you still know. Because if you're fighting Tyson for one last paycheck, you shouldn't do it unless the money is right. But if you know you can beat him, let's make the fight. Now, how sure are you?'"

"One hundred percent sure," Holyfield answered.

Nineteen hours later, the deal was done. The rest is history.

"I thought Mike Tyson was a great fighter," explains Thomas. "But his style was perfect for Evander. Evander has always done well against aggressive fighters. The strategy against Mike was to hit him, lock him up, turn him. Hit him, lock him up, turn him. You could see Mike getting more and more frustrated, particularly when he felt how physically strong Evander was and understood that Evander wasn't afraid of him. Both times against Tyson, Evander knew for sure that he was going to win."

And what about Holyfield-Lewis? Did Evander "know for sure" that he was going to win then too?

"It wasn't the same kind of feeling," Thomas answers. "When Evander is in character, he's very quiet, not at all braggadocious. That prediction of a third-round knockout bothered me. Evander said it in a moment of pique. He was on one of those teleconference calls with reporters, and someone asked him about a comment Lennox had made. Lennox had called Evander a hypocrite because of the situation with Evander fathering two children out of wedlock. It was a difficult situation; and the fact that it was two children made it ten times worse than if it had been one. Evander knew he had done wrong, but he was aggravated by the use of the term 'hypocrite' because he had admitted his mistake. So he blurted out that he was going to knock Lennox out in the third round. And then he decided, 'Well, if the thought just came to me like that, it must be God's will.'"

Thomas feels that, against Holyfield, Lewis won five rounds by a substantial margin; Evander clearly won one; and the other six were "very close." He attributes much of the controversy that followed the bout to the HBO broadcast, which he describes as "a shameless infomercial for Lennox Lewis." As for the future, he fully expects Holyfield to prevail in a rematch against Lewis this fall.

And after that?

"I don't know," Thomas answers. "That would be a landmark time for Evander to retire. If he continues to fight, there are the mandatory defenses. And Tyson III is a possibility, although that's a fight Evander would be taking just for the money."

Roy Jones Jr.?

"Evander doesn't want to do that," Thomas responds quickly. "Evander had dinner with Roy about a year ago. And he told him, 'Roy, I used to be your size. Fighting as a heavyweight is really really different.' The truth is, Evander just doesn't think it would be a competitive fight."

Meanwhile, Jim Thomas currently devotes roughly two-thirds of his professional life to Evander Holyfield. Evander has been "self-managed" since 1995, when he terminated his contract with Shelly Finkel. Thomas is his advisor and legal representative. Initially, he was paid on an hourly basis. In mid-1996, that changed to a percentage of Holyfield's purses. "A small percentage," adds Thomas. "Right now, Evander has the best bargain of any fighter I know of."

Thomas also now serves as an advisor to heavyweight challenger Michael Grant. Recently, he was named commissioner of a new women's senior golf circuit for LPGA members over age forty. And he spends an increasing amount of time on Holyfield's outside-the-ring ventures. There's a record company, clothing company, restaurant, and charitable foundation, as well as the need to oversee the work of various investment advisors and financial planners. "Evander takes some risks I might not like," Thomas acknowledges. "But he knows what the risks are and chooses to take them because it gives him control where each of his businesses is concerned. Overall, Evander's portfolio is weighted toward solid real estate investments and large cap stocks. By any reasonable standard, he's financially secure for life."

In sum, Jim Thomas is doing for Evander Holyfield what Mike Trainer did for Sugar Ray Leonard and Fred Levin does for Roy Jones Jr. If there's a difference, it's that Thomas came to Holyfield relatively late in the game, whereas Trainer and Levin were with their charges from the start of their respective professional careers. Still, Thomas's services are invaluable.

"I think Jim Thomas is an honorable guy," says Lou DiBella of HBO Sports. "We've been in some difficult situations where we've found ourselves on opposite sides of the negotiating table. But he's a good representative for Evander. His loyalty is to Evander. And let's face it. If a fighter gets to the level of Roy Jones or Oscar De La Hoya or Mike Tyson or Evander Holyfield, there's no need to pay a manager twenty or thirty percent; particularly not a manager who's loyalty is split five different ways and who's in bed with one or more promoters. A lot of fighters would be well-advised to go out and get themselves a Jim Thomas."

HBO has changed the way sports documentaries are made. The man most responsible for that change is Ross Greenburg.

Ross Greenburg and
Sports of the 20th Century

On August 17, HBO will premiere the latest in a decade-long line of documentaries known as *Sports of the 20th Century*.

"Ali-Frazier I: One Nation . . . Divisible" revisits a fight that can truly be called the "Fight of the Century." The bout, which occurred on March 8, 1971, featured two fighters, both undefeated, each with a legitimate claim to the heavyweight championship of the world. But Ali-Frazer I was more than a prizefight. It was an event of extraordinary social and political importance. Everyone in America—and indeed, the world—seemed to be taking sides. There was no middle ground.

Now HBO tells the story of how Frazier won the battle but lost the war. It's an ambitious project, but the documentary succeeds admirably. First, it sets the stage with insightful commentary and wonderful archival footage. Then there's the fight itself. Fifteen glorious rounds. And the undertaking is particularly strong when it recounts the drama from Joe Frazier's personal point of view.

This was the bout where Ali branded Frazier an Uncle Tom and sought to characterize him as an ignorant house nigger. "I swallowed a lot of razor blades," Joe says reflecting back on the hurt of those times. "And sometimes they cut inside."

Joe's son, Marvis, elaborates on that hurt and anger. Recounting how his father prayed in the dressing room before the bout, Marvis remembers, "I asked him, 'What did you pray?' He told me, 'God, help me to kill this man, because he's not righteous.'"

Journalistic ethics require that a columnist reveal any interest he has in the subject matter he's writing about, so I should note here that I'm one of the "talking heads" on screen in the documentary. I was also a paid consultant to the project. Having said that, I should add that I wish I could

A BEAUTIFUL SICKNESS

take credit for the finished product, but I can't. That goes to HBO, Joseph Lavine (who served as producer), the entire production staff, and Ross Greenburg.

Greenburg is best known to boxing fans as the executive producer of HBO's boxing telecasts, but his reach extends well into other areas of the HBO empire. Born in Texas in 1955, he grew up in the white collar suburb of Scarsdale, New York. After graduating from Brown in 1977, he worked for ABC Sports on a freelance basis for eight months. Then he was told that he wouldn't be offered permanent employment. "So I went to the Greenwich Public Library," he remembers, "looked up 'sports cable' in some directories, and came up with a company called HBO. I fired off a blind resume, got an interview, and was hired as a production assistant."

The world of cable was different in 1978. HBO was in five hundred thousand homes and had a total staff of ninety people, only three of them in the sports department. By contrast, there are now eleven hundred employees in HBO's New York office alone and the network reaches twenty-eight million homes.

Shortly after starting, Greenburg became HBO's "associate producer" for sports. "But it wasn't really a promotion," he explains. "There were only two of us in production." He is now senior vice president and executive producer for HBO Sports with a number of accomplishments to his credit, but he's proudest of the network's *Sports of the 20th Century* documentary series.

HBO Sports had produced documentaries in the 1980s, but in 1990 it embarked upon something new. "I'd just seen the Ken Burns documentary on the Civil War," Greenburg remembers. "It was superb, and I asked myself why it was that sports documentaries seemed to throw footage and interviews against the wall with no rhyme or reason."

"When It Was A Game" (about major league baseball in the 1930s and 1940s) was HBO's next documentary effort. It marked a turning point for the network and launched a new style for HBO—putting sound effects to film, using actors to voice over, and commissioning original music. But the key to it all was the massive amount of new material involved. "In addition to everything else," Greenburg recalls, "we combed the attics of America and came up with a treasure trove of original footage. That meant we were able to show people Babe Ruth and Lou

Gehrig in color. It was like we were giving our viewers a new kind of eyesight. Toward the end of production, I gathered the staff together and told them, 'Guys, savor every second of what we're going through because we'll never experience anything like this again.' We knew we'd created something special."

"Ali-Frazier I: One Nation ... Divisible" is the twenty-seventh documentary in HBO's *Sports of the 20th Century* series. To date, the programs have won eighteen Sports Emmy Awards and assorted other honors. Greenburg has final say over the subject matter of each documentary. "We look for subjects with greater meaning than the individual personality or event that we're covering," he explains. "We want subjects where the American public says, 'Wow, that looks interesting; tell us more.' We ask ourselves, 'Is this story compelling; does it have a dramatic arc?' In the end, we go on gut instinct; and so far, our instincts have been pretty good."

Many of HBO's documentaries have been intertwined with the 1960s. "That's because the sixties are fertile territory for any sports historian," says Greenburg. "Sports was a great backdrop for the turbulence of those times, and it's a privilege to document the era."

In keeping with HBO's emphasis on boxing, *Sports of the 20th Century* productions have also included "Sugar Ray Robinson: The Bright Lights and Dark Shadows of a Champion," "Sonny Liston: The Mysterious Life and Death of a Champion," "In This Corner: Boxing's Little Giants," and "In This Corner: Boxing's Legendary Heavyweights" in addition to "Ali-Frazier I: One Nation ... Divisible."

"We've never given any of our subjects one second of editorial control," Greenberg continues. "They don't get to see rough cuts. They don't tell us who we can, or can't, interview. Bill Russell approached us and said he'd decided that it was time for him to speak to the American people and tell them his story. That was the only time one of our documentaries originated with the subject. But I green lit Johnny Unitas before he decided to speak with us. We did DiMaggio without ever getting DiMaggio's cooperation." A look of bemusement crosses Greenburg's face. "So many adjectives have been thrown at DiMaggio. Aloof, mythical, unique. You can add 'strange' to the list. Like I said, he wouldn't cooperate with us; but when the documentary was complete, he asked for a tape. I sent it to him along with a poster for the show. Then he asked for fifty-five more posters, and we sent them to him. After he died, I saw that eBay was selling our posters from a so-called 'limited edition' of fifty-six, each one of them signed by DiMaggio."

HBO now produces four *Sports of the 20th Century* documentaries annually. Subjects currently in production include "Sex and Sports in American Society"; the 1972 United States Olympic Hockey Team; and the 1951 National League pennant race between the New York Giants and Brooklyn Dodgers that ended with Bobby Thomson's miracle home run. The average *Sports of the 20th Century* television premiere attracts viewers in approximately 1,250,000 homes. But as Greenburg notes, "Ratings are less important to us than branding. After all, you have to remember our message to the world: 'It's not TV; it's HBO.'"

As a general rule, Showtime plays Avis to HBO's Hertz. The man in charge of that uphill battle is Jay Larkin.

Jay Larkin

Jay Larkin carries a weighty title: "Senior Vice President, Sports & Event Programming, Showtime Networks, Inc." That means he's responsible for all of Showtime's boxing telecasts. But the forty-nine-year-old Larkin is hardly your typical television sports executive.

Born in Brooklyn, Larkin grew up on Long Island and was drawn to theater as his first professional love. His education credits include stints at the Boston Conservatory of Music and UCLA School of Theater, Film and Television, as well as a degree in theater and directing from C.W. Post. He has played the lead in a national tour of *Hair*, and been part of such Broadway productions as *Sweeney Todd* and *Sunday in the Park with George*. TV soap opera devotees might remember him from his roles on *All My Children* and *The Doctors*. For good measure, he has sung in an a cappella doo-wop group.

Larkin began working at Showtime in 1984. He is now Viacom's version of Seth Abraham, Lou DiBella, and Ross Greenberg rolled into one. But his budget is a lot smaller than that of his HBO counterparts, and Showtime has come in for its share of criticism on a number of fronts.

For starters, there's the perception in some circles that Showtime's production values are somehow inferior to those of HBO.

"I find that infuriating and heartbreaking," Larkin says in response. "HBO does very high quality work most of the time, and we do very high quality work most of the time. Their cameramen can't be any better than ours, because we use the same cameramen. Their sound people can't be any better than ours, because we use the same sound people. I'll match Steve Albert, Ferdie Pacheco, Bobby Czyz, and Jim Gray against the HBO commentators anytime."

Well and good. But there's also the matter of Showtime's association with Don King. For almost ten years, Don King Productions was the sole supplier of boxing to the network. That monopoly ended recently when Showtime began taking fights from other promoters on a card-by-card basis. But DKP will still provide the network with a dozen regular shows in 1999 plus an undetermined number of bouts on pay-per-view. A lot of people feel that Showtime has been saddled with inferior fights as a consequence of its reliance on Don King.

"Not so," says Larkin. "The decision to go exclusively with Don was a de facto process that came about as a result of the limitations of our budget. Don had Mike Tyson; Mike Tyson was the center of the boxing universe; and we could afford Mike Tyson by dealing with Don. In essence, we gave Don a budget for a given number of fights per year, and Don provided us with shows subject to our approval. Sure, we've had some bad fights over the years, but we've also had our share of great ones. And if you look at the competition—Oscar De La Hoya versus Patrick Charpentier, Roy Jones against Ricky Frazier—the competition has had its share of stiffs, too."

Which brings us to the present. Larkin isn't entirely pleased with the current situation. "Don has two fighters in the public consciousness," he notes: "Evander Holyfield and Felix Trinidad. And we're now watching both of those fighters on HBO. I won't lie to you; we're not happy about it. But I don't think we can blame Don. At Showtime, we deal with promoters. Except for Mike Tyson, we don't have a long-term contract with any fighter. HBO, on the other hand, has locked in a number of fighters, including Oscar De La Hoya and Lennox Lewis. So if Felix wants to fight Oscar and Evander wants to fight Lennox in order to fulfill their respective goals as athletes, there's really no place else for them to go but HBO. Don has had a long relationship with Showtime," Larkin continues. "And that relationship is still a work in progress. Like any marriage of volatile personalities, we've had our ups and downs. But overall, the relationship has been productive and uncontentious, and Don remains an important supplier to this network. In fact, I'll go a step further and say that, as strange as it might sound, if I was in trouble and needed to call someone for help, Don would be at the top of the list. He's not a saint. But believe in him, give him the benefit of the doubt, be fair with him, and Don will respond in kind. In a business situation, Don is a very difficult adversary, but he's my friend."

Meanwhile, if all goes as Larkin plans, the star of Showtime boxing entering the next millennium will be Mike Tyson.

"When Tyson is fighting," says Larkin, "everything else stops. I'm not saying that the relationship is free of problems. Working with Mike Tyson can be frustrating and aggravating. The most difficult part is the unpredictability. But the Tyson world is very dramatic and it's exciting as hell. If you're in boxing, you want a presence. And there's no bigger presence in boxing than Mike Tyson."

By all accounts, Jay Larkin is a good guy. In fact, noted curmudgeon Michael Katz goes a step further, saying, "Jay Larkin is a terrific guy. He's had his hands tied because he's never had the freedom or the budget to compete with HBO. But he's caring; he's honest; he's intensely loyal. Hey, do you know Jay Larkin's wife? How many guys in boxing are married to a ballet dancer?"

Meanwhile, Larkin continues to savor both the good and the bad of his profession. Sometimes, they occur simultaneously. "One of the worst moments of my life," he recalls, "was when they stopped the second Holyfield–Tyson fight. It was shaping up as such a tremendous fight, and the way it ended was terrible. I felt cheated. I was angry at Tyson. But that moment triggered something extraordinary. Right then in the truck, we stopped being presenters of a boxing match and became reporters of news. We were as objective and as thorough as any news organization could have been under those circumstances. I'm very proud of the way we handled ourselves that night. It was Showtime's finest hour."

Not long after I wrote my profile of Jay Larkin, Showtime made some significant changes. It started signing fighters to long-term contracts, and it axed Ferdie Pacheco.

Ferdie Pacheco Moves On

On June 3, 2000, Showtime began a month of heavily-promoted heavyweight boxing with David Tua versus Obed Sullivan, live from Las Vegas. Shortly after the bout ended, Jay Larkin (Showtime's senior vice president for sports and event programming) asked Ferdie Pacheco if he could speak with him in private. Pacheco is on the far side of seventy years old. He rose to fame as Muhammad Ali's ring physician in the 1960s and '70s, and had been Showtime's on-camera boxing analyst for fourteen years.

The two men retired to what Pacheco later described as a makeshift alley between TV trucks and the exterior of the building where Tua–Sullivan had just occurred.

"This is the worst thing I've ever had to do," Pacheco remembers Larkin telling him. "Tonight was your last regular broadcast."

"After fourteen years of working for Showtime," Pacheco said later, "my end came in a mugging in an alley. And I was completely alone. My wife wasn't with me. Nobody in the crew knew. It was one of the worst nights of my life. People are always getting run over and left for dead in boxing. Mostly, it happens to other people. That night, it happened to me."

Ferdie Pacheco's first appearance as a television analyst came on November 18, 1977, when Leon Spinks battled to a ten-round draw against Alfio Righetti. The bout was broadcast on CBS, and Pacheco's broadcasting partner was Brent Musberger. Three months later, Pacheco was behind the microphone again when Spinks successfully challenged Ali for the heavyweight crown. Then, in 1980, he moved to NBC as the network's de facto boxing czar. He made the fights, and he commentated on them. That struck some as a conflict of interest and there was grumbling about a Duva–Duff–Pacheco triangle, but Ferdie's public persona kept growing.

Throughout the 1980s, Pacheco was paired at NBC with Marv Albert. "Marv was great," says Ferdie. He was the guy—the only guy—who taught me about broadcasting. I thought all a TV analyst had to do was get behind the microphone and talk. Boy, did Marv teach me a thing or two."

Albert, for his part, responds in kind, saying, "Working with Ferdie was a terrific experience. I admired his passion for boxing. He had a different way of looking at the sport, and we just clicked."

Together, the tandem of Albert and Pacheco covered two Olympics and countless professional fights. "But it's strange," Pacheco remembers. "My most vivid memory as a TV analyst is a tragic one. I was in Montreal for the first Leonard–Duran fight. Cleveland Denny was on the undercard fighting Gaetan Hart. Denny got knocked out, and you could see right away that he was in serious trouble. For some reason, there was no physician at ringside, so I left the microphone to do what I could as a doctor to help him. He lingered for a while after that, but for all intents and purposes, he died in my arms that night."

My own relationship with Ferdie Pacheco began in 1989. I'd been chosen by Muhammad Ali and his wife to author what we hoped would be the definitive Ali biography. I'd begun work on the project and had compiled a list of two hundred people I wanted to interview. Because of his role as Ali's ring physician, Ferdie was among them.

Competition is a funny thing among writers. During the course of my research, I encountered many literary lights who had written or were contemplating Ali projects of their own. Some of those authors refused to talk with me about Ali, saying that we were competitors and they didn't want me to steal their thunder. Others were extraordinarily generous with their time and knowledge. Ferdie fit into the latter category. Even though he'd written one Ali book and was planning another, he sat with me for hours. *Muhammad Ali: His Life and Times*—and hence, the historical Ali record—is more complete because of Ferdie's gracious cooperation. And I came away from my Ali endeavor with the belief that there are two men who followed Ali from the beginning until the end of his ring career, who know what happened and have the ability to put it all in proper historical context. One of those men is Jerry Izenberg. The other is Ferdie Pacheco.

Meanwhile, Pacheco's dismissal sounds a disquieting note for the future of televised boxing. It was a painful end, although, in truth, one could see it coming. Over the past few years, Ferdie's role on Showtime's boxing telecasts had been dwindling. First, Jim Gray took over the post-bout interviews with fighters. Then Bobby Czyz was given the task of breaking down fight strategy before each bout. "It was like a series of amputations," Pacheco acknowledges. "First, they took a toe; then a foot; then my leg up to the knee. After a while, you're tempted to say, 'Why not get it over with.'"

The reasons for Pacheco's dismissal are unclear. Showtime executives have said privately that they felt he'd begun to slip a bit behind the microphone. But Ferdie understands boxing well and remains a first-rate communicator. Thus, one has to look to other factors. Personal tensions within the Showtime family are one possible contributing cause. It's also not beyond the realm of reason that the powers that be at Showtime were unhappy with Pacheco's penchant for calling a mismatch a mismatch before, during, and after each such bout. But one would have to be pretty foolish not to consider another motivation. More and more often these days, television is looking to project a "young" image. And that means old-time "boxing guys" like Gil Clancy and veteran commentators like Al Bernstein are being pushed aside to make room for folks like Max Kellerman, Ed Lover, and Fran Charles. Maybe that makes for higher ratings. And let's face it; on occasion, new blood is good, particularly if it's new blood like Teddy Atlas. But as far as a full appreciation of boxing by the general public is concerned, something is being lost in the process.

Pacheco maintains that he didn't have a written contract with Showtime. It was a handshake agreement for twelve shows per year. Regardless, Showtime says it will honor its financial obligations for the remainder of 2000. Ferdie will do spot promotional work for the duration of his contract, and the network will also televise a Pacheco project—*The Twelve Greatest Rounds in Boxing History*—later this year.

As for what comes after that, Pacheco has no intention of retiring. After all, he's a Renaissance man in the truest sense of the word. During the course of his life, he has been a physician, an artist, and the author of eleven books running the gamut from novels and short stories to cooking and art. He's fluent in Spanish, can get by in Italian. And, oh yes, he's still a pretty good boxing analyst. So who knows where Ferdie Pacheco might show up next as a television commentator.

Meanwhile, Pacheco surveys the scene and says simply, "I look back at it all and consider myself a very lucky guy. Television has allowed me to stay in a sport I love dearly for another twenty years of my life. What could be better than traveling all over the world and seeing a good fight from a front-row seat at the end of each trip? I've been incredibly blessed. Are my feelings hurt by being fired? Of course, they are; and right now, my vanity doesn't feel so good either. But Showtime brought me great joy for fourteen years, and there's really nothing I can do or say except to wish everyone there the best in the future."

To many knowledgeable observers, the glue that holds HBO's boxing telecasts together is Jim Lampley. In January 2000, I viewed Roy Jones versus David Telesco through his eyes.

Roy Jones and Jim Lampley: One Night, Two Professionals

Shortly after 9:45 on the evening of January 15, HBO viewers heard an authoritative yet pleasing and familiar voice: "Since Radio City Music Hall first opened its doors back in 1932, more than three hundred million people have witnessed concerts, theatrical performances, and the Rockettes on the giant stage. Tonight . . ."

The occasion was Roy Jones Jr. versus David Telesco, headlining the first athletic competition ever held at Radio City Music Hall. The site, which opened at the height of the Great Depression, was once the largest indoor theater in the world. It may still be the most spectacular thanks to a recent $70,000,000 renovation. The event was sold out. It was HBO's first boxing telecast of the new millennium. And Jim Lampley was on the air.

Lampley's journey to the ranks of sportscasting's elite began in his home state of North Carolina. He did his undergraduate and graduate work at the University of North Carolina, and graduated with a masters in communications in 1974. Then, luck being the residue of design, Lampley got lucky. ABC wanted to hire an announcer who was close to college age for sideline reporting on its college football broadcasts. There were national auditions and Lampley prevailed. At age twenty-five, he was on network television.

Lampley spent twelve years at ABC, upgrading to football play-by-play, spanning the globe for *Wide World of Sports,* and handling blow-by-blow commentary for professional boxing after Howard Cosell abandoned the sport. In 1987, he moved to CBS where, in addition to sports, he co-anchored the evening news for KCBS in Los Angeles. Then it was on to NBC for NFL football, Wimbledon, and the Olympics. He began calling fights for HBO in March 1988, and has been doing it ever since.

Asked for his "best moment" in boxing, Lampley cites two occasions.

"The night George Foreman knocked out Michael Moorer, as Moorer was being counted out, I asked myself why I wasn't the kind of announcer who sits down before a fight and thinks of lines to use in the event of a major occurrence. You know, 'Do you believe in miracles?' That sort of thing. Then the count hit ten; it was an extraordinarily powerful moment. And what came out of my mouth was, 'It happened! . . . It happened!' I think that was pretty good. And perversely," Lampley continues, "the other moment that comes to mind was at the end of the first Holyfield-Lewis fight when Jimmy Lennon announced the third judge's scorecard. The impact was just starting to sink in when Ross Greenberg (then the executive producer of HBO Sports) said three words to me from the control truck: 'Go for it.' That gave me a good feeling because it confirmed what I've always felt: that HBO values honesty and objectivity in covering fights, and that it trusts me to provide them."

And Lampley's worst moment?

"Holyfield-Moorer I," he acknowledges. "I try to discipline myself not to root when I call a fight. If I do, it affects my call, so I try to root for the fight to be exciting; that's all. But that night, I let my heart get to me. I had such admiration for Evander as a fighter and as a person that I miscalled the last few rounds. I knew it, and I think a lot of people who watched the telecast that night knew it."

Lampley's most important pre-fight preparation is the sum total of the experiences and impressions that he has accumulated over the years. Beyond that, HBO sends him tapes and a large clipping file on each boxer before every fight. On the morning of Jones-Telesco, he had breakfast with HBO executive vice president Lou DiBella. Then he went back to his hotel room, and spent the next four hours reviewing the written material HBO had sent him earlier in the week and thinking about points he might make on the air that night. At 3:00 P.M., he went for a walk and bought a new tuxedo shirt. An hour later, he returned to the hotel, put on his tuxedo, and walked over to Radio City Music Hall. "Whitney Houston is singing 'God Bless America' before the main event," he explained. "She's rehearsing now, and I have an urge to meet her."

Meanwhile, the night's telecast had been carefully broken down by HBO's production team into thirty-five segments. A welcome by New York City mayor Rudy Giuliani had been taped the night before. Roy Jones's opening of the show onstage with a dozen Rockettes had been rehearsed. Cameras were in the lobby to record arriving celebrities, including the cast of *The Sopranos*. Everything was scripted into precisely-calibrated time segments except the fights.

Derrick Jefferson versus David Izon was HBO's opening fight, and it was a strange bout, a slugfest with Jefferson doing most of the slugging. For seven rounds, he beat up on Izon, winning every round and throwing his best shots with abandon. In round seven, the pummeling was so bad that Lampley opined, "This is available for a stoppage any time." Larry Merchant added, "The fight should be stopped; David Izon is taking too much punishment." And George Foreman said simply, "I agree." That made it unanimous. Then, in round eight, Jefferson punched himself out and fell to the floor, more from exhaustion than any punch. He survived to the bell and made it eleven seconds into round nine before succumbing. In truth, it was a curiously unsatisfying ending. Izon did little to turn the tide of the bout in his favor other than survive. Jefferson, in effect, knocked himself out.

Then came the main event. In one corner, Roy Jones Jr., the undefeated undisputed light-heavyweight champion of the world, pound-for-pound, the best boxer on earth. And in the other corner, David Telesco from Port Chester, New York, with a record of 23 wins, 2 losses, and 19 KOs.

Telesco had gone through the pre-fight rituals with an attitude. Part of that was the result of his feeling disrespected by HBO, which had put only Jones's image on the early newspaper advertisements and fight posters. ("I know he's the champ," Telesco grumbled, "but he's fighting someone.") And part of it appeared to come naturally to him. After all, this is a man who not long ago spent three years in prison for dealing cocaine, which gave rise to the question, "What is your definition of hard time: three years incarceration or listening to Murad Muhammad talk for ninety minutes at a press conference?" Regardless, Telesco showed up for the final pre-fight press conference wearing a reversible mink-and-leather jacket, showy sunglasses, and a enough gold jewelry to make Don King jealous. "We all make mistakes in life," he told reporters by way of explaining his criminal conviction. "Some of us get caught, and some don't."

As for the fight itself, Telesco might be the toughest guy in Port Chester, but Roy Jones Jr. is the best fighter in the world. There's a difference. Fans at Radio City Music Hall were treated to the usual array of Jones artistry, some of it, the champion later claimed, occasioned by the fact that he'd broken his left hand in a motorcycle accident three and one-half weeks before the fight. There was dancing, lightning-fast punching, a vicious body attack. And as he's done in the past, at times Jones turned southpaw, which is a little like Michelangelo (who was a natural southpaw) painting the ceiling of the Sistine Chapel with his right hand.

Telesco brawled in spots. His best moments came when Jones retreated to a corner and the challenger threw punches in bunches. On a number of those occasions, he also used his head as a weapon. And in round eight, he threw a flagrant elbow, which drew shouts of "elbow" from the crowd, although referee Arthur Mercante appeared not to notice. Telesco should have brawled more. The only way he could possibly have beaten Jones was to make a street fight out of it and take his chances. He was going to get hit anyway, so why not go for it. But whenever he tried, he took a lot of punishment. As the fight progressed, staying on his feet became a matter of honor for Telesco. And although Jones won every round on the scorecards of all three judges, he couldn't knock the challenger down. Everything considered, it was probably Telesco's best fight. It's a measure of Roy Jones's dominance that an opponent can lose every round to him and come out of the fight with increased market value.

Simply put, it was another great performance by Roy Jones Jr. and another seamless night for one of the best announcers in sports, ending with the sign-off: "For Larry Merchant, George Foreman, and Harold Lederman, I'm Jim Lampley saying so long from Radio City Music Hall in New York City."

Harold Lederman is living every boxing fan's dream.

Harold Lederman

It's March 11, 2000, in London. Prince Naseem Hamed is defending his title against Vuyani Bungu in a bout televised by HBO. At the start of round four, HBO blow-by-blow commentator Jim Lampley asks a question that seems innocent on its face: "Harold Lederman, how do you have it scored?" At which point, viewers are treated to a shouting nasal voice that makes Dick Vitale seem calm and Howard Cosell sound like Mozart.

"JIM!!! THREE TO NOTHING; THIRTY TO TWENTY-SEVEN, PRINCE NASEEM HAMED. YOU KNOW, JIM . . ."

Harold Lederman is doing his thing.

Lederman was born on January 26, 1940, and grew up in the Bronx. His father was a pharmacist who owned a small drug store.

"My father had two passions," Lederman remembers. "Theater and boxing. Each year when I was growing up, we'd go out to the Rockaways and rent a house on the beach for the summer. The next town over was Long Beach, where they had fights every Friday night. My father would go with his friends. They'd throw me in the back of the car. Teddy Brenner was the matchmaker, and I saw some great fights. Sandy Saddler, Tommy Bell, Paddy DeMarco, Roland LaStarza. That's where my love of boxing started."

After graduating from high school, Lederman followed in the footsteps of his father, grandfather, and uncles on both sides of the family by entering a four-year pharmacy program at Columbia University. The school was located at Broadway and 68th Street, several miles from Columbia's main campus, but only two blocks from boxing's famed St. Nicholas Arena.

"I became a regular at the fights," says Lederman, "and I always kept score. Then, in 1963, I got married, and my father-in-law was an inspector for the New York State Athletic Commission so I asked him about becoming a judge. He told me to go down to the commission and apply for a license, but the commission said I needed more experience, so I went to the amateurs."

From 1965 through 1967, Lederman judged amateur tournaments. Then, in June 1967, he got his professional license.

"They had shows almost every Friday night at the Audubon Ballroom, where Malcolm X had been assassinated," Lederman continues. "It was on 165th Street and Broadway; and to be honest, a lot of judges didn't want to go there because it wasn't the safest neighborhood in the world but I didn't mind. So that's where I made my pro debut, and I got sent there almost every Friday night."

Thirty-three years later, after judging an estimated six hundred shows and attending thousands of fights as a fan, Harold Lederman is still hooked on boxing. His most memorable moment came in 1976, when he, Barney Smith, and Arthur Mercante awarded Muhammad Ali a unanimous decision over Ken Norton in Ali–Norton III. "I had it dead even going into the last round," he says, "and I gave the last round to Ali. I got a lot of criticism on that one. My phone didn't stop ringing for a month, but I still think we were right."

Then, in 1986, Lederman's boxing stock skyrocketed. "I was at home watching Tim Witherspoon versus Tony Tubbs on television," he remembers. "And what the commentators were saying and what I was watching on the screen were two different things. So I telephoned Ross Greenburg [then the executive producer of HBO Sports] and told him he needed someone to score the fights. Ross said he'd call me, and I figured that was the end of it. You know how those things are. But two weeks later, I was behind the pharmacy counter at work when Ross called and asked, 'Harold, how would you like to work a show?' I knew there'd be some criticism of my doing it because I was still an active judge. But New York wasn't doing much boxing at the time, and I figured what the heck."

Lederman made his television debut in Las Vegas at the Pinklon Thomas versus Trevor Berbick WBC heavyweight championship fight. "Thomas was a heavy favorite," he remembers. "Everyone figured he'd knock Berbick out in two rounds and that would be the end of my TV career, but I got lucky. For the first and only time in Berbick's career, Eddie Futch was in his corner. Somehow, Eddie managed to teach Berbick enough tricks to go twelve rounds and win the fight. And I gotta tell you, every time I see Eddie Futch, I tell him, 'Eddie, I owe my career to you.'"

Harold Lederman is now a star of sorts, and the secret to his success is simple. With most television commentators, there's a sense that something separates them from the rest of us. Jock credentials, special knowledge, fluent diction, good looks. But Harold is "everyman." He could be any one of us.

"Harold is Harold," says HBO boxing analyst Larry Merchant. "Sometimes, I disagree with him on scoring. I'm inclined to lean toward the guy who's doing the most damage; the guy who puts the most hurt on the other guy in a given round. Harold puts a different cast on it, but he knows what he's doing. He's consistent, and he absolutely loves boxing. Harold is the kind of guy who shows up for the weigh-in early and stays late. He'll go anywhere at any time for any fight, and he's filled with wonder for it all."

Jim Lampley echoes Merchant and says, "Nobody cares more; nobody has seen more; and nobody would go to the ends of the earth for a fight more willingly and joyously than Harold Lederman. His enthusiasm for boxing is a supernatural force."

And HBO Sports executive vice president Lou DiBella adds, "As strange as this might sound, Harold has actually become a cult figure. He's enormously popular with our viewers and he deserves it, because he's a perfect goodwill ambassador for boxing."

So there you have it. Harold Lederman is a nice guy, and Harold Lederman loves boxing. His celebrity status is fun for him. It opens doors, but isn't so overwhelming as to become a burden on his privacy. Except for his television gig, he no longer judges fights. After the recent IBF indictments, the higher-ups at HBO suggested that he cut his ties with the sport's outside power brokers and Harold complied. But he can still often be found behind the pharmacy counter at the Shoprite supermarket in Carmel, New York, where he works as a registered pharmacist. And if you engage him in conversation, be prepared for some thoughts on "clean punching, effective aggressiveness, defense, and ring generalship." Because, first and foremost, Harold Lederman is a fan.

"Judging on HBO has gone ten times further for me than I imagined it would in my wildest dreams," Lederman says in closing. "And I love every minute of it. I love going to the fights. I love spending time with boxing people. I love it when I walk through a hotel lobby and total strangers stop to talk boxing with me. I gotta tell you something. I'm a very lucky guy."

Arthur Curry is one of many people behind the scenes who keep HBO Boxing running smoothly. But his story is more compelling than most.

Arthur Curry

Arthur Curry was born in Harlem on February 18, 1960. His life began in a single-parent home with his mother and two older sisters. A younger brother was born in 1962.

"I have no idea what my mother did," Curry says, reflecting on his early childhood. "She was just a lady I saw from time to time. And I met my father once in my life, when I was in a foster home."

When Arthur was four, he and his siblings were placed in separate foster care facilities. Two years later, his natural mother was brutally murdered. Not long after that, his father drank himself to death.

For twelve years, Arthur Sheppard (which was his name as a child) moved from home to home. Looking back, he recalls, "I was in group homes; I lived with families; I stayed with friends. There was a lot of pain. But one thing I remember was, every summer, the foster agency sent us to a summer camp, where they had arts and crafts, chess, canoeing, activities like that. And each year, that camp gave me a vision of hope, a belief that life could be better than what I was going through. So even at a young age, I felt there was a better way."

The defining moment for Arthur Sheppard came at age sixteen. A jazz singer named Edward Curry and his wife Lise (an investment advisor) wanted to adopt a newborn child. But Arthur's social worker prevailed upon them to adopt Arthur.

"For the first time in my life," Curry remembers, "there was someone who had confidence in me and believed in me. I experienced love for the first time, and everything changed. Without my new parents, I don't know what would have happened to me. Before them, I'd been in constant pain. I'd always felt that I had an inner beauty, but I'd never had a foundation to build on. There was so much I had to make up for, and they opened a whole new world for me. School had always been a matter of survival; that's all. But they taught me to rededicate myself. I graduated from high school. Then I enrolled at Fashion Institute of Technology, because I'd always been interested in art. And when I turned twenty-one, I changed my name to Curry. That was important; it erased a lot of negatives. I wanted to honor my parents, and I was proud to be a Curry."

At age twenty, Arthur Curry took a part-time job in the mailroom at what was then Time-Life. Three years later, Curt Viebranz (a Time-Life vice president) took a mentoring interest in the soft-spoken young man who delivered his mail and suggested he move to the company's art department, where Curry spent the next six years. In 1989, at the suggestion of Seth Abraham, he moved to HBO Sports as a production assistant. "I had great teachers at HBO," Curry acknowledges. "Seth Abraham, Janet Indelli, Lou DiBella. They gave their heart and soul to educate me."

In 1996, Curry assumed his present position as manager of HBO's Sports Talent Relations. Officially, his primary responsibility is described in the corporate manual as "building and maintaining relationships with boxers, support staff, and entourage." Beyond that, he acts as a goodwill ambassador for HBO at various charity events, is actively involved in HBO's "Reaching Beyond The Ring" community program, serves on the board of directors of the Retired Boxers Foundation, and keeps his finger in creative design. But it's in his friendships with boxers that Curry shines most brightly.

"Very few people understand how much Artie does for the fighters," says Lou DiBella. "To the fighters, Artie's not a suit; he's their friend. He cares deeply about them and really tries to find out what they need. Even though he works for HBO, they know he has their best interests at heart."

Curry describes his role as follows: "I'm the hands-on guy with the fighters. Whatever they need, I'm there for them. Part of it is entertainment, taking them to ballgames, shooting pool. But it's also listening to them, helping them. I've been a fighter all my life, so I understand these guys. I'm real with people all the time, so the people who know me trust me. That's the strength of my position."

Curry's work intensifies in the days before an HBO bout. That's when fighters are most on edge, their needs are greatest, and they're likely to be a bit suspicious of someone who's friendly with the other side. "I've learned to stand back," Arthur says, explaining how he handles the tensions of those times. "The guys know I'm there if they want me, but I don't force myself on them. I go into both dressing rooms before and after the fight. During the fight, I don't root for either guy. When you care about both fighters, you just have to look at it as a business and hope that no one gets hurt. The most difficult fight for me to watch was Arturo Gatti against Ivan Robinson, both times. And there's a special place in my heart for Roy Jones. I love Roy; I can see myself growing old with him. But there's so many guys I care about that I don't want to start naming names, because I'm sure I'd forget a name and leave someone out."

Roy Jones, for his part, responds in kind, saying, "Artie Curry is one of the best friends a person could have. He does his job. He's a true professional. But he's a whole lot more than that. Sometimes, when it feels like the whole world is against me, Artie will say, 'Look, brother, keep your head high; do what's right and everything will be okay.' And he tells me what he thinks is right, whether or not he agrees with me, which is the way friends should be. Artie is never this way today and another way tomorrow. There's no slippin' and slidin', no games, just straight-up real honesty. The man is family. Artie Curry is a blessing to me."

So that's Arthur Curry. A remarkable man, and a very lucky man because he is able to pursue causes he's passionate about and follow the rhythms of his heart. He is embraced by some of the finest athletes in the world, and he regards them as some of the finest people in the world. Their relationship is more than business. They're friends.

There are a lot of negatives in professional boxing. Arthur Curry is on the positive side of the ledger.

Ron Borges knows his trade as well as any boxing writer in the country.

Ron Borges

Ron Borges was out on a limb. Mike Tyson was about to do battle with Evander Holyfield for the first time, and Borges was the only major boxing writer in the country picking Holyfield to win.

What could have occasioned such insanity?

"I was talking with Evander about a week before the fight," Borges explained later. "And Evander asked me with genuine puzzlement in his voice, 'Why would you try to intimidate someone who can't be intimidated?' That did it for me. I told myself, 'I might look very foolish when this is over, but I think this guy is going to win.'"

Ron Borges doesn't look foolish often. He was born in 1949, and grew up on Martha's Vineyard, where he delivered Red Smith's groceries when the dean of American sportswriters summered on the island. Currently, he covers boxing for the *Boston Globe*.

Borges is more than a reporter. He's a writer who can put his stories in context. "My mom and dad drilled a message into me to love words," he says, recounting his journey. "And they taught me to remember that there's a world beyond the arena of fun and games."

As for boxing, "We didn't have a television when I was growing up," Borges recalls. "But I used to go over to a neighbor's house and watch Friday night fights. I fought a little as a kid, starting when I was about twelve. They weren't formal amateur fights. We'd put up a makeshift ring on someone's lawn or the street and wear headgear and gloves. One day, some kid was popping me in the face repeatedly. I went back to the corner and my brother, who was trying to motivate me, asked, 'Don't you want to fight this guy?' I said, 'Not particularly.' He pushed me out for the next round anyway and I won, but that was my last fight."

After graduating from high school, Borges worked at a series of manual jobs, returned to school, and graduated from Brandeis with a degree in English in 1974. "The first summer after college," he remembers, "I put my degree to good use by delivering Table Talk pies and potato chips to stores and restaurants. Then the editor of a weekly newspaper on Martha's Vineyard asked if I'd cover some local town meetings for fifteen dollars a night." Borges liked it, and a career was born.

The following year, Borges moved to California "without a job to follow a woman." In 1976, he began writing sports for the *Sacramento Union*. At the time, Sacramento and Stockton were hot boxing towns with local heroes like Pete Ranzany, Bobby Chacon, and Yaqui Lopez. "One of the first fights I covered," Borges remembers, "was Pete Ranzany against Randy Shields. It was a great fight; one of those fights that's so good that, when it's over, the fans throw money into the ring. Afterward, I asked Pete, 'Did you get the twenty bucks?' He said, 'What are you talking about?' So I showed him a picture one of our photographers had taken of his trainer picking up a twenty dollar bill in the ring. But that's the way it is in boxing. The fighter fights, and most of the money goes to other people."

In 1978, Borges moved north to the *Oakland Tribune*. "Better job, more money," he acknowledges. "One of my most vivid memories from that period," he continues, "is a trip I took to Lincoln, Nebraska. I was changing planes in Omaha, and there was this huge guy in the airport; he must have weighed 380 pounds, wearing bib overalls. It was George Foreman, looking like a man without much money. He was in Nebraska to preach, and no one in the airport outside of myself seemed to know who he was."

In 1982, Borges moved back east to take a job with the *Baltimore News American*. One year later, he accepted a position as a staff writer with the *Boston Globe*. While football takes up most of his time during the NFL season, boxing remains his first love.

"My favorite people in boxing are the fighters," Borges says. "I find them to be the most honest of all athletes, and there's a nobility about them that goes far beyond their skill and athleticism. Evander Holyfield is the embodiment of what an athlete should be. He's fearless, always prepared. I love George Foreman and Larry Holmes, both of them. In my part of the country, you don't want to say too many nice things about Larry Holmes because of his Marciano comment ("Rocky Marciano couldn't have carried my jockstrap"). But Larry was a great fighter, and

I think he's a good guy. I like Oscar De La Hoya. A lot of people don't, but I do. Shane Mosley is a great kid and a great fighter. And then there are guys like Vinny Pazienza, who I might not like a whole lot but I genuinely admire. Vinny is a guy who to me embodies what boxing is all about. He has limited skills. If you think you're going to see Monet when Vinny fights, you're wrong because Vinny Pazienza is a house painter. But he'll stay on the job for his full shift. Vinny has never stolen a dime from anyone who bought a ticket to see him fight."

As for the people Borges doesn't like, you can start with promoters. "If this were the 1700s, most of them would be in the slave trade," he offers. "Although I have to say, I kind of like Cedric Kushner. From what I can see, he's honest with his fighters. Most managers remind me of promoters," Borges continues. "And the state athletic commissions and world sanctioning bodies are awful. They should be helping the sport and protecting the fighters. But in the end, they all acquiesce for the right amount of money for the right fight on any given night. After a while, the corruption starts to dull your senses. Look at the decision in the Chavez-Whitaker fight. Not one person I know was surprised that they stole it from Pernell. If it had been the World Series or the Super Bowl, it would have been a national scandal. But everyone just shook their head and said, 'That's boxing.'

"The sport is the worst advertisement for itself," Borges says in closing. "But I found it fascinating as a young man and still do. If you can't write boxing, you can't write. You don't have to be a great writer to write boxing. All you have to do is put down on paper what you see in front of you."

The people at MediaWorks have an often thankless job. But they perform it with class.

MediaWorks

It's fight day in Atlantic City, and Ed Keenan is under siege. The thirty-seven-year-old former Florida State University student is in the press room at the Trump Taj Mahal, putting the final touches on an intensive effort that began when Main Events hired MediaWorks to handle publicity for the heavyweight bout between Michael Grant and Andrew Golota. Now Keenan is answering questions from reporters and handling last-minute requests when what he really wants to do is watch the drama that's unfolding on the television to his left. Florida State (the top-ranked team in the country) is locked in a riveting struggle with arch-rival Florida in a game that will determine whether the Seminoles play for college football's national championship. "I got to see most of the game," Keenan remembers. "But I missed the end because it was getting close to fight time." Then he adds reflectively, "I'm sorry I missed the end. I love watching Steve Spurrier lose."

MediaWorks is largely the creation of two people. Pam Sinderbrand was a publicist for Trump Plaza in Atlantic City. In the late-1980s, she left her job to found a small PR agency that she operated out of her home. Dave Coskey was senior vice president for marketing at Trump Plaza. After the 1991 heavyweight championship bout between Evander Holyfield and George Foreman, Dan Duva of Main Events told Coskey that, if he started a public relations firm, Main Events would help with the financing and give him its business on pay-per-view fights. Coskey joined forces with Sinderbrand, and MediaWorks was formed. The company is now located in Linwood, New Jersey, and has a fulltime staff of seven. Roughly seventy percent of its business is related to boxing, with the bulk of that work performed by Keenan, Divena Freeman, and Brian Little.

Keenan grew up in New Jersey, and worked for the Philadelphia

76ers in ticket sales before joining MediaWorks in 1994. Freeman came on-board a year later. When Vinny Pazienza fought Roberto Duran in Atlantic City, MediaWorks needed someone who was fluent in both English and Spanish to build bridges between Duran's camp and the media. Freeman worked the week leading up to the fight as media coordinator for the Duran camp, and was particularly active in promoting the fight with the Hispanic media. Later that year, she began to work at MediaWorks fulltime. "The best part of the job for me is getting the story out in a way that serves my people," she says with pride. "At one time, everyone in the Hispanic community who loved boxing had to go to the Anglo papers to read about their favorite sport. Now they have alternatives." Little was an intern at MediaWorks while going to school at the University of Delaware. When he graduated in 1996, he was offered a fulltime job.

MediaWorks handles publicity for about a dozen major fights each year. As a general rule, the task involves formulating a comprehensive publicity plan, preparing press kits, contributing to an advertising strategy, and coordinating personal appearances by the fighters from the opening press conference through fight week. In doing their job, staff members rely on a database that includes 1,500 media contacts and is cross-referenced to target media outlets by geographic region, language, print versus television versus internet, etc.

Not everything runs smoothly.

"The hardest part of the job is getting the fighters to accept their role," says Little. "It's easy to make plans, but harder to implement them. You have to make sure that the fighters get places on time and do the right interviews. Most of them are cooperative, but they all have their days."

For example?

"Andrew Golota hates TV interviews," Keenan acknowledges. "They make him nervous. Before Golota fought Lennox Lewis, we had a media day. There was a chair for Golota, a chair for Lou Duva, and eight or nine television crews waiting. Golota took one look and started shaking me by the neck, back and forth, back and forth, asking, 'Do you think we have enough television here?' He was kidding, I think. He was kidding, but he was aggravated. Another time, two days before a fight in Wildwood,

New Jersey, we had a round-card girl contest to help promote the fights, and only one girl showed up."

But those problems are nothing compared to the headaches caused by the demand for ringside press credentials. For a major fight, there can be literally thousands of requests, and often, the press section is limited to 150 or 200 people. When MediaWorks handles credentials, it's Keenan who has the final say on who sits where. "I'd love to put everyone who works for a legitimate media organization at ringside," he offers. "But sometimes that's not possible. There are times when we have a cut-off, so what I do in those situations is ask the promoter for more space, and then I explain to the media what our limitations are."

As for who gets credentials, "Personal favoritism doesn't enter into it," Keenan continues. "We go largely by how large a newspaper's circulation is; how big an audience a particular TV or radio show or website is expected to reach; and what the overall impact of a given story will be. We also look to ongoing relationships, like who has given us good pre-fight publicity and how much a story about a particular fight will create interest in the next one."

Major fights with international appeal cause extra credentials headaches. By way of example, the Polish media doesn't sell tickets in North America. People in the United States don't turn on HBO just because there's an article about Andrew Golota and Michael Grant in a newspaper in Poland. But as Keenan notes, "During fight week, you have people complaining, 'Look, I flew all the way from Warsaw for this fight,' so we try to accommodate them. Our biggest problem is with photographers," Keenan says in closing. "They all want to be on the ring apron, which is understandable but also impossible."

Eric Gelfand (director of sports public relations for Madison Square Garden) has worked with MediaWorks on numerous occasions. "They're very good at what they do," says Gelfand. "They're polished; they set up tours very well; and they're a particularly strong asset during fight week."

Ray Stallone (director of media relations for HBO Sports) echoes Gelfand's comments. "They're good people," says Stallone. "And they execute; they get the job done. I think one of the keys to their success is that, on top of everything else, the people who work there are fans. They're not just in it for the paycheck, and that shows through."

Meanwhile, noted curmudgeon Michael Katz (who is also the much-respected dean of American boxing writers) sums up for his brethren with the observation, "The folks at MediaWorks aren't perfect, but they try very hard to help you out. They're absolutely wonderful people. In fact, they're so nice, I don't think they belong in boxing."

The year after I wrote about MediaWorks, Divena Freeman was driving alone when her car skidded on a patch of black ice, careened off the highway, and came to rest underwater. By the time Divena was brought to the surface, she was in a coma from which she never recovered.

Divena Freeman: An Appreciation

In 1995, when Vinny Pazienza fought Roberto Duran in Atlantic City, MediaWorks needed someone who was fluent in both English and Spanish to build bridges between "Manos de Piedra" and the media. Thus, it hired Divena Freeman to work the week leading up to the bout as media coordinator for the Duran camp. Soon she was working fulltime at MediaWorks, thrust into the vortex of boxing.

Divena died last month in the aftermath of a traffic accident. Now, as boxing's elite ready for Lennox Lewis versus David Tua, those in the media who worked with Divena remember her fondly:

JAY SEARCY (*Philadelphia Inquirer*): Divena had a gift for recognizing human interest stories. She always got beneath the surface of the press-conference attitude to tell you what was real about fighters. And she tried so hard to be helpful. With a lot of people, if you ask them for something, they immediately start thinking of all the reasons why they can't do it. But if you asked Divena for something, she'd immediately start thinking of all the ways she could help.

ED SCHUYLER (Associated Press): She was always honest, which is very refreshing in boxing. And she always had a smile for you, no matter how hectic things were for one or both of you at the time. She was a lovely lady.

ED KEENAN (MediaWorks): She had a great heart. Everyone could see that; the media, the promoters, the fighters. And her work ethic was incredible. Whatever she did, she put one hundred percent into it. She wanted everything to be perfect.

TIM SMITH (*New York Daily News*): I was at a press conference in Las Vegas right before De La Hoya versus Trinidad. Felix had spoken with particular passion in response to a question, and the guy who was interpreting for him gave us the most bland cliche-ridden answer imaginable. You knew from Felix's passion that this wasn't really what he'd said. But if you didn't speak Spanish, what could you do about it? And I'll never forget, Divena pulled me aside and told me, "Tim, that's not what Felix said." And she then proceeded to give me some of the best quotes I've ever gotten at a press conference. She understood writers and what our job was.

LEE SAMUELS (Top Rank): She was kind and gentle. There aren't many people like her in this business, or any other business for that matter. Certainly, she helped us penetrate the Latin market. But what impressed me most was the way the fighters respected her. She was an unsung hero.

KEVIN FLAHERTY (HBO): I'm going to tell you what everyone else in boxing will tell you. Divena was one of the nicest people you could possibly meet. I used to look forward to seeing her in the press room. When she said, "Good to see you," she said it like she meant it.

STEVE FARHOOD (CNN/SI): She was always smiling and, at the same time, very professional. In the pressurized atmosphere of ringside for a big fight, she was unfailingly friendly and helpful. That should be the norm for someone in the position she had, but unfortunately it isn't. Divena was special.

BRIAN LITTLE (MediaWorks): I started at MediaWorks in 1996, and Divena was my mentor. She was very organized. I saw how she did her job. But what impressed me most was the way she treated people. To Divena, all people were important, regardless of which newspaper or which television network they worked for. That might be the most important thing I learned from her. But the truth is, I admired everything about her.

MARK TAFFET (HBO): There's a saying, "Good things come in small packages." And with Divena, that was true. In a business where people have good days and bad months, she was always smiling. She was the first person in the press room each morning and the one who locked up at night. Sometimes, when you work for a company like HBO, you begin to think that the large license fees you pay entitle you to cooperation. And Divena showed you can also get cooperation by treating everyone with respect. She set an example for all of us to follow.

ANTHONY CARTER PAIGE (WFAN): I saw her at ringside three weeks before she died. We sat and talked like we always did. That's the way Divena was. She always found time for a kind word with everyone. And now, this. It's like a reigning champion died.

RAY STALLONE (HBO): This is a tough business with lots of pressure. But whatever was going on, Divena was always the essence of professionalism and kindness. When I heard the news, it was awful, just awful. You can replace a person in a job, but not in your heart.

RON BORGES (*Boston Globe*): She always went to bat for the media to help us get what we needed; and at the same time, she was protective of the fighters. That's a fine line to walk, but she walked it. And she treated writers from small publications as nicely as she treated writers from big ones. It was never, "You work for a little magazine, so I can't help you."

GEORGE KIMBALL (*Boston Herald*): What set her apart from most people in the business was Divena never learned to lie. She always told you the truth. And if she didn't know the answer to a question, it was never "I don't know." It was, "I'll find out."

HAROLD LEDERMAN (HBO): It's interesting. A lot of PR people aren't very nice. You'd think they would be, but they're not. Some of them are real nasty. And Divena was nicer than nice. She was the kindest person I've ever known. You felt so good when you walked into the room and saw her sitting behind that desk. God, it's a shame. We'll all miss her.

ERIC GELFAND (Madison Square Garden): Divena was—I can't believe I'm saying "was"—Divena was unique. She was unbelievable. She bridged the gap between fighters and the media, between Anglo and Hispanic, as well as anybody in the business. And she was an absolute sweetheart.

MICHAEL KATZ (Housefboxing.com): People in boxing always write nice things about you after you're gone. Divena was nice when she was alive.

Wilt Chamberlain was never a professional boxer. But at one point in his career, he came awfully close.

Wilt Chamberlain
August 21, 1936–October 12, 1999

At first glance, a boxing magazine might seem like a strange place to write about Wilt Chamberlain. But the fraternity of great athletes transcends any one particular sport. And as Jerry West recently observed, "Wilt Chamberlain was one of those fabulous players who defined sports."

Chamberlain entered the NBA in 1959, and changed the way the game was played with his unique combination of size, agility, and strength. He was the league's dominant player for fourteen years, first with the Philadelphia Warriors (who later moved to San Francisco), then with the Philadelphia 76ers and Los Angeles Lakers. Along the way, he rewrote the record book like no athlete in any sport has ever done.

When Chamberlain entered the NBA in 1959, the league record for points in a single season was 2,105. As a rookie, Wilt scored 2,707. In his third season, he raised the standard to 4,029 and averaged 50.4 points per game. He led the NBA in scoring in each of his first seven campaigns, during which he averaged 39.6 points per contest. To put that number in perspective, no one else in NBA history has averaged more than 37.1 points per game over the course of a season.

When Chamberlain entered the league, the best single-season field goal percentage ever was .490. Wilt's rookie mark was .509. In 1972–73, he shot a staggering .727 from the floor. He led the league in field goal percentage nine times, and once made thirty-five consecutive field goals in NBA play. His Achilles heel, of course, was free-throw shooting. Over the course of his career, Chamberlain registered a mediocre .511 from the charity line. Yet ironically, he also holds the record for the most free throws ever in an NBA game. That occurred in Hershey, Pennsylvania, on the night of March 2, 1962, when he converted on twenty-eight of thirty-two foul shots en route to scoring 100 points against the New York Knicks, the most points ever scored in an NBA contest.

When Chamberlain entered the league, Bill Russell held the single-season NBA record for rebounds with 1,612. As a rookie, Wilt pulled down 1,941. One year later, he raised the standard to 2,149. The top seven rebounding seasons in NBA history belong to Wilt Chamberlain. He led the NBA in rebounding eleven times. He also leads the league in career rebounding with 23,924. He once had 55 rebounds in a single game, and averaged 22.9 rebounds per game throughout his career. Again, to put that number in perspective, over the course of his career, Kareem Abdul-Jabbar averaged 11.4 rebounds per game.

In 1967–68, Chamberlain was the only center ever to lead the league in assists. He once averaged 48.5 minutes per game for an entire season. That's four full quarters plus a bit of overtime per game. Chamberlain averaged 45.8 minutes per game throughout his career. He once played forty-seven consecutive complete games.

And oh yes, he never fouled out of an NBA contest.

In fourteen seasons, Chamberlain's teams made the playoffs thirteen times. They played for the NBA championship on six occasions, winning twice. Two of those championship losses were to the Boston Celtics, who also defeated Chamberlain-led teams in the conference finals five times. His rivalry with Bill Russell stands as history's greatest personal rivalry within a team sport.

Moreover, Chamberlain's athletic prowess wasn't limited to basketball. He was a magnificent track and field competitor. He was perhaps the finest volleyball player ever. And beyond that, for a brief period in 1971, he was at the vortex of professional boxing. In fact, in early 1971, Wilt and Muhammad Ali actually signed a contract to fight one another. But then Ali lost to Joe Frazier and the contract had to be renegotiated.

"I took it seriously," Chamberlain later recalled. "I spent some time training with Cus D'Amato. I believed I was capable of going out there and representing myself in a way that would not be embarrassing. I thought I could acquit myself reasonably well. I didn't have to learn how to become a complete boxer. I was going to learn for eight or ten months how to apply my strengths and skills against one person. One of the first things Cus said to me was, 'You're going to learn how to fight one man, that's all. We're going to have all the tapes of Ali. We're going to know all the things you have to do and what you possess to do it with against this one person. And there's no way that Ali can train to fight you. He won't know anything about you as a fighter, because there's only one of you and no tapes.'

"That was my edge," Chamberlain continued. "Ali would be coming in blind. He'd have no idea what he was facing, whereas I'd know what to expect. And of course, I had God-given strength, size, and athletic ability. If I'd been the odds maker, I'd have made Muhammad a ten-to-one favorite. But I thought a man as great at his job as Ali was might take me lightly. I could see that happening. And because of his nature, he'd want to have fun with this particular fight, which might give me an opening. I truly believed there was a chance for me to throw one punch and take Ali out."

Ultimately, the fight never took place. Chamberlain said that renegotiations failed over economic issues. Ali's promoter, Bob Arum, claimed that Wilt simply chickened out. Bill Russell offered what was perhaps the best epitaph for the bout when he said simply, "I can't speak for Wilt. I just know that I personally would never challenge a champion in his field of expertise. I would never get in a boxing ring with Ali or on the football field with Jim Brown or on a track with Carl Lewis. I would never impose my thoughts or motivations on someone else. But for me personally, that's just not the way I am."

But it was the way Wilt was. The title of his 1973 autobiography—*Wilt: Just Like Any Other 7-Foot Black Millionaire Who Lives Next Door*—said it all. Wilt was different. His thoughts often ran against the grain, and he spoke his mind regardless of whether or not his views were popular. He even had the temerity to challenge the prevailing view that Muhammad Ali in the 1960s was a spokesman for black America.

"I knew Muhammad fairly well during his time of glory," Chamberlain once declared. "I liked the man; I still do. And I applauded some of the stands he took, for example, his refusal to go into the war. But when Muhammad was held up as a spokesman for black people, I thought that was ludicrous because Muhammad was a guy writing lightweight poetry who happened to be a tremendous athlete, who was not educated in areas where somebody who speaks for a group of people should be. If somebody like Muhammad was speaking for black America, then black America was in bad shape."

Wilt Chamberlain was so strong and so physically gifted that at times he seemed impervious to the physical afflictions that beset lesser men. To see the life leave such a physically imposing figure so prematurely reminds all of us that we're mortal. Meanwhile, athletes around the world are in mourning with the words, "We'll miss you, brother."

Round 4

Issues and Answers

Nothing in boxing makes me angrier than the exploitation of fighters. One of the reasons this exploitation continues is that government agencies like the New York State Athletic Commission don't do their job properly.

How Not to Run a State Athletic Commission

Earlier this month, the New York County District Attorney's office served a subpoena on the New York State Athletic Commission. The subpoena was designed to gather information regarding the weigh-ins that preceded the February 26, 2000, fights at Madison Square Garden. It has been alleged that both Oscar De La Hoya and Arturo Gatti weighed in above their contractually required weights, and that one or more commission officials were guilty of criminal conduct in conducting a fraudulent weigh-in. Anyone who saw Joey Gamache lying on the canvas for seven minutes after being brutally beaten by Gatti understands the seriousness of the allegation.

But questions regarding the New York State Athletic Commission go far beyond a single weigh-in. It has also been alleged that, during the reign of New York governor George Pataki, the commission has become a microcosm of incompetence and corruption. The first step in this process was the appointment of a man with serious intellectual deficits to be chairman of the commission. Floyd Patterson was a courageous fighter. But at the time of his appointment, he had serious memory problems and was totally unqualified to head a government agency. Patterson was forced to resign in March 1998 when a deposition revealed that he didn't know such basic information as his office address and sometimes couldn't even remember the name of his wife. But by then, the damage had been done. Using Floyd as a cover, job after job at the commission had been filled with people who knew next to nothing about professional boxing but were politically well-connected. The result was—and still is—that fighters are not being properly protected and boxing is not being properly regulated in the State of New York.

The New York County District Attorney's investigation is thought to be fairly narrow in scope. However, the FBI is now beginning a broader probe. It is believed that the FBI will focus on the alleged misuse of tax-payer dollars by the New York State Athletic Commission in return for political contributions and other political favors to Republican Party candidates and causes. In that regard, it's worth comparing New York and Nevada.

The Nevada State Athletic Commission is far from perfect. But it's executive director—Marc Ratner—is one of the most respected men in boxing. In 1999, Nevada hosted forty-two fight cards, and the total budget for the Nevada Commission was $325,000. That comes to $7,738 per show. By contrast, during the past four years, New York has hosted roughly thirty fight cards per year. The total budget for the New York State Athletic Commission is unclear, because commission officials have repeatedly refused to release complete financial information. Indeed, last September, New York State assemblyman Scott Stringer was so frustrated by the commission's refusal to release financial data that he filed a Freedom of Information Act request for information. The numbers that Stringer requested have still not been provided. However, best indications are that the New York State Athletic Commission costs taxpayers in excess of $1,400,000 per year. That comes to more than $87,000 per boxing show.

The commission currently has ten appointees on full salary reaching as high as $101,600 per year. One of the questions the FBI intends to ask is, "How many of these are 'no-show' jobs." The commission also employs seventy-seven inspectors, nine advisory board members, eight "special assistants," and numerous other personnel on a per diem basis. It would be interesting to know how much money and how much work these employees and their relatives contributed to Republican Party candidates and causes.

NYSAC officials seek to justify their budget on grounds that the commission pays certain medical expenses not covered in Nevada and that New York is one of a handful of states that still regulate professional wrestling. But medical costs account for only a small portion of the budget differential between New York and Nevada. And everyone understands that professional wrestling is a sham. The only motivation for regulating it is to create more patronage lucre.

There are a number of honest, knowledgeable, hard-working men and women affiliated with the New York State Athletic Commission. Their service is tarnished—and boxing is tarnished—by the corruption around them.

Midway through 2000, the situation at the New York State Athletic Commission worsened with the resignation of Bob Duffy.

From Bad to Worse:
The New York State Athletic Commission

Last week, Bob Duffy resigned from his position as boxing coordinator for the New York State Athletic Commission. In a blistering letter to Chairman Mel Southard, Duffy spoke of the idealism with which he once viewed the commission and wrote, "It was not long before I realized that what I hoped for was an illusion. People were hired to work for the Commission with little or no knowledge of the sport of boxing. Not only did this compromise the integrity of the Commission, it also placed combatants directly in harm's way . . . The morale of the Commission is at an all-time low and . . . I foresee no positive change for the Commission in the near future. I believe I was a loyal, trustworthy, and knowledgeable employee and also a true asset to the Commission. It is apparent that I am not the type of individual you are seeking to keep in your employ."

Duffy is a lifelong New Yorker, who has spent more than three decades in government service. He has been a Deputy United States Marshal and a detective for the New York City Police Department. His resume includes two years with the FBI and fourteen years with the NYSAC. Most recently, he was responsible for coordinating and supervising the conduct of all professional boxing shows in the State of New York.

Duffy's resignation comes at a time when the NYSAC is mired in scandal. During the reign of New York Governor George Pataki, the commission has become a microcosm of incompetence and corruption. Its current chairman is Mel Southard. The other two commissioners are Jerry Becker and Marc Cornstein. James Polsinello is a special assistant to the chairman. Tony Russo is executive director. In 1999, the commission spent in excess of $1,400,000 to regulate sixteen fight cards and professional wrestling in the State of New York. It has been alleged that much of that total was expended on "no-show" jobs and other political patronage plums.

Earlier today (September 13), Duffy broke the self-imposed silence that followed his resignation from the Commission and spoke with Houseofboxing.com. Here is some of what he had to say:

• "Everybody knows what's going on at the commission. To get a job, it helps to know someone in the Republican party, contribute money to the Republican party, or work for the Republican party."

• "Mel Southard is an okay guy; Mel is a gentleman. But he puts up with a lot of things that he shouldn't have to put up with. I said to Mel a hundred times, 'Let's go to the Governor and tell him what's going on.' Mel said he agreed with me, but it never happened. I think he's under a lot of pressure and his hands are tied."

• "Right now, almost no one at the Commission has a good working knowledge of boxing. There a still a few good people there, but some of the people are in over their heads and others are corrupt. There are certain people at the Commission on full salary who are supposed to come to work every day, and I almost never saw them."

• "At the first Holyfield-Lewis fight, I chose two inspectors for each corner. Bill O'Malley and George Ward were supposed to work one corner, and Mike Fayo and Harold Townes were supposed to be in the other. Then Polsinello came to me and said, 'I'm assigning the corners.' There was a lot of yelling, and he overruled me. So Chris De Fruscio and Mike Pascale worked Lewis's corner, and Marc Cornstein and Jerry Becker were assigned to Holyfield. This was Pascale's first fight in the corner. You don't start your career as an inspector in the corner at a fight for the heavyweight championship of the world. I complained to Becker, and Gerry told me, 'Hey, Duffy; you don't understand. We won the election.'"

• "The safety of the fighters and the financial wellbeing of the fighters is more important to me than anything else. Let's face it. The fighters today are mostly black and Hispanic. A lot of them are poorly educated. If they can't go to the Commission for protection, where else can they go? But right now, the people who run the Commission don't care. They might tell you they do, but they don't."

Sometimes, things have to get worse before they get better. At present, three government agencies (the FBI, the New York State Inspector General's office, and New York County District Attorney's office) are investigating the New York State Athletic Commission. On Thursday, September 21, Bob Duffy will sit down with representatives of the New York County District Attorney and continue telling them what he knows. It should be an interesting session.

Duffy, by the way, is a Republican who voted for George Pataki twice. "But the Democrats were never this bad," he says in closing. "What's going on now is a total disgrace. At the commission today, you have to be more Republican than American, and that's not what good government is about."

New York is among the worst offenders. But as I noted in June 2000, problems with state regulation of boxing are widespread.

A Culture of Lawlessness

Bob Arum began testifying this week in a federal court in New Jersey. He's a government witness in the criminal trial of IBF president Robert W. Lee Sr. Arum has admitted paying $100,000 demanded by Lee in exchange for the IBF agreeing to sanction a world heavyweight championship fight between George Foreman and Axel Schulz. Don King, Cedric Kushner, and other promoters have been discussed at length in connection with the proceedings. But this isn't a column about any of them; nor is it about the WBC, the WBA, or the IBF. This is about the regulators; the various state commissions that have ignored, and in some instances played an active role in, the culture of lawlessness that pervades boxing today.

Let's start with the Nevada State Athletic Commission, which is considered one of the better commissions in the United States. Marc Ratner, its executive director, is a respected administrator. Ratner is a good guy.

On May 6, 1992, Joseph A. Maffia (the comptroller of Don King Productions for five years) swore under oath as follows: "Under Nevada law, the maximum percentage a manager can take from a fighter's purse is 33-1/3 percent. Yet in many cases, Don King promoted fights in Nevada in which one or more of the fighters was managed by Don's son, Carl King of Monarch Boxing, Inc. Oftentimes, in those instances, the fighters were required to pay Carl King a fifty percent managerial share, and false declarations were filed with the Nevada State Athletic Commission."

A copy of Maffia's statement was sent to the Nevada Commission. What did the commission do in response? "That's a fair question," says Ratner. "And I don't know how to answer it. I remember the allegation, but there was no follow-up, possibly because we never had a complaint from a fighter." However, Ratner does add, "Boxing is big business in Nevada."

How about New Jersey, home of the IBF and the site of boxing's current showcase trial? New Jersey allowed Stephan Johnson to fight in Atlantic City despite the fact that he was under medical suspension in Canada. Johnson died from injuries sustained in a bout against Paul Vaden last November. Larry Hazzard is chairman of the New Jersey Board of Athletic Control. What lessons has Hazzard learned from the Johnson tragedy? "I'm not going to talk about that," Hazzard answers. How did Hazzard feel when he learned of Arum's admission that bribes had been paid in exchange for title-bout sanctions and rankings? "I was a bit surprised," he says. And then Hazzard adds, "If that, in fact, happened." One wonders if Hazzard thinks that John Ruiz's number-one ranking has been honestly arrived at.

Then there's Virginia, where boxing is under the control of the Department of Professional and Occupational Regulation. Rather than regulate boxing itself, the department chose to enter into a contract with Doug Beavers, who was charged with administering the sweet science as a private contractor. Beavers was also chairman of the IBF Ratings Committee. Last November, a federal indictment revealed that Beavers had admitted to engaging in a pattern of systematic corruption by accepting bribes on behalf of Robert W. Lee Sr. in exchange for preferred rankings and title-bout sanctions. It took five months before the Commonwealth of Virginia got around to terminating Beavers's contract.

And of course, there's New York. Call the Pennsylvania State Athletic Commission, and Executive Director Greg Sirb will answer your questions. Call the Nevada State Athletic Commission, and Executive Director Marc Ratner will speak with you. Call the New York State Athletic Commission, and a good portion of its personnel are in hiding. Maybe that's because many NYSAC personnel are currently under investigation by the FBI for the alleged sale of jobs and "no show" jobs. Scott Trent (a press official) recently articulated the position of the commission as follows: "We will only answer written questions. Submit written questions, and we will answer those that we deem appropriate."

When pressed for comment, Mel Southard (chairman of the NYSAC) declared, "I can't talk to you about boxing. That's the policy." However, Southard was willing to talk about the hundreds of thousands of dollars in taxpayer's money that the commission spends each year to "regulate" professional wrestling. "If you saw what goes on around the ring at some of those wrestling matches," says Southard, "you'd know why we have to be there."

There were sixteen fight cards held in New York last year. The latest estimate is that, during the same period, the New York State Athletic Commission cost taxpayers in excess of $1,400,000. Throw out the bogus wrestling regulation, and the NYSAC cost taxpayers roughly *$87,500 per card*.

Meanwhile, the NYSAC recently issued a press release declaring that the Empire State has become "the first state in the nation to implement comprehensive boxing reform." Foremost among these "reforms" is limiting boxer-promoter contracts to *five* years. The "reforms" also call for referees to be paid up to $9,000 and judges up to $6,000 each for officiating at championship fights. And henceforth, these patronage plums will be handed out, not by the naughty world sanctioning organizations but by, you guessed it, the New York State Athletic Commission. Nine thousand dollars for one night's work. Nah! No chance that anyone would kick back to the Republican Party for that kind of bonanza.

But back to Bob Arum for a moment. The man is a licensed promoter. He has admitted that he paid $100,000 to get George Foreman versus Axel Schulz sanctioned by the IBF as a world championship fight. The fight was held in Las Vegas. So what's the Nevada State Athletic Commission doing about it?

"The process is simple," explains Ratner. "The State Attorney General wanted to talk with Arum when the story broke. But on the advice of his lawyers and at the request of the U. S. Attorneys Office, Arum asked for a delay until after he had testified at the trial in New Jersey. There will come a time when we sit down and talk with him. Then the commission will meet. We could take away his license, put conditions on his license, fine him, or do nothing. But it wouldn't be equitable to single out one person, because there are a lot of problems out there and this is just one of them."

In other words, everyone does it so why pick on Bob? And the sad thing is that, in this particular instance, Ratner is probably right. The regulators have condoned and, in many instances, been part of a culture of lawlessness for so long that it's virtually impossible for an honest promoter to compete in boxing anymore. The playing field simply isn't level. And it isn't always easy to discern which promoters are the corrupters and which promoters are the victims of extortion.

So what's the solution?

No one state can clean up boxing. If a single state tries to regulate the sport properly, the big fights will simply go somewhere else.

The Muhammad Ali Boxing Reform Act is inadequate on its face.

And the Association of Boxing Commissions isn't the answer. The ABC is a confederation of forty-six member states, the District of Columbia, and five native American tribes. Its president is Greg Sirb, who also serves as executive director of the Pennsylvania State Athletic Commission. The ABC's primary accomplishments to date, according to Sirb, are implementation of a boxer identification card program, creation of a medical suspension list, and the promulgation of uniform rules for championship bouts held in the United States. He also notes that, under the Muhammad Ali Boxing Reform Act, the ABC is expected to establish guidelines for boxer-manager and boxer-promoter contracts and objective criteria for rankings.

But let's get real. Marc Ratner is executive vice president of the ABC. Here's what Ratner said recently about the organization: "Whatever the ABC tries to do, enforcement will be a problem. The structure just isn't there. To try to run this thing as a mom and pop organization out of the Pennsylvania State Athletic Commission for an hour a day won't do the job. And in addition to lacking structure, the ABC doesn't have funding."

Also, the ABC is simply a collection of regulators, many of whom have shown a disinclination to do the job right in the first place and can't even police themselves.

In sum, boxing, like every other major professional sport, needs a centralized governing body. Boxing needs a federal commission.

Among the many ills that boxing faces today is ringside judging that, too often, is biased, incompetent, and corrupt.

Judging the Judges

HBO's recent welterweight festival was great for boxing. Oscar De La Hoya passed his "I.Q. test" when he decisioned Ike Quartey. And Felix Trinidad looked superb in a bout that marked the end of Pernell Whitaker's reign as a great fighter. But in addition to answering some questions about the welterweight division, the bouts highlighted several issues regarding the way fights are judged.

The first issue centers on the notion some people have that, once a bout begins, the champion is entitled to special consideration.

De La Hoya versus Quartey was a close fight. The point here isn't who should have won. It's that, after the bout, a lot of people said they thought Oscar deserved the decision because Quartey hadn't done enough to take the title from a champion.

Gil Clancy helped train De La Hoya for the Quartey fight. Despite his allegiance to Oscar, Clancy said recently, "Once the bell rings, the title is up for grabs and there's no longer a champion. Whoever wins the fight wins the fight."

That's the way it should be. If the scorecards balance out at the end of a championship bout, the champion retains his title on a draw. That's his edge; and it should be his only edge. Or looked at from a different perspective, suppose it was De La Hoya rather than Quartey who'd been stripped of his title for refusing to fight a mandatory defense in lieu of this bout. Would that have meant De La Hoya (who fought cautiously for most of the night) didn't do enough to take the title from Quartey?

The second issue concerns "geographic distribution." Felix Trinidad comes from Puerto Rico. Pernell Whitaker hails from Virginia. Therefore, the New York State Athletic Commission approved judges from Puerto Rico, Virginia, and New York for the Trinidad-Whitaker bout. That's a lousy way to choose judges.

A spokesman for the commission says that the IBF submitted the names of the Puerto Rican and Virginian judges, while the NYSAC designated the referee and third judge. But listen to what Marc Ratner (executive director of the Nevada State Athletic Commission) has to say about the selection of judges for title fights.

"In Nevada," explains Ratner, "we insist on appointing the judges. As soon as a title fight is signed, I'll confer with the president of the sanctioning body and ask for the names of six or seven judges. Then we choose three; and we prefer to have all neutral judges. If you have a Mexican fighter against a Colombian fighter, it doesn't make sense to have one Mexican judge, one Colombian judge, and one American judge, because right away you're assuming that two of the three judges will judge with their hearts."

Ratner is putting it politely. Geographic distribution increases the chances that two of the three judges will be biased. The way things worked out, there was no dispute regarding the judging in Trinidad-Whitaker. But Whitaker was victimized by two of the worst decisions in memory when he fought Jose Ramirez and Julio Cesar Chavez. Suppose Trinidad-Whitaker had been close? What sort of pressure would have been on the judges then?

And last, there's a serious issue regarding the quality of ring judging in general.

"We have a vested interest in quality judging," says Ratner. "Apart from the obvious fact that we want things to be fair, there's a lot of money bet in Nevada on fights. And if people can't trust the judging, it hurts the entire gaming industry, not just boxing. So after every fight card in Nevada, large and small, I sit down with the judges and referees to talk about the fights. We pay particular attention to anything unusual that happened, which includes significant variations in the scoring and decisions that people think were just plain wrong. If there's doubt about a decision, I might ask the judges, 'What impressed you in that round? How influenced were you by that cut?' I have the records of every ring judge who has worked in Nevada since 1983, so I know who the good ones are, and those are the ones we appoint."

That doesn't explain why Ken Morita (who had Mike Tyson ahead of Buster Douglas after nine rounds in Tokyo) was approved by the Nevada commission as a judge for De La Hoya versus Quartey. Still, Nevada's reputation for judging is pretty good. But what about New York, where the quality of judging will become increasingly important as Madison Square Garden continues its quest to once again be the "Mecca of Boxing."

Teddy Atlas is one of the most knowledgeable people in the sweet science. He's not afraid to voice his opinions, even though his candor often puts him at odds with others who can help him or hurt him.

"The judging in New York is a joke, especially in the small local fights," says Atlas. "It's almost as though some people at the commission are in bed with the promoters and the other money people; and the guy they're backing has to win so there can be more fights in New York. When there's a bad decision, it can be the result of incompetent judging or corrupt judging. In New York, you have both. Sure, there are some good judges in New York. But too often, you have these horrible decisions because the judges know that, if they don't decide a certain way, they'll get less work. And I'll tell you something: real boxing fans are disgusted by those decisions. If you're going to do things that way, you might as well not even have judges. Just say in the rules that, if the guy the promoter wants to win is standing at the end of the fight, he gets the decision."

As Atlas acknowledges, there are some good judges in New York. Overall, the quality of judging in the Empire State may well be no better and no worse than the rest of the country. But perhaps the saddest thing about it all is that, when a horrendous decision comes down the pike, people in boxing don't even get excited about it anymore. They just shrug their shoulders and say, "That's boxing." Maybe they even have a good laugh.

Don Elbaum tells a story about a fight he promoted years ago. One of his fighters was making his pro debut against an opponent named Richie DeJesus. "It was a great bout," Elbaum remembers. "Every round was a war; but clearly, my guy won the fight. Then they announced that DeJesus had won on a split decision. I went bonkers, I mean, really nuts. I started screaming at the judges. 'How could you do this to me? You're total incompetents. That's the worst decision I've ever seen.' And all that happened was, one of the judges looked at me and said, 'Don, I'm sorry. I thought DeJesus was your fighter.'"

Funny story? Yes. But also troubling. These are *judges*.

This article created a dilemma for me. I've always admired Arthur Mercante. He's one of the best referees in boxing history and a true gentle- man. But I felt that, at age seventy-eight, it was time for him to retire from the ring. In March 1999, Arthur was being prominently mentioned as a candidate to referee the first championship bout between Evander Holyfield and Lennox Lewis. I wanted to have my say, but I didn't want Arthur to think I was stabbing him in the back. So I wrote the follow- ing article. And then, before it was posted on the Internet, I telephoned Arthur and read it to him. When I was done, Arthur thanked me for the nice things I'd written about him; he said he'd take my thoughts under advisement; at age eighty, he's still refereeing; and he's still a gentleman.

The Third Man in the Ring

Arthur Mercante was born in Brockton, Massachusetts, in 1920. In 1954, he refereed his first world title fight—Benny Paret versus Federico Thompson. He has now been the third man in the ring for 133 cham- pionship bouts and is enshrined in the International Boxing Hall of Fame.

What made Arthur great?

For starters, he's a man of absolute integrity who ruled in the ring without fear or favor.

He has a thorough knowledge of boxing's rules and regulations, coupled with sound judgment and the ability to act decisively and force- fully in a crisis.

He has always been a master at positioning in the ring. And that's crucial, because the job demands being able to see whether a blow was above or below the belt; whether a cut was caused by a punch or a head butt; whether a man on the canvas was knocked down or slipped.

Also, Arthur has always kept himself in the best possible physical con- dition. Even today, at age seventy-eight, he begins each morning with a series of stretching exercises and fifty abdominal crunches. Then he does ten chin-ups and fifty push-ups. At night, he works with weights. At 170 pounds, he weighs only ten pounds more than when he joined the Navy in 1942.

All of which brings us to the present.

I like Arthur Mercante. I think he's a gentleman. He's one of the finest referees in the history of boxing, and he's still better than most refs. He knows what he's doing in the ring and does it well. But like all of us, Arthur has gotten older.

Joe Louis once described the frustration inherent in being an aging athlete. "I saw openings I couldn't use," the Brown Bomber acknowledged after his 1947 fight against Jersey Joe Walcott. "A man gets old, he don't take advantage of those things as fast as he used to."

Unlike Joe Louis at the end of his career, Mercante is still capable of performing at a high level. But at age seventy-eight, everything takes longer. At seventy-eight, a man moves more slowly in those crucial split-seconds when he must intervene to save a fighter who's helpless from absorbing further punishment. At seventy-eight, a man shouldn't be in the position of having to break two extremely physical athletes in their twenties apart. At seventy-eight, a referee can get hit and badly hurt. Also, sometimes there are unavoidable tragedies in fights. And if one of them were to happen on Arthur's watch, fairly or unfairly, it would be blamed on his age.

I know that John Glenn went into space at age seventy-seven. But here, as with Arthur, the exception proves the rule. No matter how good Arthur Mercante still is, it would be bad for boxing to have other seventy-eight-year-old referees in action around the country. Being a boxing referee is far more demanding than being a baseball umpire, and there are no seventy-eight-year-old umpires in major league baseball.

There's a lot that Arthur Mercante can still contribute to boxing. He would be superb at the helm of any state athletic commission or other regulatory organization. No one is better equipped to teach the craft of refereeing to young officials and supervise their performance. In the past, Arthur has been a good television commentator, and he could be again. He would make a spectacular ring judge. I just question whether he should be refereeing into the next millennium.

Evander Holyfield and Lennox Lewis are scheduled to meet for the heavyweight championship of the world on March 13. It will be the biggest fight at Madison Square Garden since the first Ali-Frazier bout in 1971. Arthur Mercante was the third man in the ring when Ali and

Frazier met on that long-ago night. And it would be the crowning achievement of his illustrious career if he were to be the third man in the ring when Holyfield and Lewis do battle. I'd like to see that happen. And then I'd like to see Arthur Mercante retire from active duty.

Rocky Marciano (who was born in Arthur's hometown of Brockton in 1923) retired when he was on top. So can Arthur Mercante.

The first Holyfield-Lewis fight took place as scheduled, with Arthur Mercante Jr. (not his father) as the referee. But the New York State Athletic Commission ceded control over the judges to the WBC, WBA, and IBF—the three organizations that were sanctioning the bout. And therein lay the rub. At night's end, the focus wasn't on the referee or, for that matter, on the fighters. It was on the judges, whose questionable scoring resulted in a draw that most onlookers thought was unduly kind to Evander Holyfield, who happened to be Don King's fighter.

King's Crowning Glory

The heavyweight championship of the world is the most coveted title in sports when it is undisputed and clear-cut. The first heavyweight championship fight contested in New York took place at Coney Island on June 9, 1899, when James J. Jeffries claimed the crown by knocking out Bob Fitzsimmons at 1:32 of round eleven. Jeffries was American; Fitzsimmons was British. And in the one hundred years since then, no Brit has held the undisputed heavyweight championship of the world. This is no small matter to the boxing faithful of England, who revere the memory of the thirty-nine men, all British, who reigned as heavyweight champion from 1719 through 1882.

On March 13, 1999, the heavyweight crown should have returned to England but didn't. For the time being, Lennox Lewis will have to make do with his WBC belt and boxing's so-called "lineal championship," which he won by virtue of knocking out Shannon Briggs, who was awarded a horrible decision over George Foreman, who knocked out Michael Moorer.

In retrospect, apart from the fight itself, two major stories surrounded the bout. The first concerns Madison Square Garden. In recent years, the Garden has been on the fringe of recommitting to the sweet science. It has hosted some of the biggest names in boxing, but the big names haven't been fighting there in big fights. Instead, it was Oscar De La Hoya versus Jesse James Leija; Evander Holyfield versus Bobby Czyz; and Roy

Jones Jr. versus Merqui Sosa, Bryant Brannon and Lou Del Valle. All of that led a frustrated Dave Checketts (president of the Garden) to proclaim, "Frankly, we're tired of hearing everyone say that the last time we had a big fight here was Ali-Frazier in 1971."

Well, the Garden has now had a big fight. And Holyfield-Lewis was as big as it was because it was in New York. New York City is the media capital of the world. When New York buzzes, the whole country buzzes with it. That's why the kick-off press conferences for major fights are held in the Big Apple. Since the 1970's, most big fights have gone elsewhere because the economics of boxing have been keyed to site fees paid by casinos. But the economics of the next millennium are likely to be different. The dollars that major fights generate will be determined more and more by pay-per-view buys, not site fees. That means the primary target audience will be millions of pay-per-view buyers around the world, rather than several thousand high rollers courted by casinos. And as Holyfield-Lewis dramatically showed, staging big fights in New York is the best way to attract pay-per-view dollars. HBO's Lou DiBella said as much, when he estimated on fight night that Holyfield-Lewis had generated an additional 250,000 buys because of the publicity emanating from New York.

But obviously, there's another story regarding Holyfield-Lewis—the judges' scorecards. The fight was boxing's biggest showcase event in years. And once again, boxing has been tarnished.

The only way boxing will ever be cleaned up is by the United States Department of Justice bringing a civil antitrust lawsuit against the world sanctioning bodies for conspiracy in restraint of trade. Two prime courtroom exhibits were on display on March 13—the judges' decision and the presence on the undercard of the WBC's number-one-ranked mandatory challenger John Ruiz. In a civil antitrust suit brought by the government, there is no jury. The court can award any equitable relief it deems proper.

Meanwhile, Don King has won again. The man is amazing.

For a long time, people thought that Larry Holmes was propping King up. Then Holmes retired, and King survived on a diet of Tony Tubbs, Tim Witherspoon, and their brethren. Next, it was Mike Tyson, who was supposed to be King's sole support. And after Tyson went to jail, Julio

Cesar Chavez was said to do the job. But the truth is, no one props up Don King. He stands on his own.

Writing about another king (Henry V), William Shakespeare penned the classic admonition, "Give the devil his due."

Don King has survived at the top of the most cutthroat business in the world for a quarter-century. Like him or not, he is one of the most charismatic, hard-working, brilliant men on the planet. That acknowledgement is his due. But if one wants to gauge Don King's impact on boxing, March 13 was truly "King's Crowning Glory."

The issue of ring judging remained in the forefront as boxing entered the new millennium.

Open Scoring . . . Consensus Scoring . . . How about Honest Scoring!

Last month [May 2000], a task force created by the attorneys general of eighteen states released a report that outlined a series of recommendations for the improvement of professional boxing. There were some things right and some things wrong with the report, but perhaps its most glaring flaw was one of omission. It failed to acknowledge that many state athletic commissions are dumping grounds for incompetent political hacks who know next to nothing about boxing. This omission was particularly noteworthy since Eliot Spitzer (who chaired the task force) is attorney general of the State of New York.

For those of you who have been on Mars for the past year, the FBI and New York County District Attorney's office are currently investigating the New York State Athletic Commission for fraud, the sale of jobs, the institutionalization of "no show" jobs, and a host of other offenses. For Mr. Spitzer and his followers to pretend that an association of state athletic commissions can clean up boxing is akin to suggesting that George W. Bush and the Republican Party lead the way on campaign finance reform. Still, one of the report's recommendations was particularly noxious and bears special mention. The task force suggested that the various state commissions consider "consensus scoring."

Consensus scoring is a method of tabulating judges' scorecards on a round-by-round basis and throwing out the score most favorable to each fighter. Let's assume that Felix Trinidad fights Bernard Hopkins. If two judges score the first round 10-9 for Trinidad and one judge scores it even or 10-9 for Hopkins, the round goes to Trinidad 10-9. If one judge scores it for Trinidad, one for Hopkins, and one calls it even, it's a 10-10 round. In other words, in each round, the median score governs. The middle judge defines the "consensus."

The task force report states that consensus scoring will "improve the scoring process" Boy, are they wrong.

Let a simple example suffice. Suppose the Trinidad–Hopkins bout goes the distance. And further suppose that Hopkins clearly wins five rounds; Trinidad clearly wins three rounds; and four rounds are up for grabs. Judge Honestman scores two of the close rounds for Hopkins. Judge Virtuouswoman scores the other two close rounds for Hopkins. But Judge Fuzzy scores all four close rounds for Trinidad. Under regular scoring procedures, Bernard Hopkins would win a split decision as a consequence of having won seven of twelve rounds on the cards of two judges. But under consensus scoring, Judge Fuzzy would be able to swing all four close rounds to Trinidad, giving Felix the decision even though the other two judges both scored the fight for Hopkins.

In sum, consensus scoring enables a single corrupt or incompetent judge to control a close fight.

"Open scoring"—which has been suggested by other "reformers"—is equally misguided.

Under open scoring, the scores of the judges are announced after each round. But several problems are intertwined with the process. First, a fighter who knows he's comfortably ahead late in a fight would be even more tempted to hold and run than is currently the case. Second, open scoring would eliminate the drama inherent in the time-honored tradition of announcing the result at the end of a fight. Third, as a fight progresses, a judge whose scoring is at odds with those of his brethren might try to bring his card closer to those of his fellow judges rather than score on the basis of what he saw in the ring. And last, under open scoring, judges would be even more susceptible to crowd intimidation than they are now.

The bottom line is simple. Forget about consensus scoring. Forget about open scoring. Boxing needs honest scoring.

Initially, I was skeptical about the accuracy of "punch stats." But after several independent counts, I came away with the belief that, properly used, they're a valuable tool in evaluating fighters.

How Reliable Are "Punch Stats"?

The statistic commonly known as "punch stats" is the creation of two men. Logan Hobson is a former sportswriter for UPI. Bob Canobbio was a researcher for *Sports Illustrated*. In 1984, they were working at a sports database company, when they saw a computer program that was capable of tracking every shot in a tennis match. That gave them the idea to try their hand at the sweet science.

"Boxing was devoid of statistics other than the end result of each bout," explains Hobson. "We felt that should change, because statistics are the lifeblood of sports. They enable fans to compare present-day athletes with one another and to compare contemporary athletes with athletes from different eras."

Working on their own, Hobson and Canobbio designed a computer program to accommodate their needs. Then, on November 28, 1984, they brought it to Atlantic City to test it out. "Trevor Berbick won a ten round decision over Walter Santemore," Hobson remembers. "When it was over, we looked at our results. We didn't know the full significance of the numbers, but we knew we had come up with something good."

Hobson and Canobbio now have a company called CompuBox that computes fight statistics for HBO, ESPN, and TNT. They cover sixty to seventy fight cards a year and churn out statistics for roughly two hundred bouts. Technically, "punch stats" is a term employed by HBO and its affiliates. ESPN refers to CompuBox's output as a "punch profile."

The CompuBox system utilizes two laptop computers, two keypads, and two operators (most often, Hobson and Canobbio). Each computer has four active keys—one each for jabs thrown, jabs connected, power punches thrown, and power punches connected. If a punch is blocked by an opponent's gloves or arms, it counts as a miss. Each operator records the efforts of one fighter. For example, at Holyfield-Lewis I, Hobson was responsible for Lewis's punch output while Canobbio was responsible for Holyfield's. At the end of each round, the computer automatically tallies the results.

"We're not in a position to judge fights because each of us is watching just one fighter," says Hobson. "During a bout, I'm totally focussed on my guy. In fact, sometimes, at the end of a round, I'll look at the screen and say, 'Wow! The other guy did better than the one I was watching.'"

The CompuBox system is far from perfect. The distinction between "jabs" and "power punches" is often irrelevant, because not all so-called "power punches" are damaging blows. Hobson acknowledges as much, and explains, "We tried a system where we broke things down into three categories; punches thrown, punches connected, and effective punches connected. An effective punch was described as a blow that stopped an opponent from doing what he was doing or had a visible effect. I liked the idea, but most people didn't. They thought it was too subjective."

And of course, there's the question of how reliable punch stat numbers really are.

The answer is, they're only as accurate as the split-second judgments of the two men entering them into their computers. Canobbio says there's "a two percent margin of error." In reality, the margin might be greater than that. "I'll be the first guy to admit that punch stats aren't one hundred percent accurate," says Hobson. "But I think we're pretty good. ESPN ran some checks on us in the early days, and found us to be highly accurate. And from time to time, Bob and I check ourselves against the tapes of fights we've covered, although I'll take our live call over our call off a tape every time."

The bottom line is, CompuBox is a boon to boxing. Punch stats might not be perfect, but neither is the official scoring of assists in the NBA. And punch stats are just beginning to be fully exploited. At the moment, analysts tend to look at statistics from one round or one fight. For example, Vinny Pazienza landed zero punches in round four of his 1995 bout against Roy Jones Jr. Michael Spinks landed 84 of 101 punches in the last round of his 1987 knockout victory over Gerry Cooney. Zack Padilla and Ray Oliveira landed more combined punches in their 1993 bout than any two fighters ever recorded.

But that's just the tip of the iceberg. More and more often, CompuBox is now being retained prior to fights to develop statistical profiles of boxers and their opponents. "We worked with Ray Leonard before the Hagler fight," says Canobbio. "We analyzed tapes of ten or twelve Hagler fights, broke them down, and found that, with the exception of Hagler-Hearns, Hagler came out very slowly in all his fights. In the first four rounds, he'd throw very few punches. Then, in the middle rounds, he'd pick things up. So the obvious strategy was for Ray to throw a lot of punches early, even if they were pity-pat blows. Stay busy, and he'd have a four-round cushion going into round five of the fight. We also worked with Emanuel Steward before Holyfield-Lewis. The numbers were obvious. In his previous fights, whenever Lennox had thrown thirty or more jabs in a round, he'd controlled the round. So Emanuel told Lennox that he had to jab."

Taking a broader look, CompuBox numbers reveal that Shane Mosley had four fights in 1998. In those fights, Mosley's connect percentage ranged from 45 percent to 60 percent, while his opponents were limited to connect percentages of 22 percent to 36 percent. Overall, Mosley had a plus/minus ratio of 31 percent over his opponents; the best ratio of any boxing superstar tracked by CompuBox in 1998.

"That tells me something," says Hobson. "It means that, on top of everything else, Shane Mosley is a much better defensive fighter than people give him credit for." To which Canobbio adds, "Wouldn't it be wonderful if we could go back in time and say that Jack Johnson had the best defensive ratio of any heavyweight champion ever; or Muhammad Ali's plus/minus ratio early in his career was the best of any fighter in history."

In sum, punch stats aren't dispositive of who won a fight, but they're a wonderful tool to help in evaluating what goes on in the ring.

"When we began, people thought of punch stats as a gimmick," says Hobson. "Now punch stats are one of the standards by which fighters are judged. Our statistics don't tell the whole story of a fight, but they say a lot."

In 1998, Michael Katz wrote an article in which he referred to promoter Bob Arum as "the Yom Kippur Whore" and said several other uncomplimentary things about Arum's decision to promote a fight on Yom Kippur night. Ultimately, the fight never took place. But Arum filed a libel suit against Katz that spurred the Boxing Writers Association of America to action. Ultimately, the case was settled without payment to Arum. Katz did not retract or apologize, but he did issue a statement saying, "My choice of words crossed a line that I myself regret."

Arum v. Katz

In the March 1998 issue of *Boxing Digest,* Michael Katz wrote an article that was critical of Bob Arum's decision last year to hold the Buster Douglas versus John Ruiz fight on the night of Yom Kippur. One can agree or disagree with the article, but the Boxing Writers Association of America believes that Mr. Katz's right to express his opinion is clearly protected by the United States Constitution.

In recent months, Mr. Arum has been an outspoken critic of Michael Katz. Much of his displeasure appears to have been occasioned by articles that Katz has written criticizing Oscar De La Hoya for not fighting the best-available opposition. Representatives of Top Rank have complained to Katz's editors at the *Daily News* about Katz's writing. Mr. Katz, for his part, believes that Arum has embarked on a campaign of harassment against him.

On March 9 of this year [1999], Arum filed suit against Katz in the Nevada district court, alleging that the aforementioned article was libelous and violated Mr. Arum's rights. We believe the lawsuit is wholly without merit from a legal point of view. However, defending against it will cost Mr. Katz many thousands of dollars. And because Arum chose to sue only Mr. Katz and not the publisher of the article, Mr. Katz will have to bear the entire cost of defending against the article on his own.

Mr. Arum's attorney summed up his client's position as follows: *"The thrust of the article is that Mr. Arum lacks the integrity to be a fight promoter."*

Mr. Arum himself demonstrated the lengths to which he will go in pursuing his case against Mr. Katz when he testified *under oath* on June 1 that he believed Katz's article in *Boxing Digest* was responsible for the disappointing number of pay-per-view buys for Top Rank's May 16 fight card featuring Genaro Hernandez and Erik Morales. Relevant portions of Arum's testimony follow:

Arum: The pay-per-view results from that fight were very very disappointing.

Q: Now is it your opinion that some of the disappointing results were attributable to the Michael Katz article that is the subject of this lawsuit.

Arum: Yes.

Q: And what do you base that opinion on?

Arum: The bad results that we had in certain urban areas that have heavy Jewish populations . . . I wouldn't say that the entire drop-off is attributable to it . . . But I do feel that some significant portion of the drop off is attributable to the article.

The Boxing Writers Association of America deplores the Arum lawsuit. We believe that it constitutes a threat to all writers and all representatives of the media. If Mr. Arum can silence Michael Katz, who is one of the most respected and influential boxing writers in the country, think what he can do to the rest of the media. We also believe that Mr. Arum's lawsuit is particularly inappropriate given Mr. Arum's penchant for making statements that attack other individuals for what Mr. Arum claims is bigotry, financial corruption, and other misconduct.

Boxing is the only major sport today that is absent from most American college campuses. Should it be a presence?

College Boxing

The year was 1960. Dressed in red, the Wisconsin Badgers entered the arena to the roar of thousands of hometown fans. Inside the Fieldhouse, the band played "On Wisconsin." The NCAA Championships were about to begin. But it wasn't basketball; it was college boxing.

Intercollegiate boxing began shortly after World War I. Bouts consisted of three two-minute rounds. As with amateur scoring today, the emphasis was on the number of blows a fighter landed rather than the power of his punches.

Wisconsin dominated college boxing the way Notre Dame once dominated college football. The Badgers won eight NCAA championships. During one five-year stretch, the smallest crowd to watch a Wisconsin boxing match at home was eighty-five hundred. Capacity crowds of fifteen thousand were common. Dick Bartman (a member of Wisconsin's 1956 NCAA championship team) later recalled, "They'd march you down the aisle with ten thousand people cheering you on. When you got into the ring, you were so pumped up you'd be embarrassed to lose."

On April 9, 1960, Wisconsin team captain, Charlie Mohr, entered the ring at the Fieldhouse to defend his NCAA middleweight championship against Stu Bartell of San Jose State. Bartell won on a second-round technical knockout. After the bout, a doctor asked Mohr if he was all right.

"I guess so," Mohr told him. "Actually, I've got a headache."

The headache was caused by bleeding in the brain. Mohr collapsed and began having convulsions. He died eleven days later. Soon after, the NCAA announced an end to intercollegiate boxing.

The events recounted above came to mind recently when Anwar Chowdhry (president of the International Amateur Boxing Association) declared, "We want to bring boxing back to the schools and colleges, like the old days. That's where our future lies."

With all due respect to Mr. Chowdhry, the NCAA isn't about to reinstate boxing. But there is a way to link college and boxing again. The solution lies in a professional league comprised of college students.

The league could start with eight teams in eight cities. The league itself would be the promoter. The New York team could be owned by Madison Square Garden, while Los Angeles could be under the aegis of the Great Western Forum. Some owners might be casinos. Under that model, the New England franchise would be based at Foxwoods or the Mohegan Sun, while Las Vegas and Atlantic City would also have franchises. Alternatively, there could be a Budweiser franchise owned by Anheuser-Busch in St. Louis or a Coca-Cola franchise in Atlanta. Each team would build relationships with colleges in its geographic area.

The teams would have sixteen fighters apiece; two fighters in each of eight weight divisions. The fighters would be professional athletes fighting four-round bouts under professional rules. There would be two matches per team per month; one at home and the other on the road. Each fighter would be trained by his team.

Now comes the key—*To compete, a fighter would have to be a full-time college student who meets the equivalent of NCAA academic standards.* Both the league commissioner's office and individual teams would be responsible for monitoring the fighters' academic progress. If a fighter became academically ineligible, he wouldn't be allowed to fight for his team.

Each fighter would have a contract with his team. Team members would be paid full tuition, room and board, and a cash stipend. Each team would be limited to the same amount of money for each fighter. While under contract, a fighter could fight only for his team.

Each contract would be for a period of four years or until the student graduated, whichever came first. If a team member dropped out of college, he would be ineligible to participate in the league. If he chose to continue fighting professionally, the league would have promotional rights to his fights for the duration of his contract at fair market value.

Looking at things realistically, this would not be world-class competition. The fighters would be young, and the definition of a "league" is a .500 fighter. But think about it for a minute. Teams could recruit in the amateurs—"We have an offer for you." Keith Mullings, who later became the IBF junior-middleweight champion, dropped out of school and entered the United States Army because he couldn't afford to go to college. Michael Bentt, who knocked out Tommy Morrison for the WBO heavyweight crown, eschewed college as a young man because he felt that his life options were limited. College boxing would attract its share of young quality fighters. And when they graduated, they'd have four years of professional experience in addition to a college diploma.

So let's look at the plusses.

College boxing would be good for the image of boxing.

College boxing would be a good investment for the franchise owners. Fans (and particularly the fighters' classmates) would come to the bouts because there would be eight competitive professional matches on each card. Opportunities for corporate sponsorships and a modest television contract would also be there.

But most important of all, college boxing would be good for the fighters. It would give them additional options in life and help improve their lives. And if one of the young men in college boxing (like a Keith Mullings or a Michael Bentt) is good enough to win a world title some day, more power to him.

I like the standing eight count. Although as far as that issue is concerned,
I seem to be in the minority.

The Standing Eight Count

The standing eight count is part of a natural progression in boxing. In the old days, a fighter who knocked an opponent down could hover over him and attack as soon as his opponent's knee left the canvas. That *modus operandi* was much in evidence on July 4, 1919, when Jack Dempsey challenged Jess Willard for the heavyweight crown. Dempsey downed Willard seven times in the first round, smashing him to the canvas again and again while the champion was rising but not yet ready to defend himself. Willard suffered a horrible beating—a broken jaw, broken nose, cracked ribs, and six broken teeth—before succumbing at the end of three rounds.

Notions of good sportsmanship dictated a rules change. Thus, over the next few years, it became common to require a fighter who had knocked his opponent down to go to a neutral corner and stay there until instructed by the referee to return to battle. Dempsey himself was the most famous casualty of the new rule. On September 22, 1927, the Manassa Mauler sought to regain his title from Gene Tunney, who had defeated him on a ten-round decision one year earlier. In round seven of their rematch, Dempsey drove the Fighting Marine to the canvas with a perfectly-timed left hook. But instead of going to a neutral corner, he lingered over his fallen foe, causing a five-second delay in the count. In all likelihood, Tunney would have been able to rise after nine seconds. But the fact that he had fourteen seconds to do it made life easier for him once he was on his feet again. Tunney won going away; Dempsey retired after the bout; and "The Long Count" became a fabled part of sports lore.

Fastforward to March 13, 1961, when Floyd Patterson and Ingemar Johansson did battle for the third time and the mandatory eight count was introduced to championship boxing. The rationale behind the rule was simple. When a fighter is knocked down, he shouldn't be penalized for getting to his feet quickly. Thus, after each knockdown, the referee should, at a minimum, count to eight before the action resumes. The new rule was considered particularly advantageous to Patterson, who was in the habit of going down often (seven times in his losing 1959 effort against Johansson). And in fact, Floyd availed himself of the mandatory eight count twice before stopping Ingo in round six of their 1961 bout.

The mandatory eight count is now universally accepted in boxing. But its most recent variation—the standing eight count—is not.

A standing eight count is administered at the discretion of the referee when a fighter is taking punishment and not properly defending himself but won't go down. For purposes of scoring, it's treated as a knockdown.

Some people love the standing eight count. Others hate it. The *Unified WBC-WBA-IBF Rules for Title Bouts* specifically states, "There will be no standing eight count." Across the country, state commissions are split on the issue. Opponents of the rule sometimes claim that standing eight counts are unnecessary because a fighter in trouble can always "take a knee" if he needs a breather. But that begs the issue. Taking a knee is not an acceptable alternative. That's like giving a fighter the opportunity to call "time out" in the middle of a round, and you can't do that in boxing. Plus, a true champion won't take a knee.

So is the standing eight count good or bad for boxing?

Arthur Mercante argues against it with the declaration, "I'm opposed to the standing eight count, because the point at which a referee is supposed to use it is precisely the point at which a fight should be stopped. The fighter's knees are weak; his eyes are rolling. So why prolong his agony? As a referee, it's my prerogative to use it or not use it, and I never will. The standing eight count is nothing but a cop out, because the referee is in doubt."

Jerry Izenberg of the *Newark Star Ledger* echoes Mercante's reservations and says, "By definition, a standing eight count saves the fighter from being knocked out, and that means it's a double-edged sword. A fighter can be an inch away from getting knocked out; then he's brought back; and then he can go an inch away from getting knocked out again. That's not good for the fighter."

And Marc Ratner (executive director of the Nevada State Athletic

Commission) proclaims, "Nevada does not have it, and I'm against it. A good referee knows when to stop a fight. The standing eight count is a crutch for a weak referee."

Also, it should be noted that, often, there's an alternative to the standing eight count. If the ropes keep a fighter from falling, technically that should be ruled a knockdown. And in many situations where a standing eight count is invoked, the fighter against whom the count is called is pinned against the ropes.

Still, the standing eight count has its share of proponents. "I like it," says trainer-commentator Teddy Atlas. "Lots of guys have come back from being badly hurt in a fight to win. If a guy gets knocked down, the referee gives him ten seconds to get up and then he gets a few more seconds to compose himself before his opponent attacks again. A standing eight count gives a fighter the same chance to recover that he has if he goes down. Denying a fighter a standing eight count and stopping the fight penalizes the fighter for staying on his feet."

Angelo Dundee concurs with Atlas, adding, "A standing eight count gives the referee a chance to evaluate a fighter and study his condition much more carefully than he'd be able to in the heat of battle."

Also, boxing fans hate to see fights that are stopped inconclusively. The standing eight count benefits the public by eliminating some of this doubt and giving them longer bouts. And it's worth remembering that, even after a standing eight count, the referee can always stop a fight.

Personally, I like the standing eight count. And for me, one bout that brings it into perspective is a fight where the referee couldn't invoke it, allowed the action to continue, and was correct in his assessment.

In the twelfth round of his bout against Oscar De La Hoya, Ike Quartey was pinned against the ropes, hurt, taking considerable punishment. Had the standing eight count been in effect, referee Mitch Halpern might well have used it. But without that option at his disposal, Halpern let the battle go on. Quartey survived, and the contest went to the judges' scorecards.

De La Hoya versus Quartey can be used to argue both ways. But to me, it supports the validity of the standing eight count. If Halpern had stopped the bout, it would have been a defensible call. Yet Ike Quartey and the boxing public would have been deprived of a satisfactory ending to a wonderful fight. Meanwhile, the absence of a standing eight count added to the danger at hand. This was a major title fight, virtually even in the final round. Mitch Halpern, understandably, wanted to give Quartey every opportunity to continue, so he let the bout go on where a less important fight might have been stopped. Still, that put Quartey at greater risk of serious harm than would have been the case if a standing eight count had been called.

Mitch Halpern did a good job that night. But there should have been one more tool at his disposal.

Some things seem like common sense to me. I still don't understand why boxing doesn't allow for a five-minute break to stem the flow of blood after an accidental head butt.

Should Boxing Have a New Accidental-Head-Butt Rule ?

It happens often. Two fighters are engaged in battle. One of them comes in low; there's a clash of heads; and suddenly, blood is flowing from an accidental head butt. Unfortunately, boxing regulations fail to deal adequately with the situation.

As a general rule, if a fight is stopped because of a cut caused by an accidental head butt and fewer than four rounds have elapsed, the bout is declared a technical draw. After four rounds, officials go to the scorecards for a decision. The WBC has a provision in its rules requiring that a point be deducted from the uninjured fighter regardless of fault. But for purposes of this discussion, that's irrelevant.

The issue here is simple. When a fighter is hit below the belt, he's given up to five minutes to recover. So if a fighter is cut by an accidental head butt, shouldn't his corner be given up to five minutes to stem the flow of blood?

"I'm not sure," says trainer and TV commentator Teddy Atlas. "I'd have to think about it a while. The five-minute rule for low blows makes sense, because after a while the pain from a blow to the groin goes away. But a cut stays with you for the entire fight, and some of those cuts are very bad."

"It's an interesting question," responds Marc Ratner (executive director of the Nevada State Athletic Commission). "And I'm not sure of the answer. A rule like the one you're talking about would have a positive impact in certain fights. Let's take the second bout between Julio Cesar Chavez and Frankie Randall as an example. That fight had an unsatisfactory ending, Chavez was cut by a butt in the eighth round of a fight that was virtually even. The cut was bloody, but not in a particularly dangerous location. Under the rules, Chavez was awarded a technical decision; but things might have been different if his corner had been given five minutes to stop the flow of blood."

The arguments in favor of a new head-butt rule are obvious. Fans like to see a fight run its natural course. It's unfair for the outcome of a bout to be determined by a cut that has been sustained by accident. No fair-minded person wants a champion to lose his title because he's trailing an opponent by a single point after five rounds. And to deny a challenger his chance for glory based on a similar whim of fate is equally unjust. Plus, blood flowing from an accidental head butt often handicaps the injured fighter by obscuring his vision if a bout is allowed to continue.

"Five minutes is an intriguing idea," acknowledges Flip Homansky, who was the presiding ring physician at the second Chavez-Randall fight. "The majority of the time that I stop a fight on cuts, it's not because of bleeding. It's because of the severity and location of the cut, so five minutes wouldn't make a difference. But there's no doubt that there are times when the rule you're talking about would make a difference. Almost any cut will stop bleeding with Avitene and five minutes of pressure. Certainly, it's an idea that warrants further discussion."

So let's have a discussion. All opinions are welcome.

The structure of professional boxing deserves criticism. But there are also some very nice things that can be said about it.

Boxing—The Open Sport

"Boxing," Seth Abraham once declared, "always has a cold. It's never completely healthy."

Actually, forget about the cold. Herpes is more like it. The sweet science has long been known as the red-light district of professional sports. Yet, for all its failings, boxing is also the most democratic and most open of all sports. Let a few comparisons suffice.

Throughout the first half of the twentieth century, baseball and boxing were intertwined in the nation's consciousness as America's only truly national sports. Indeed, one of boxing's most treasured moments—the Dempsey-Tunney "long count" of September 22, 1927—occurred a mere eight days before Babe Ruth's mythic sixtieth home run. Yet if one compares racial progress in the two sports, the contrast is clear. Joe Gans, Jack Johnson, Henry Armstrong, Joe Louis, and Sugar Ray Robinson all held world championships before Jackie Robinson set foot on a major league baseball field. Were the odds stacked against black fighters? Absolutely. But at least they had a chance to prevail.

The second half of the twentieth century has witnessed black dominance on the playing field in many athletic endeavors. It has been twenty-two years since a white player led the National Basketball Association in scoring. Last season [1998–1999], sixteen of the top seventeen scorers in the NBA were black. It has been thirty-seven years since a white player led the National Football League in rushing. Last year, there were twenty one-thousand-yard rushers in the NFL. All of them were black.

Yet for all these statistics, the residual effects of old prejudices remain. Doug Williams is the only black quarterback to have led his team to victory in the Super Bowl. At the start of the 1997 season—a full fifty years after Jackie Robinson's debut—only eight black pitchers had been credited with a victory in World Series play. And perhaps more important, the ownership councils in baseball, football, basketball, and hockey are almost exclusively white, as are the television executives and other behind-the-scenes power brokers.

Contrast that with boxing. Don King, the sport's dominant power broker over the past twenty years, is black. Larry Hazzard and Wilbert McClure are among the state athletic commission chairmen who are black. Bob Lee, Murad Muhammad, and numerous other fistic powers that be are black.

Boxing, more than any other sport, offers open access. One doesn't need eight hundred million dollars to buy a franchise. A college education is unnecessary to manage or promote. All you need is a dollar and a dream. On March 8, 1971, Don King listened to reports of the first Ali-Frazier fight from a prison cell in Marion, Ohio, where he was incarcerated for manslaughter. Four years later, King co-promoted Ali-Frazier III.

My own experience with professional boxing confirms its open nature. In 1983, I finished writing a book about Beethoven. Being a life-long sports fan, I wanted to write next about sports. But which sport? Baseball was my first love. But I couldn't just walk into Yankee Stadium and start talking with Don Mattingly. I was a basketball fan, but there was no way I could go to Madison Square Garden for an in-depth conversation with Larry Bird when the Celtics were in town. Bill Parcells? No way. Wayne Gretzky? Not a chance. But I could walk into any gym in the city and start talking with fighters.

My first day out, I visited the Times Square Gym. Davey Moore and Saoul Mamby (both former world champions) were training there. Each man spoke with me for an hour. The next day, Emile Griffith came by. Soon, I was on a first name basis with Ray Arcel, Gil Clancy, Arthur Mercante, and dozens of others who populated the sweet science. John Condon gave me a press credential so I could sit at ringside at Madison Square Garden. Writers like Michael Katz and Jerry Izenberg shared their knowledge with me. One year later, I had written *The Black Lights*.

Over the years, I've authored two dozen books and hundreds of articles on a wide range of subjects. But the sweet science is never far from my heart. It has taken me around the world with Muhammad Ali and seated me at ringside for some truly great fights. It has introduced me to some of the best people I've ever met and, also, to some of the worst. But whatever happens, I'll always appreciate the fact that the door to the sport was open to me. It's one of the reasons I agree with fight manager Mike Jones, who once said, "You can knock promoters; you can knock trainers, managers, even fighters. But don't knock boxing. It's the purest sport there is; and anyone who's ever been involved will tell you, it's an honor to be associated with boxing."

Some of the best times I've had in boxing have been at small club fights.

Go to a Fight

I assume that you (the reader of this column) are visiting the HBO Boxing website because you like boxing. Therefore, I have a suggestion to make.

Go to a fight.

I'm not talking about toughman contests or a kickboxing tournament or some other form of imitation boxing. I'm talking about real boxing between professional fighters. Television covers the sport well, but there's no substitute for live action. A club fight will do. In fact, a club fight is best.

Club fights are the lifeblood of professional boxing. A handful of fighters come out of the amateur ranks with such a high level of skill and attendant publicity that they can skip club fights and go directly to the bigtime. But for every Roy Jones Jr. or Oscar De La Hoya, there are hundreds of young men who turn pro the blue collar way. These young men have the same dreams as Olympic medalists. And they ply their trade in small venues against other no-name fighters with no titles at stake and no television.

The purpose of club fights from the promoter's point of view is twofold. Number one, there's money to be made from the live gate. And number two, the cards are designed to garner experience and get some publicity for fighters under contract to the promoter. There are times when every bout on a club card is a set-up for the house fighter. On those occasions, there's no point in a true boxing fan being in attendance. But when club fights feature competitive bouts, they're well worth the price of admission.

Why should you go to a club fight?

For starters, there's the atmosphere. A club fight will take you back to boxing the way it used to be in the 1930s and '40s before the advent of television and casino glitz.

Second, at a major fight, the only way to get close to the ring is to be a member of the media or a high roller with a thousand-dollar comp ticket. But at a club fight, spectators are right on top of things. They can feel the action and see the pain etched on a fighter's face. It's a unique experience that can't be fully appreciated without being there.

Third, club fights offer good action. Local fighters against local fighters before a local crowd. The skill level isn't world-class, but you do see some pretty exciting fights.

And last, if you're lucky, you might witness history in the making. Many great fighters began their respective professional careers as club fighters. Think about it. What would it mean to have been in Holyoke, Massachusetts on March 17, 1947, when Rocky Marciano made his pro debut against Lee Epperson or in Scranton, Pennsylvania, on March 21, 1973, when Larry Holmes stepped into the ring for the first time as a professional against Rodell Dupree.

Not all club fights are entertaining. But some promoters are known for putting on consistently good shows. Don Elbaum has promoted, or otherwise been involved with, over a thousand club fight cards over the years. Joe DeGuardia's Star Boxing is becoming a fixture in the New York metropolitan area. Don Chargin in California, Bobby Hitz in Chicago, Red Fourtner and Tom Harmon in Tennessee, Fred Berns in Indiana, and Tuto Zabala in Miami have a reputation for putting on action fights. In fact, in the eyes of boxing maven Johnny Bos, "Club fights are the only pure boxing left. Most everything else is a set up," Bos opines, "because you get to a certain level and no one wants to put his guy in a competitive fight unless there's a million dollars on the table."

So check it out. Good club fights represent the heart and soul of boxing every bit as much as big-name championship bouts.

Naseem Hamed is a talented fighter. But after his United States ring debut against Kevin Kelley in 1997, I drew a distinction between marketing and ring greatness.

Hype and Glory

It's not often that a fighter makes his United States ring debut as the featured bout at Madison Square Garden. But HBO is committed to developing Prince Naseem Hamed into a media sensation in the United States, and romancing the New York media is essential to that process. Thus, the Garden and the fifty-by-twenty-foot billboard in Times Square featuring a sneering Hamed, coupled with giant ads on bus shelters throughout the Big Apple. Also, advertisements on radio and television; national print advertising; an endless stream of luncheons, bus trips, and open workouts; even a forty-foot banner in Los Angeles; all designed to raise Hamed's profile in America from ground zero to the sky at a cost in excess of one million dollars. The week before the fight, Michael Jackson showed up at one of Hamed's training sessions. And on fight night, 150 seats were removed from the Garden's normal seating plan so the Prince could dance down a two-hundred-foot runway amidst flashing strobe lights and confetti before somersaulting over the top rope into the ring. Hamed might be a lousy dancer, but he sure eclipsed Michael Buffer's, "Let's get ready to rumble."

Hardcore boxing fans already know about Hamed. This was a reach for something more, an effort by HBO to create a franchise fighter with crossover appeal. And The Prince understands his role. He's quick-witted and quite savvy when it comes to marketing, which is one reason he's already a sensation in England with fight purses and endorsement income that place him ahead of such stars as Wayne Gretzky and Brett Favre on *Forbes* magazine's list of the world's top-grossing athletes. It's too early to tell what the response to Hamed will be in the United States. After all, it's hard to make a hero out of a five-foot-three-inch featherweight with an arrogant public persona and ears the size of Dumbo's. But HBO is giving him every opportunity to make it big. A simple comparison puts things in perspective. Look at what Showtime has done for Ricardo Lopez as opposed to what HBO is doing for the Prince.

So what lies ahead? Most likely, the success or failure of HBO's marketing campaign will depend on how well Hamed can fight. He has exceptional power in both hands, and the powers that be put him in tough on December 19. But let's not forget that Kevin Kelley was life-and-death against Troy Dorsey and Smoke Gainer. The Prince might be an extraordinary talent, but he still has a lot to prove before he's recognized as great. And before he makes it really big, he'll have to learn to couple his boasts with a wink.

The show outside the ring should get boring pretty quickly. The show inside the ring will be interesting to watch.

Bob Yalen of ESPN told me that he got hundreds of e-mails after this article ran on Houseofboxing.com. I assume that at least some of them agreed with my thoughts.

ESPN2 *Friday Night Fights*

In autumn 1998, boxing fans waited with anticipation as ESPN2 launched *Friday Night Fights.* The network promised a studio show that would lift its telecasts toward the level of other major sports with news updates and the innovative use of classic fight films. And it promised good fights. Now, almost two years later, there are questions regarding the extent to which ESPN2 has kept its promises.

ESPN2 reaches seventy million homes. Bob Yalen is its director of brand management; the "brand" in this case being boxing. Yalen controls the budget for *Friday Night Fights* and has quality control over the fights themselves. Russell Peltz, who reports to Yalen, helps make the matches and serves as on-site coordinator.

Reviews for the studio show have been mixed to date. Instead of Terry Bradshaw and Howie Long, ESPN2 has given us Brian Kenny and Max Kellerman. Kenney serves as an affable traffic cop. And Kellerman? Well, Max is Max.

"I get to pontificate, and I love it," Max says. "Am I aware of the fact that some people criticize me? Sure, and some of the criticism might be valid in terms of my style. But I don't like it when people who dislike my style carry it over to criticizing the content of what I say. To me, that's just player-hating, jealousy, because hardcore boxing fans understand that I know what I'm talking about."

Not everyone agrees.

It's not Max's fault," says Teddy Atlas, who handles ringside analysis in tandem with blow-by-blow commentator Bob Papa. "Max's enthusiasm is healthy for the program, but sometimes the producers let him venture into areas where he doesn't have the expertise to go."

Meanwhile, no matter how you dress it up, ESPN2 needs good fights.

The heart of the show is fisticuffs. And while *Friday Night Fights* might not require a heart transplant, an angioplasty would help. There have been some good matchups recently, but far too many of the fights have been disappointing. Compared with Gillette's legendary *Friday Night Fights* of the 1950s and 1960s, ESPN2 simply doesn't measure up.

Kellerman acknowledges as much when he says, "We need more competitive matchups with significance; but right now, we're talking about an either/or situation. In fact, one reason I like being in the studio is that I don't have to be at ringside commentating if it's a lousy fight. And let's be honest, we've had stretches where the fights have been less than good."

One reason for the disappointing nature of the fights is that ESPN2 pays a relatively modest "rights fee" for each show. The maximum it has paid to date is $145,000 for Dana Rosenblatt versus Vinny Pazienza, and the average runs in the neighborhood of $65,000. That means the network pays TV production costs and gives the promoter $65,000 for the right to televise a given show. The promoter then adds this rights fee to revenue from ticket sales, on-site sponsorships, and other sources of income before paying the fighters and other promotional expenses. $65,000 is not a lot of money to pay for two quality fights. By contrast, HBO averages roughly $200,000 for *KO Nation* and $750,000 for *Boxing After Dark*.

Also, there have been allegations that Top Rank and Dean Chance (a Bob Arum ally) receive more money than other promoters and aren't held to the same standards of quality for fights. "It's no secret," says Kellerman, "that Bob Yalen and Bruce Trampler (Arum's matchmaker) are very close." However, Yalen vigorously dismisses the suggestion of preferential treatment, saying, "Arum is treated the same as everyone else. Nothing at all is different. Whoever comes up with the best fights gets the date."

Nonetheless, critics point to several fight cards—including the May 19, 2000, telecast from the Playboy Mansion, and ask if these bouts constituted "the best fights." The Playboy card—featuring Vasiliy Jirov, Butterbean, and Mia St. John—was promoted by Top Rank and was horribly non-competitive. "That card deserved criticism," opines Kellerman. "I love real boxing, but those bouts were awful. Mia St. John and

Butterbean can't fight. Jirov was in against a non-opponent. That night wasn't about competitive matchups. It was about ratings and having fun at the Playboy Mansion, which is okay, I suppose, if you put it in perspective for viewers, which we tried to do."

Yalen, for his part, acknowledges paying more than the norm for the Playboy card, but defends his choices with the observation, "We were using the Playboy site to bring in sponsors and affiliates, and we put on what we thought the public wanted to see."

However, this is one area where Teddy Atlas is in accord with Max. "We've had some good fights," says Atlas. "But we've had more bad ones, and there's no justification for that. Unemployment is very high among fighters, and there's a limited number of available TV dates. That means ESPN2 can demand that managers and promoters put their fighters, good fighters, in competitive fights on a regular basis. If we demanded more, we'd get more, because there's nowhere else for them to go. But what happens is, you start doing favors and making soft matches for one promoter, and then no one wants to go in tough. You have to develop a philosophy of matchmaking, and then you have to live by it. And I think, if Russell Peltz was given proper authority, he'd do that."

However, Peltz doesn't have that authority. It's no secret that the job he has now isn't the one he thought he was being hired to do.

"My philosophy of matchmaking is to make the best action fights possible," says Peltz. "I'm against putting on big names simply to get a rating if all that happens is the big name whacks out his opponent in a round or two. I'd much rather put on fights like the ones I have in Philadelphia. We sell out every show at the Blue Horizon, because people know they're coming to see good fights and the guy in the blue corner has as much of a chance to win as the guy in the red corner. But that's not always what television wants."

The fear among hardcore fight fans is that Peltz won't be around ESPN2 for long. In the interim, ratings for ESPN2's *Friday Night Fights* have remained fairly constant, averaging around .85, which translates into 540,000 homes per week. The network plans to add thirteen additional dates on Tuesday nights in the summer of 2001. "We're still looking at broadcast teams," says Yalen. "We'll want to do something to differentiate the show from *Friday Night Fights*."

Meanwhile, ESPN2 is the only weekly televised show in boxing, and that makes it important. It represents boxing to the entire country. And too often, what it's telling the public now is that boxing is a mediocre sport. If this were the National Football League, NFL officials would be working with the higher-ups at ESPN to give the public better matchups. But boxing has no controlling authority, and, when boxing dies on ESPN2, the network will simply go on to the next sport.

Still, let's give the last word to Bob Yalen, who says, "I want people to be entertained by *Friday Night Fights*. I want to hear what they like and don't like, and which fighters they realistically want to see. My e-mail address is bob.yalen@espn.com. Tell your readers to send me their thoughts."

You heard him.

The first time I talked at length with Lennox Lewis was on July 4, 2000. This article was the result.

Lennox Lewis: An Appreciation

On June 9, 1899, James J. Jeffries claimed boxing's heavyweight crown by knocking out Bob Fitzsimmons in the eleventh round. Jeffries was American, and Fitzsimmons was British. More than one hundred years passed from that date until an Englishman again held the undisputed heavyweight championship of the world.

Now the heavyweight champion is English-born. And the Brits ignore him. They holler about Naseem Hamed. They fixate on Mike Tyson. They wax nostalgic about Henry Cooper. Hey gang, wake up and smell the roses. Lennox Lewis is boxing royalty.

The standard knock on Lewis is that he's dull. Some perceive him as aloof, moody, and arrogant. Others see him as shy. Either way, Lennox's trainer, Emanuel Steward, acknowledges, "Lennox is kind of reclusive. When he's not with his friends, he likes to sit in his room, watch TV, and be by himself."

But let's take a look at what Lennox Lewis brings to the table.

First, Lewis is a quality fighter. Over the years, he has beaten the likes of Evander Holyfield, Michael Grant, Andrew Golota, Razor Ruddock, Tommy Morrison, Ray Mercer, and Frank Bruno. In 1993, when Lewis was the mandatory challenger, Riddick Bowe relinquished his WBC heavyweight crown rather than face him. In 1996, Mike Tyson did the same. The sole loss on Lewis's record is a second-round knockout at the hands of Oliver McCall in 1994. And although Lewis was in trouble at the time, the stoppage was premature.

As for his personal side, Lennox Lewis one-on-one has a genuine warmth about him. His voice is soft and, at times, lyrical. He has a good sense of humor and considers himself "a citizen of the world." "After all," he notes, "I'm British by birth; my parents are Jamaican; I was brought up in Canada; and I spend a lot of time in the United States. That makes me a true world champion."

Lewis also offers the following:

• "I want to be a special person; someone with a positive gleam about me, so I can do special things and make people happy. Sometimes I fantasize about having special powers—flying like Superman or having ESP—so I can zoom in and save people in distress."

• "I'm a goal setter. When I was growing up, my mum and I didn't have much money and I wanted a waterbed that cost $450. So I went out and put together a dance. My mum worked the kitchen; I sold tickets; and I made five hundred dollars."

• "Watching the news on television makes me sad. It's all about people being raped and killed and suffering and war."

• "My heroes are people who have done positive things. My mother, Nelson Mandela, Bob Marley. Bob Marley gave an entire island an identity and made its people proud."

• [When asked whether he would rather be heavyweight champion of the world, the international chess champion, or a rock star] "That's a good question. Let me hear the choices again. Wow, that's a tough one. I guess, heavyweight champion first; world chess champion second; and a rock star third. But all of them are good."

• "I like nature, and I love animals. I hate hunting. I don't understand why anyone would want to kill an animal for sport. Isn't it enough to enjoy the beauty of them? It was great to go to Africa and not see a single animal in a cage."

• "I met the Queen. She's very petite. She kind of looked up at me and said, 'My, you're a big fellow.'"

• [Regarding his famous dreadlocks] "Now and then, I go for a steam and get my hair tightened. There's one place I go to in New York, another in London, and one in California. But there are very few people I let touch my hair. There might be some Delilahs lurking around, so I have to be careful."

Much of the public's lack of interest in Lewis stems from the fact that he's a private person. "I am what I am," he says in response. "I don't want to be an open book. I'm happy to be the one who's watching and observing. I enjoy partying, but not in limelight places. I don't need cheap publicity like Mike Tyson. The public doesn't know me yet, but that's all right. Eventually, people will get to know me. And I hope, when that happens, I'll be known for my good qualities. But I want it to happen naturally."

In this age of confessional television and Monica Lewinsky telling Barbara Walters about Bill Clinton's sexual proclivities, that's a refreshing attitude. And it underscores the tiresome nature of the public inquiry into Lewis's own sex life, which he has every right to consider private. I mean, let's get real. Mike Tyson stares at Razor Ruddock at a press conference and says, "I'm going to kiss your fat lips and make you my girlfriend"— and people ask whether or not Lennox is gay?

Still, that does bring us back to Tyson, whose presence shadows Lewis's life. It's Tyson, of course, who has threatened to rip Lewis's heart out, eat it for dinner, and then feast on Lewis's children (he has none) for dessert. Tyson today is a train wreck waiting to happen. But he remains the best one-punch knockout artist in boxing, and Lewis-Tyson would be a perilous fight.

"In chess," Lewis observes, "even the simplest moves are dangerous." The same can be said about any move that one makes in the ring with Tyson. In the past, Lennox has had problems with stamina. He has looked his best against tall opponents. And his overhand right takes longer to deliver than Tyson's hook. A lot of people don't want to see Lewis-Tyson happen. Ironically, Tyson might be among them.

Meanwhile . . . Pay attention, England! Who would you rather have your children look up to and model themelves after—Lennox Lewis or Mike Tyson? Who would better represent the world of boxing—Lennox Lewis or Mike Tyson? You don't have to worry about picking up the newspaper and reading about Lennox Lewis and drugs, or Lennox Lewis and some woman who was assaulted in a bar or raped in a hotel room. With Lennox Lewis, there are no ugly histrionics; just decency, dignity, and grace.

Evander Holyfield brings a lot of positives to the table. But it was hard to overlook the negative when he sought to have Lennox Lewis stripped of the WBA title and then claimed that beating John Ruiz would give him a legitimate claim to the heavyweight championship.

Evander Holyfield: A Tarnished Legacy?

For sixteen years, ever since Evander Holyfield burst upon the scene at the 1984 Olympics, the key to his image has been the public's perception of his character. In the ring, Holyfield has been a warrior, giving his all in glorious bouts against Dwight Muhammad Qwai, Riddick Bowe, and Mike Tyson. Outside the ring, he has become more confident and verbal, sharing his thoughts with humor and grace.

There have been problems along the way. As of last year, Holyfield had nine children: three by his first wife, one by his second wife, and five out of wedlock by four different women, including two during his second marriage. But people were willing to overlook this personal failing because of the belief that, when it came to boxing, Holyfield was a warrior who pursued the sport with a sense of absolute integrity. Because of our belief in his character, we forgave him the draw against Lennox Lewis. Evander would never be part of a rigged decision. All he did was fight.

But now, Holyfield's image is in jeopardy. On August 12, he will enter the ring to do battle against John Ruiz for the WBA heavyweight crown. John Ruiz has never beaten a quality opponent. His main claim to fame is that he was knocked out in nineteen seconds by David Tua. He is in the tradition of the last New Englander to fight for the heavyweight title: Tom McNeeley. Meanwhile, Holyfield hasn't won a fight since 1998. However, none of this has kept Evander from proclaiming, "A victory over Ruiz means I would be four-time heavyweight champion of the world."

Right! And a victory over Brian Nielsen made Dickie Ryan heavyweight champion. Let a simple analogy suffice.

Suppose David Stern had announced the matchups for the final round of this year's NBA playoffs as follows: the Chicago Bulls versus the Los Angles Clippers. Strange, you say. The Bulls are a once-proud franchise that lost sixty-five games this season, and the Clippers lost sixty-seven. But that's the way things work in the convoluted world of professional boxing. Thus, Henry Akinwande, who was disqualified for cowardice in his 1997 bout against Lennox Lewis, was the WBA's mandatory challenger for Lewis's unified crown until it was determined that he was medically unfit to fight because of hepatitis. At that point, the WBA simply moved John Ruiz into the number-one slot and elevated Holyfield to number two.

Meanwhile, as the WBA was doing its thing, Lewis contracted to fight Michael Grant. Give Lennox credit. Once he won the title, he sought out the best available opponent. But there was a hitch. In order to get a rematch with Holyfield after their disputed draw, Lewis had been required to sign a contract that read in part, "If Lewis wins the rematch, the parties understand and agree that Lewis's next bout after the rematch shall be against the WBA's mandatory challenger, or its leading available contender, pursuant to the rules and regulations of the WBA. Provided further that, if Lewis chooses not to fight such WBA mandatory challenger or leading available contender, Lewis shall vacate the WBA title."

With the FBI breathing down its neck, the WBA chose to interpret its "rules and regulations" in a manner that allowed Lewis to defend his title against Michael Grant before taking on Ruiz. However, by then, a series of ill-considered moves by Lewis's legal team had landed the matter in the United States District Court for the Southern District of New York before Judge Lewis Kaplan. Kaplan ordered Lewis to relinquish the WBA crown as a precondition to fighting Grant, despite Lewis's offer to fight Ruiz in July.

The most disappointing aspect of the whole mess is the role that Evander Holyfield played in it. Evander attended the court hearing and advocated stripping Lennox Lewis of the WBA title. Moreover, in late April, he issued a two-thousand-word statement which boils down to one simple sentence: "I believe that the rules of the sanctioning bodies should be consistently applied to all fighters."

But the WBA rules are a sham. Its points-based ratings system was tailor-made to set up a title bout between Holyfield and Ruiz. The absurdity of it all is underlined by the fact that, under the system, Ruiz winning the so-called WBA Regional North American heavyweight title is worth more points than a fighter winning and unifying the heavyweight championship of the world. The system wasn't put into effect by the WBA until March of this year (on the eve of the Lennox Lewis versus Don King litigation hearing). And the WBA doesn't even apply its own system to every weight division.

The result? On August 12, the two men Lewis refers to as the "Mother Theresa of Boxing" and "Johnny Louise" will fight for the WBA heavyweight championship.

And so it seems that, for Evander Holyfield, the Ten Commandments are dwindling to seven. We've lost "Thou shalt not commit adultery" and "Thou shalt not covet." Quite possibly, "Thou shalt not steal" will be the next commandment to go. Evander might not have stolen the WBA title, but one can make a pretty good argument that he was an accessory to the theft. And come August 12, he'll be in possession of stolen goods.

In sum, the "Real Deal" is in danger of becoming the "Real Steal." There's right, and there's wrong. And for Evander to say, "A victory over Ruiz means I would be four-time heavyweight champion of the world," is just plain wrong. Whoever wins on August 12 will have as much legitimacy and credibility as Bruce Seldon did when he was WBA heavyweight champ.

It's in the best interests of boxing that the heavyweight championship be unified with its crown resting upon the head of one man. Right now, that man is Lennox "The Real Champ" Lewis. Thus, a word of advice to Evander Holyfield: When you beat John Ruiz on August 12, you should take the WBA belt and present it to Lennox Lewis. If you do that, you'll be remembered in history with boxing immortals like Muhammad Ali, Joe Louis, and Rocky Marciano. But if you keep the belt, you'll be linked forever with Gilberto Mendoza and Jimmy Binns.

It's a test of character.

When Mike Tyson fights, inevitably the story goes beyond the bound-aries of boxing. That was certainly the case before his October 2000 bout against Andrew Golota in Auburn Hills, Michigan.

Tyson, Michigan, and Zoloft

Zoloft will be in the news a lot over the next two months. That's because Mike Tyson is expected to apply for a license to fight in the State of Michigan.

Zoloft is an inhibitor that increases the availability of serotonin in the brain. Serontonin is a neurotransmitter that transmits impulses and regu-lates mood. Zoloft blocks the reuptake of serotonin so more is available in the brain.

How important is Zoloft to Mike Tyson?

During an October 1999 hearing before the Nevada State Athletic Commission prior to Tyson being given a license to fight Orlin Norris, doctors testifying on Tyson's behalf stated that he suffered from "deficits in executive function that make him prone to impulsive behavior." However, the doctors voiced the belief that Tyson's condition could be controlled through psychotherapy and medication.

When Tyson was sentenced on February 5, 1999, for assaulting two motorists following a traffic accident in Maryland, his lawyers told the court that he needed Zoloft as part of his therapy. Tyson, the court was told, had begun taking Zoloft regularly and been taken off the drug only briefly, in January 1999 while preparing for his fight against Frans Botha. However, once in prison, Tyson refused to let a prison psychologist exam-ine him and was denied access to Zoloft. The result was a violent tem-per tantrum during which Iron Mike became enraged and threw a television set, leading to his being placed in a five-by-eight-foot isolation cell as punishment.

Tyson is reported to have been taking Zoloft for about two years. During that period, he has had fights against Frans Botha, Orlin Norris, Julius Francis, and Lou Savarese. It is believed that he has gone off Zoloft prior to each of those bouts, and, in them, he has (1) tried to break Frans Botha's arm off at the elbow; (2) hit Orlin Norris on the break twice; the second time, after the bell; (3) fought foul-free against a human punching bag named Julius Francis; and (4) punched referee John Coyle so he could punch Lou Savarese some more after Coyle had stopped the fight.

And of course, outside the ring without Zoloft, Iron Mike is reliably reported to have punched promoter Frank Warren. The prevailing view is that it wasn't Warren who initiated the fisticuffs.

Plus, Houseofboxing.com has learned that Tyson exploded while his deposition was being taken in a civil lawsuit filed on his behalf against Don King. At that deposition, which was conducted at the law offices of Peter Fleming (King's attorney), Tyson became agitated and demanded to know why King was staring at him. He then threw a sheaf of papers at his former promoter. Another of King's attorney's, Michael Murphy, demanded that Dale Kinsella (who represents Tyson) control his client, at which point Tyson threw a glass of water at Murphy, attacked him, and had to be restrained by security personnel who were in the room.

Also, let's not forget that Iron Mike has been convicted of rape and bit Evander Holyfield twice.

Thus, it seems logical to ask, "If Mike Tyson is licensed to fight in Michigan, will he be on or off Zoloft for the fight?"

"I can't comment on that," says Tyson advisor Shelly Finkel.

"Is there anyone who can?"

"No," Finkel answers.

So let's present the dilemma plain and simple. There's not a lot of medical literature on the issue of whether or not Zoloft affects world-class athletic performance. Certainly, being on the drug does nothing to increase strength or reflexes. If anything, it hampers aggression. But a person taken off Zoloft is likely to suffer from withdrawal symptoms for several weeks. That means, during the initial period without Zoloft, a patient is likely to experience more anxiety and rage than would be the case if he, or she, had never been on the drug to begin with.

In other words, the State of Michigan is about to import a man who, while within its borders, will be denied the medication that keeps him from acting like a psychopath.

The Michigan State Athletic Board of Control has nine members, all of whom have been appointed by Governor John Engler. Its chairman is Dave Sebastian, who said last month that Tyson wouldn't be licensed to fight in Michigan without a hearing. However, in reality, boxing in Michigan is regulated by the Department of Consumer and Industry Services. The Athletic Board of Control is only an advisory body.

Moreover, according to David Mayo of the *Grand Rapids Press,* the Michigan Athletic Board of Control is a "spurious governing group" whose nine members are all political appointees. Michigan law requires that six of the nine board members be "license-holding professional box- ing workers." The rationale for this requirement is that boxing should be run by people who know something about boxing. However, Mayo reports that three of the "professional" board members, including Chairman Sebastian, have fulfilled their requirement by simply acquir- ing a timekeeper's license at the time of their appointment. "Anyone can become a licensed timekeeper," writes Mayo. "You pay thirty-five dollars per year, and you get a license. If you need someone to stare at a stop- watch for three minutes and then ring a bell, you've got the right group."

I happen to be among the small group of boxing commentators who think that Mike Tyson is still one of the best heavyweights in the world. I also think that the people who are supposedly looking out for Tyson's best interests should ask themselves whether Iron Mike would be better off if he avoided high-stress situations like prizefighting without Zoloft.

"I think it's crazy," says Dr. William Hoffmann, a psychiatrist with experience in the athletic arena. "If you go on and off Zoloft, you're mess- ing around with a patient's neurotransmitters. To get the maximum bene- fit from Zoloft, you have go on it and stay on it long-term. To put a patient on Zoloft and take him off Zoloft and put him on and take him off is abusive."

"This is an ongoing issue for boxing, not just because of Mike Tyson but also because of Ike Ibeabuche and a number of other fighters," adds Flip Homansky. Homansky served as chairman of the Medical Advisory Board to the Nevada State Athletic Commission until recently when he was appointed to the commission itself. "My view," Homansky contin- ues, "is that, if someone needs a drug like Zoloft, then they shouldn't be taken off it to get them into the ring or make them better in the ring or make them more aggressive in the ring. That's simply not the right thing to do in terms of the welfare of the individual."

Also, putting aside Mike Tyson's best interests for the moment, the interests of society at large must also be considered.

In opposing Tyson's request for a visa to fight Lou Savarese in Scotland this past June, Roseanna Cunningham told fellow members of Parliament, "With Tyson, the message is that no matter what the crime, the level of violence, the fact that your behavior has included rape, you can go on, live your life, make mega-bucks, be a hero, be surrounded with all the trappings of success, and gain preferential treatment from official-dom. If we do not challenge that image head-on in every way we can, then we collude by default in that image."

The primary reason Mike Tyson will be allowed to fight in Michigan is because millions of dollars are involved. That means the State of Michigan, like too many of our governmental entities these days, has one set of rules for the very rich and another set of rules for the rest of us.

Prior to Mike Tyson versus Andrew Golota, the focus was on who might refereee the fight and how that lucky soul would go about his work.

Pity the Poor Referee

On an autumn night in 1969, a largely unknown comic named Woody Allen walked onstage at Madison Square Garden. New York mayor John Lindsay was running for re-election. Lindsay was widely credited with keeping New York City calm at a time when riots were sweeping America's inner cities. But his first term had been plagued by crippling labor strikes, inept snow removal, and numerous other failures.

Lindsay's campaign consultants had decided on a humble approach. Time and time again, the mayor told prospective voters, "I made some mistakes, but I've learned from them." And then, to emphasize the complexity of the job—second only to the Presidency of the United States—the mayor's *mea culpa* was coupled with the tag line for his campaign: "It's the second toughest job in America."

But would it fly with the electorate? The mayor's campaign was badly in need of funds. A major fundraising rally was scheduled for Madison Square Garden. Looking out at the assembled throng, Woody Allen spoke the words that would make him a household name in New York and were credited with reviving the flagging Lindsay campaign: "Being mayor of the City of New York is the second toughest job in America. The first toughest is performed by Spiro Agnew's wife every night."

Thirty-one years later, being mayor of the City of New York might still be "the second toughest job in America." The first toughest will be performed by some unfortunate soul on the night of October 20. Someone has to referee the fight between Mike Tyson and Andrew Golota.

For those of you who have forgotten, as summarized here last month, in his last five fights, Mike Tyson has (1) bitten Evander Holyfield twice; (2) tried to break Frans Botha's arm off at the elbow; (3) hit Orlin Norris on the break twice; the second time, after the bell; (4) fought foul-free against a human punching bag named Julius Francis; and (5) punched referee John Coyle, so he could punch Lou Savarese some more after Coyle had stopped the fight.

Andrew Golota is best known for having been disqualified twice for low blows in bouts against Riddick Bowe. He has also flagrantly head-butted Danell Nicholson and bitten Sampson Pouha. To put Golota in perspective, referee Wayne Kelly recalls giving the Polish giant instructions in the dressing room at Madison Square Garden before his first bout against Riddick Bowe. "I told him, 'Andrew, I want you to know something. I've seen you fight, and I'm aware of your tactics. I expect a clean fight tonight, and I expect you to obey my commands at all times.' All Golota did was look at me and say, 'I do what I have to do to win.' That's a direct quote; I'll never forget it. And I told him, 'Not in my ring.'"

In other words, in terms of job desirability, refereeing Tyson-Golota would seem to rank right up there with serving as a marriage counselor for Bill and Hillary Clinton, being employed as George Foreman's dietician, and working as an image consultant for Jeffrey Dahmer. This bout gives new meaning to the phrase "protect yourself at all times." However, four of the best referees in boxing, past and present, say that it would be a wonderful assignment. And the similarity in their thinking is remarkable.

Arthur Mercante has refereed 137 world title bouts. He was the third man in the ring for two Tyson fights—a three-round KO of Steve Zouski and Iron Mike's second-round stoppage of Tony Tubbs in Japan. "In the second round," Mercante recalls, "Tyson knocked Tubbs down and took another shot at him just after he went down. If that punch had connected, he could have been disqualified."

"Some referees would be unable to handle Tyson-Golota," Mercante continues. I'd come on very authoritatively with both fighters in their dressing rooms before the fight. I'd say to each of them, 'Based on your past performance, it's clear that this fight could end in a disqualification. You haven't always abided by the rules in the past, and this time I expect you to obey them. I'm going to be very tough on fouls. I won't hesitate to take a point away early or disqualify either fighter.' I'd remind them of that when I gave them their final instructions in the ring, although the final instructions are mostly window dressing. Then, when the fight started, I'd be more demonstrative than might ordinarily be the case. The first time there was a foul, even if it was accidental, I'd call a time out, bring the fighters together, and tell them both that no breach of the rules would be tolerated. But in terms of taking points away from either man, I'd call it the same as any other fight. I'd love to have that fight," Mercante says in closing. "It would be a wonderful challenge."

Joe Cortez has refereed 134 world title fights. He was the third man in the ring for Andrew Golota versus Lennox Lewis, as well as for Tyson-Holmes, Tyson-Tillis, Tyson-Frazier, and three Tyson preliminary contests. "In some of those bouts," Cortez remembers, "my instructions lasted longer than the fight, but they were basically clean fights."

"For a fight like this," Cortez continues, "the referee has to be prepared mentally as well as physically. In the dressing room beforehand, when I gave Tyson and Golota their instructions, I'd tell each man, 'We're starting with a clean slate. I know what's happened in the past, and I'm not going to hold it against you. But I'm a no-nonsense referee. I'm not here to play games. If you commit a foul, you'll be penalized. If you retaliate outside the rules, you'll be penalized. I'm here to enforce the rules. You're here to obey them. Don't try to take advantage of me."

But in a fight that's expected to end in a knockout, would the threat of deducting points make a difference?

"Absolutely," Cortez answers. "Sometimes, the best knockout artist in the world has to go the distance. Look at what happened in Tyson-Tillis. I'd remind both fighters of that in their dressing rooms. I'd tell them, 'Look, guys, one point could be the difference between your next fight being for ten million dollars and tonight being just another loss on your record. And I'd remind them that a disqualification, if that's what happened, could cost them their license. I'd also talk to the cornermen for each fighter. I'd tell them, 'You know your fighter better than I do. I won't tolerate any violation of the rules or any unsportsmanlike conduct, so keep your fighter in line.'"

As for the fight itself, Cortez says, "It's like any other fight. You have to take control at the start. That means, the best time to take a point away is early to set the tone for both men. Once the fighters know you mean business, they'll respect you. But if there's a foul and you don't step in, particularly with these two guys, you're almost guaranteeing that things will get out of hand and there will be a disqualification."

Would Cortez like to referee the fight?

"Absolutely," he answers. "I love challenges."

Former heavyweight contender *Randy Neumann* has refereed twenty-four world title fights and been the third man in the ring for Tyson versus Carl Williams and Michael Grant versus Golota.

"As a referee, you don't want to go into a fight with any biases," says Neumann. "But here, both sides are hyping the fight by saying it could get dirty. And my response to that is, 'No kidding!'"

"In the dressing room before the fight," Neumann continues, "I'd tell each fighter, 'Look, I was a fighter myself. I'm not going to tell you how to fight. You can do it inside; you can do it outside. But you will follow the rules.' Other than that, any instructions I give them would be humorous because, if they don't know the rules by then, they never will."

"As for the fight itself, I suppose I'd be more inclined than usual to take a point away early. Normally, for something like a low blow, you give two warnings and then, the third time, you take away a point. But here, because of their histories, if you don't set the tone early, there could be trouble. But you have to remember there are low blows, and there are low blows. How soon you take a point away depends on intent. So if one of the guys drops his shoulder and brings up a left hook or uppercut to the crown jewels . . . well, you get the picture."

"The main problem I see in terms of controlling the fight is that both guys are capable of flipping out," Newman says in closing. "Both men have a history of insane conduct. You don't deliberately foul a guy at the risk of disqualification when you're winning, but Golota did that against Riddick Bowe twice. And biting off part of someone's ear like Tyson did against Holyfield, if you did that in a bar, you'd be facing a pretty stiff criminal charge. But I have to tell you, I'd love to referee this fight. I was a fighter. Boxing is my love. And to be involved, to make a difference, it's what I love to do."

Mills Lane refereed 102 world title fights before retiring last year. His resume includes serving as third man in the ring for Holyfield-Tyson II, where he disqualified Tyson for biting Holyfield's ear, as well as Tyson's bouts against Trevor Berbick, Bonecrusher Smith, Tony Tucker, Razor Ruddock (their second fight), Peter McNeeley, and Frank Bruno (their second contest).

"It's going to be a tough fight," Lane says of Tyson–Golota. "Mike is rough on the inside. If you let him get away with it, he hits low, uses his elbows, and throws punches after the bell. The first thing I'd do before anything else is, as soon as I was assigned, I'd go to the state commission and say, 'If I have to do something to keep this from getting out of hand, I expect you to back me on it.' The final instructions in the center of the ring don't matter. That's just ceremonial. But in the dressing room before the fight, I'd tell each fighter, 'Look, you're a pro. This is your business, and I expect you to act professionally tonight.' With Tyson, I'd say, 'Mike, I've been in with you seven times, and I know what you do when you get frustrated. It will cost you dearly if you step out of line tonight.' And with Golota, I'd tell him, 'Andrew, I've watched you fight, I know your history, and I know your reputation. I've read all the newspaper talk leading up to this fight and I'm telling you now, I'm not putting up with any violation of the rules by either fighter.'"

"But they key to it all," Lane says, "is what you do in the ring once the fight starts. You can plant a seed in a fighter's mind in the dressing room but, once the fight starts, you have to make good on your word in order for the tree to grow. That means, if there's anything out of line, you come down hard, quick, and early. And in this particular fight, you have to be a little quicker on the trigger in issuing warnings and taking away points than might ordinarily be the case, because otherwise things will get out of hand. The early part of the fight will probably be the most difficult part for the referee. That's when both fighters will be trying to establish their turf. And Tyson is a different fighter in the first six rounds of a fight than he is in the later ones. If Tyson doesn't get you out early, he becomes a much less aggressive fighter."

"The thing that worries me most about this fight," Lane acknowledges, "is what I call 'the nut question.' You've taken all the proper precautions. You've done all the right things. Now what do you do if things still get out of hand? There's a danger here that one or both fighters will give in to their lesser impulses. And if that happens, you'll need a strong competent referee who isn't afraid to disqualify one of the fighters. But anybody who likes refereeing would want this fight. If you like what you do, you want to be challenged. And no doubt about it, this one will be a challenge."

It seems as though every time I write something critical about Mike Tyson, I get a spate of e-mails calling me a racist mother———er. But if one is serious about writing boxing, some things have to be said.

The Intimidation Factor

With all the talk about Mike Tyson's bizarre behavior at his recent [October 2000] press conference in Los Angeles, one moment has been all but lost in the shuffle. Talking about Lennox Lewis, Tyson raged, "He tried to bully me once, and he's kind of big. He makes me kind of nervous without his gloves and shorts on, so if he ever tries to intimidate me again, I'm gonna plant a bullet in the back of his motherfucking skull."

Lennox Lewis bullying Tyson? "If he ever tries to intimidate me again . . ."?

And something in my mind clicked. The same day that Tyson had his meltdown in Los Angeles, I spent some time alone with Lewis while he was in New York to promote his November 11 championship bout against David Tua. Inevitably, our conversation turned to Tyson, and Lennox said he'd had a confrontation with the ex-champ recently in Las Vegas. "He called me a bitch," Lewis said. "I thought about going after him, and then I figured, 'Why bother?' But next time, I might do it."

At that point, we were interrupted by the scheduling demands of an HBO photo shoot. I wasn't sure how seriously to take Lennox's remarks. Now, judging by Tyson's rant, it appears that I should have taken them very seriously. For the moment at least, Lennox Lewis seems to be winning the war of intimidation against Mike Tyson.

Fear is a funny subject among fighters. Cus D'Amato, who did more than anyone else to mold Tyson as a fighter, often waxed eloquent on the subject. "Heroes and cowards feel exactly the same fear," D'Amato said once. "Heroes just react differently to it."

Once upon a time, Tyson was a master intimidator. He's still awfully good at it. But Buster Douglas took a large chunk out of Iron Mike's aura of invincibility, and Evander Holyfield destroyed it. Now Tyson might actually be intimidated by Lennox Lewis rather than the other way around.

None of this is to pre-judge the outcome of Lewis-Tyson, which would be a competitive fight. Also, it's worth noting that, before we get there, Tyson has to beat Andrew Golota; Lewis has to beat David Tua; HBO and Showtime have to work out a deal—and at least one more important question has to be revisited: Should Mike Tyson be allowed to fight?

Tyson's conduct, in and out of the ring, is a matter of public record. But even veteran Tyson-watchers found his comments in Los Angeles to be chilling: "I don't care about living or dying. I'm a dysfunctional motherfucker . . . Bring on Golota; bring on Lewis. They can keep their titles. I don't want to strip them of their titles, I want to strip them of their fucking health . . . I'm in pain, so I want them to be in pain. I want their kids to see pain . . . I don't care about his (Lewis's) children, if he has any. Fuck 'em . . . You don't know me; you can't define me. I'm a convicted rapist, a hell-raiser, a father, a semi-good husband. I raise hell. I know it's going to get me in trouble or killed one day, but that's just who I am. I can't help it . . . Listen, I'm a nigger. No, really, really, listen to me. I'm a street person. I don't even want to be a street person; I don't like typical street people. But your grandchildren will know about me. They'll be like, 'Wow, wasn't that a bizarre individual?'"

Greg Garrison is a former prosecutor who was retained by Marion County, Indiana, authorities to serve as lead counsel in the 1992 prosecution of Mike Tyson for rape. Garrison tried the case and won a "guilty" verdict that led to Tyson being incarcerated for three years.

Garrison has been fairly silent on the subject of Mike Tyson as of late, but that doesn't mean he's without opinions on the subject.

"I don't care if Tyson is allowed to fight again or not," Garrison told Houseofboxing.com last week. "He's made such a complete fool of himself, it doesn't really matter. But the way people are talking about him, it's as though you have some racehorse or gamecock and you're giving it whatever it needs to compete. Zoloft is supposed to be what keeps Tyson from going completely nuts. At least, that's what the doctors who give it to him say. I'm not sure if he's a psycho or if he's just no damn good. But if they're going to take him off Zoloft to get him ready to fight, it seems to me that, if he has to be that nutty to be in the ring, then he shouldn't fight."

When the subject of Zoloft was raised at Tyson's press conference in Los Angeles, Tyson told the assembled media, "I'm on it to keep from killing you all." He then added, "I don't want to be on it. I'm jacked up. My sex life is jacked up. My dick don't work."

Garrison had this to say in response: "The last thing that's going to quit working on Mike Tyson is his dick. So if his dick isn't working anymore, he's in really bad shape."

There are rumors that Garrison has been contacted in recent years with regard to several sexual assaults that Tyson is alleged to have committed after the Desiree Washington incident, and also with regard to another rape that Tyson is alleged to have committed prior to his encounter with Washington. At least one of these cases has reportedly been settled for a substantial amount. "I'm familiar with a couple of those incidents," Garrison acknowledges. "Some I can talk about; some I can't. In fact, it's probably better if I don't talk about any of them."

"I just wish he'd go away," Garrison says about Tyson in closing. "He's not worthy of all the attention. All he is, really, is another ex-con who can't stay on the right side of the law. But I suppose, the way things are, for the time being, we'll keep seeing pictures of Mike Tyson mowing his lawn, Mike Tyson playing with his children, Mike Tyson shooting his neighbors, or whatever else Mike Tyson feels like doing on any given day."

Meanwhile, the self-described "baddest man on the planet"—the fighter who once denigrated opponents with the taunt, "How dare they challenge me with their primitive skills?"—has been reduced to threatening to sneak up behind Lennox Lewis and "plant a bullet in the back of his motherfucking skull."

I have as much respect for Roy Jones Jr. as a fighter as I do for anyone in boxing. But as the year 2000 came to a close, I questioned whether Roy was still entitled to boxing's mythical "pound-for-pound" crown.

Pound-for-Pound 2001

As another year comes to an end, it's time to revisit the issue of "pound-for-pound." That is, who's the best fighter in the world today? For years, Roy Jones Jr. has been deserving of the honor. Now he faces two worthy challengers in Felix Trinidad and "Sugar" Shane Mosley.

Let's start with Jones. The first time I saw him fight in person was on January 10, 1992, at Madison Square Garden. It was Roy's sixteenth pro fight, and he stopped Jorge Vaca with a picture-perfect left hook at 1:45 of round one. He was a superstar in the making, and a slew of victories followed. Impressive wins over Bernard Hopkins and James Toney solidified his credentials. And in January 1996, after watching Jones demolish Merqui Sosa, I wrote, "It's not just that Jones is undefeated, it's the way he wins that's so impressive. With an arsenal that includes blinding speed, lightning reflexes, uncanny timing, and devastating power, Jones does things in the ring that no one has done since Muhammad Ali in his prime."

Nine months later, I elaborated on that theme after Jones demolished Bryant Brannon in two rounds: "Pound-for-pound belongs to Roy Jones," I wrote. "Nobody else can fight like he does, and nobody else is as good. At times, his bouts look like a Sugar Ray Robinson highlight film. And if Jones's performance against Brannon is an indication of what the future holds, the gap between him and the rest of the field is widening. Boxing fans should enjoy Roy Jones Jr. while they can. He's a fighter for the ages."

Throughout the 1990s, Jones dominated the middleweight, super-middleweight, and light-heavyweight divisions in a way that few fighters ever have. And even more telling, you could have gone to a hundred professional boxers; asked them to name the best fighter in the world pound-for-pound; and virtually all of them would have answered "Roy Jones Jr."

Jones is now 43 and 1 with 35 knockouts. The sole loss on his record (a 1997 disqualification suffered against Montell Griffin) was avenged by a first-round knockout four-and-a-half months later. He was the reigning "pound-for-pound" champion as the new millennium began, but things have changed since then.

There are three reasons to consider deposing Roy Jones Jr. from his "pound-for-pound" throne. Number one is the absence of a defining fight since Jones outclassed James Toney in 1994. In fairness to Roy, over the years, he has fought the best in three weight divisions. There are very few fighters who can test him, and he shouldn't be blamed for not fighting heavyweights, men who are forty pounds larger than he is. Nor is Dariusz Michalczewski (who some accuse Jones of ducking) a credible challenger. Michalczewski would pose less of a threat than many of Jones's past foes. But sooner or later, Roy Jones in the 1990s got around to fighting everyone under two hundred pounds who mattered, and he's not doing that anymore. He simply isn't entering the ring against the best available competition as one would hope and expect of a fighter seeking a top spot in boxing history.

Reason number two is the fear of injury. I remember a conversation I had with Roy shortly after his 1996 bout against Eric Lukas. I asked him when the last time was that he'd cried. And he answered, "I cried this morning. I was thinking about Gerald McClellan."

McClellan, of course, is the former middleweight champion whose life has been turned into a living hell by extensive brain damage suffered in a 1995 bout against Nigel Benn. All fighters are aware of the risks inherent in their trade. Jones is particularly open about them. "Most people who talk about boxing have no idea what it's like to be on the receiving end of what goes on in a boxing ring," he once said. And before he fought Eric Harding, Jones acknowledged, "You never know which guy you're in with where something bad could happen to you."

In recent years, this awareness of injury has been reflected in Jones's choice of opponents and, more significantly, in his fighting style. He no longer commits to his punches as frequently and forcefully as when he was young. He's a different kind of fighter now, even if the difference is only incremental.

And that leads to point number three. Roy Jones has slipped a bit as a fighter. He hasn't been blowing out opponents the way he did in the past. He's getting older and, perhaps more important, he hasn't been training like he once did. Also, Jones has been content to go about his business against mandatory challengers like Ricky Frazier and Richard Hall, which isn't the best way to stay on top pound-for-pound unless one believes that a fighter can turn his skills on and off at will.

If Jones returns to the gym, starts working his butt off, and rehones his talents against tougher opponents, he can get back to where he once was. Meanwhile, he might still have his alphabet-soup belts, but he has relinquished his pound-for-pound title. "I'm the only one who can beat me," Roy Jones Jr. once said. He's done just that.

Next on the list is Felix Trinidad, whose credentials are well-known: 39 wins, no losses, and 32 knockouts on a resume that includes decisive victories over Oba Carr, Pernell Whitaker, David Reid, and Fernando Vargas.

Trinidad is pure fighter. "A killer robot," Emanuel Steward calls him. He's better at his new weight of 154 pounds than he was at 147. And he's better pound-for-pound at 154 than he was at 147.

The Reid and Vargas fights showed how good Trinidad is. But the fly in Trinidad's ointment is Oscar De La Hoya. The truth is, no matter how the judges scored it, Oscar beat Felix. Yes, he retreated for the last three rounds. But overall, he outlanded Trinidad 263 to 166.

Suppose you're at a horse race. Horse #1 is winning by ten lengths and falters down the stretch but still finishes a length ahead of Horse #2. Horse #1 is the victor. The same should be true when scoring a fight. Trinidad can't be number one pound-for-pound because he was outclassed by De La Hoya, although it should be added that the Reid and Vargas fights also showed why Oscar ran the last three rounds.

That then brings us to Shane Mosley. "Sugar" Shane's record is 36 and 0 with 33 knockouts. Over the past fifteen months, he has moved from 135 to 147 pounds without missing a beat. And as with Roy Jones, it's not just that Mosley keeps winning. It's the way he wins that makes him so special.

After Mosley's fifth-round knockout of Eduardo Morales at Madison Square Garden in 1998, I wrote, "Great athletes look different from the rest of the field in the way they go about their work, and Mosley has moved into that class. His bouts are now part competition and part performing art. He's a complete fighter; fast, well-schooled, and he punches with power. On those occasions when he suffers a defensive lapse, he takes his punishment well. Outside of Roy Jones, no one active in the sweet science today has more pure physical talent. Shane Mosley has the right to use the name. A new 'Sugar' has been crowned."

Also, Shane Mosley beat Oscar De La Hoya, whereas Felix Trinidad didn't.

So there you have it. Roy Jones Jr., Felix Trinidad, and Shane Mosley. All three men are doing what they have to do to win. Jones is doing it the most easily of the three. But at the moment, Mosley is doing it best.

Pound-for-pound at the start of 2001, it's Mosley, Jones, and Trinidad in that order.

Some Thoughts on Boxing

Fighters get old in a particularly cruel way.

When a fighter loses three fights in a row, either he's being badly managed or he should retire from boxing—or both.

People talk about the pressure that a "big fight" atmosphere puts on a fighter. But the pressure doesn't come from everything that surrounds a big fight. It comes from the fact that top-quality fighters aren't used to fighting an opponent who's as good as they are.

Boxing is a great sport and a lousy business.

In the ring, a fighter can submit to pain or he can resist it.

Some words of wisdom from Angelo Dundee: "Boxing isn't the same anymore. The romance is gone. The true boxing guys are being pushed aside at every level of the sport."

A competitive fight isn't necessarily an entertaining fight. That's why matchmakers are so important.

If John Ruiz is the top-ranked heavyweight challenger in the world, then a heavy bag at Gleason's Gym deserves to be ranked second.

I can't imagine Roy Jones Jr. sitting on his stool the way Gennaro Hernandez and Julio Cesar Chavez did against Oscar De La Hoya. Jones is beatable, but he's the hardest person in boxing to beat since Muhammad Ali in his prime. When Roy Jones Jr. is at his best, bad things happen to the other guy.

Fighters get careless. But the truly great fighters do it less often than the rest and take they advantage of their opponents' mistakes.

Some words of wisdom from Evander Holyfield: "If you hit someone, they're gonna hit you back. My momma taught me that when I was a little boy."

Confidence is important for any athlete, and that's particularly true of fighters.

There will be controversy as long as there's boxing. The only way to end the controversy is to abolish boxing, and I really don't want that to happen.

A heavy underdog has to go into the ring asking himself, "How do I beat this guy?"—not, "How do I keep from getting hurt?"

Some words of wisdom from Sugar Ray Robinson: "You always say, 'I'll quit when I start to slide.' Then, one morning, you wake up and you've done slid. You can't choose your ending in boxing."

In a street fight, the combatants always look for an edge: a gun, a knife, the first punch, whatever. In the ring, the playing field is supposed to be level. But too often, it isn't. Too many people in boxing learn the rules simply so they can break them without getting caught.

The young Mike Tyson was a great fighter. He could hurt you with any punch in a combination. He could hurt you with every punch in a combination. And when he hurt you, it was like a shark smelling blood. The young Tyson was relentless in his assault. His opponents were in danger of being knocked out every second of every round. Sure, if you took him into the seventh or eighth round, he might get a bit tired. But by then, you didn't feel so good either. And by the way—even today, the consequences of making a mistake against Mike Tyson can be devastating.

Cruiserweight means loserweight.

Some words of wisdom from George Foreman: "Look at what happens to the head in boxing. The head is what's getting hit. There aren't any push-ups or sit-ups or roadwork you can do to get the head in shape. Just pure determination not to lose."

There's a law in the State of New York that decrees, "No licensed promoting corporation or matchmaker shall knowingly engage in a course of conduct in which fights are arranged where one boxer has skills or experience significantly in excess of the other boxer so that a mismatch results with the potential of physical harm to the boxer." The New York State Athletic Commission should enforce this law more often. And the same principle should take hold in other states.

There's no way that Arturo Gatti will lose a fight on cuts again. He's all out of blood.

In boxing, as in the rest of life, you can't rush experience.

Some words of wisdom from Billy Costello: "A champion doesn't have to measure himself against the world. All he has to do is measure himself fight by fight against one opponent at a time."

A fighter should only continue his career if he can make enough money by fighting to fundamentally change his life.

Aging fighters are like aging lovers. As their bodies get older and their physical prowess wanes, they try to get by on technique.

Most boxing writers have a story to tell about seeing a fighter killed in the ring. This is mine.

A Dangerous Game

When I started writing about boxing, Mike Jones told me something that always stayed with me: "If you go to the fights often enough, eventually you'll witness a tragedy."

Mike had been in Wilford Scypian's corner on November 23, 1979, when Scypion fought Willie Classen at Madison Square Garden. Classen was knocked out in the tenth round and died several days later. I mentioned to Mike that I'd seen Emile Griffith pummel Benny "Kid" Paret on television in 1962 and Ray Mancini against Duk Koo Kim, again on the small screen, twenty years later

"It's different when you're there in person," Mike told me.

On November 20 of last year, Mike Jones's prophecy came true for me. I witnessed a tragedy. Stephan Johnson suffered injuries in a fight against Paul Vaden that led to his death two weeks later. I've said many times that television cosmetizes a lot of what goes on inside a boxing ring. On November 20, there was no filter. When Johnson collapsed to the canvas, I was sitting with Spider Bynum (a NABF official on site that night) at the edge of the ring apron. We were as close to Johnson as it was possible to be.

Stephan Johnson was a decent man, who had been fighting professionally for twelve years. Given the fact that he was under medical suspension in Canada at the time of his death, there are serious questions as to whether he should have been in the ring against Vaden. But that's an issue for another time. The point to be made here is that, even under the best of circumstances, boxing is a dangerous sport.

Ironically, boxing is also a marvelous showcase for the brain. Skilled fighting requires balance, coordination, speed, reflexes, power, instinct, discipline, memory, and creative thought. These assets enable a professional fighter to deliver blows that smash an opponent's head backward and twist it violently from side to side. The human brain is a jellylike mass suspended inside the skull in cerebrospinal fluid. A hard blow shakes the brain, sending it careening off the inside of the skull. In extreme cases, blood vessels snap and the brain begins to bleed. Since there is no room inside the skull for anything except the brain and cerebrospinal fluid, the pressure of the added blood compresses the brain, causing unconsciousness, coma, and sometimes death. Fighters understand this. They know that getting punched in the head is an integral part of their business and that sometimes bad things happen. "People say a lot of things," Roy Jones Jr. once noted. "But most people have no idea what it's like to be on the receiving end of what goes on in a boxing ring."

Personally, I believe that, when boxing is properly regulated, its risks are acceptable in relation to what is gained. Yes, it's inherent in the sport that some people will take a beating and others worse. To discount this danger is to deny young men like Stephan Johnson the full measure of credit they deserve for the courage they display every time they step into a boxing ring. But it would be a disservice to the memory of Stephan Johnson to use his death as an argument against the continuation of boxing.

There was a time in our nation's history when young men enlisted in the military for glory. Now they do it as a job. Fighters, like soldiers, fight for glory and money. One can argue that war is necessary, whereas boxing is not. But the truth is, many of our nation's wars have been avoidable, with both sides fighting for economic gain or some other nonessential cause. The "good wars" such as the Allied effort in World War II have been few and far between.

However, Stephan Johnson's death does put further into perspective the ugliness of corruption in boxing. Every time a sanctioning body takes a bribe to raise a fighter in its ratings, every time a ring judge renders a biased decision, every time a state athletic commission gives a job to an inept political appointee who doesn't know the first thing about protecting fighters, those powers that be will desecrating the memory of Stephan Johnson, who made the ultimate sacrifice in pursuit of his dream.

Round 5

Curiosities

*One of the challenges in writing is to find a subject that hasn't been cov-
ered a thousand times before and then to write about it in an informative and entertaining way. I think I did that when I conducted "the first
interview ever with the ring canvas at Madison Square Garden."*

Hello, Mr. Ring Canvas

Q: Hello, Mr. Ring Canvas. How are you today?

RC: Very good, thank you.

Q: Let's start with a few basic questions. What are you made of?

RC: What do you think I'm made of?

Q: Canvas?

RC: Duh.

Q: Don't be a wisenheimer.

RC: Okay, I'm sorry. Actually, I'm made of cotton. They weave the
fibers very closely together. That's what gives canvases like
me our texture.

Q: Fine; let's move ahead. Tell me a little more about yourself.

RC: Well, the first thing you should know is that they change me for
almost every fight. The ring at Madison Square Garden is
old. The posts, girders, and stairs have been around since the
mid-1920s, when the third Madison Square Garden is built
at Eighth Avenue and 49th Street. And since then, they've
only changed the red velvet ropes a few times. But because
of different promoters and sponsors, I'm constantly being
replaced.

Q: How big are you?

RC: That's a tricky question. The ring at the Garden is well-
engineered, but it's not a conventional ring. Normally, ring
posts are on the edge of a ring canvas. But at Madison Square
Garden, all four posts are recessed. That means I'm 23-feet-
6-inches squared, but the posts are only 20-feet-3 inches
apart and the area enclosed by the ropes is a relatively small
18-feet-3-inches on each side. Also, because the posts are

recessed, you can't just lay me down like you would with a normal ring canvas. I need circular cut-outs in each corner so I can fit over the posts.

Q: That sounds complicated.

RC: It's not too bad. Everlast has all the specs up in the Bronx, and generally they do a great job. Of course, every now and then, there's a screw up.

Q: Such as?

RC: I don't want to say.

Q: Come on, this is for the HBO Boxing website.

RC: Well, all right. Listen, do you think you could get me George Foreman's autograph?

Q: Tell me about the screw-up.

RC: It wasn't much. On the morning of the Holyfield-Lewis fight, someone discovered that Everlast had put one of the post holes in the wrong place. So the Garden brought some woman with a big sewing machine into the ring to cut me apart and sew me back together again. As I said, it wasn't much. All it did was create total panic and chaos for about four hours.

Q: So Everlast makes you and ships you directly to the Garden?

RC: Negative. Nowadays, because of advertisements, it's usually the promoter who brings me in. What happens is, Everlast cuts me to size and ships me out to be painted. If Budweiser is the lead sponsor, I go to Hogan Paint in St. Louis. If it's a Don King fight sponsored by Corona, they send me somewhere else.

Q: How much do you cost?

RC: That's a personal question.

Q: Don't be coy.

RC: All right. Generally, Everlast charges $2.80 per square foot, although the Garden and major promoters get a wholesale discount.

Q: How big a discount?

RC: About fifty percent, although the Garden pays a little more for me because I'm a special cut.

Q: How much do you weigh?

RC: Seventy-five pounds at birth. But I'm very porous and most promoters put a lot of paint on me, so usually I'm around 150 pounds by the time a fight starts.

Q: What happens to you after a fight?

RC: The Garden treats me nicely. In the old days after a fight, they'd clean me and hang me from the rafters to dry. Then they'd use me again. But now, because so much stuff is painted on me, they just stick me in storage. Every now and then, I get scared that maybe they'll cut me up and sell me to collectors after a big fight. But so far, that hasn't happened.

Q: So basically, you just lie around all day. Sounds like a pretty soft job.

RC: That's what you think. This job is hard. Do you have any idea what it's like to have Michael Grant lumbering around on top of you. I mean, the guy is a sweetheart, but he weighs a ton. And then, there are the indignities. I didn't mind it in the 1970s when they changed me from white to blue to absorb the television lights. But how would you like it if someone painted Don King's logo on you? Or an ad for Midas mufflers? There are times when I look like Dennis Rodman.

Q: Any other complaints?

RC: You bet. The job comes with a lot of pressure. I'm always worrying about screwing up.

Q: How can a ring canvas screw up?

RC: For starters, I'm brand new for every major fight. That means fighters slip on me. The promoters are supposed to put some kind of granules in the paint to make me sticky, but sometimes they forget. Fortunately, the preliminary fighters scuff me up before the main event. But if someone slips on a Budweiser logo because Bob Arum was too cheap to use the right kind of paint, who do you think gets blamed for it.

Q: What's the worst thing that ever happened to you?

RC: Once, after one of his fighters won on a knockout, Lou Duva kissed me. Do you have any idea what it's like to get kissed on the lips by Lou Duva.

Q: So overall, do you like the job?

R.C: Oh, yeah. Most of the time, it's great. I'm part of history. Over the decades, I've seen some wonderful fights. Joe Louis, Sugar Ray Robinson, Rocky Marciano, and Muhammad Ali have all fought on me. And sometimes, after a really big fight, some reporter will write, "Last night, the eyes of the world were focused on a small square of illuminated canvas." That's neat.

Q: So you like boxing.

R.C: I love boxing. Particularly that moment, just after the referee has given the fighters their final instructions and they're in the corner, dancing up and down on me, waiting for the bell to start round one. I love that moment. It gives me chills.

A Simple Solution

As Bill Clinton's impeachment problems dragged on, not a day went by without someone suggesting that the president make "a dramatic gesture" of one sort or another. And it occurred to me that it would be quite "dramatic" if the president punched Kenneth Starr in the stomach.

I suspect that, at this point in Mr. Clinton's life, punching Starr would be immensely satisfying. Whether or not it would be proper is another matter. Michael Katz (the esteemed boxing writer for the *Daily News*) advises me that such a blow would be appropriate "as long as it's above the waist." However, Teddy Atlas (who knows a thing or two about punching people) takes a contrary view.

"There are times when circumstances enable you to feel self-righteous even if you do something that's not accepted by society," Atlas informs me. "But you need purity in your heart to be justified in punching another person. And if the president is being honest with himself, it would be hard for him to feel self-righteous given the fact that it was his own conduct that enabled Starr to attack him."

I'm inclined to agree with Atlas, which leads me to another question. Why don't Bill Clinton and Kenneth Starr meet in a boxing ring?

"Certainly, it's a fight we'd look at," says Lou DiBella of HBO. "It's a classic matchup between a slick boxer and a puncher."

"As a boxing guy, it's a fight I'd love to see," adds matchmaker Johnny Bos.

Thus, I bring you tomorrow's news in the form of the following newspaper report:

Bob Arum announced today that Bill Clinton and Kenneth Starr had agreed to settle their differences in a boxing ring. The two men will do battle in a twelve-round bout scheduled for July 4. It wasn't clear how the warring camps had come to select Top Rank as their promoter. But sources close to the rivals said that both sides were impressed by Arum's much-quoted statement, "Today I'm telling the truth. Yesterday I was lying."

At a press conference held at the Friars Club to announce the bout, Arum expressed delight with the impending confrontation and proclaimed, "This fight will be more politically charged than Joe Louis versus Max Schmeling and Muhammad Ali versus Joe Frazier. Those contests were candidates for the Fight of the Century. This will truly be the Fight of the Millennium."

Starr will be trained by Kevin Rooney, who told reporters, "As long as Ken remembers to move his head like I'm teaching him, he'll do all right." Clinton will be trained by Lou Duva, who declared, "We know Ken Starr can dish it out, but I don't think he can take it. And no matter how hard my guy gets hit, he's impossible to knock out."

Arum said that Clinton will enter the ring to the sound of "There Is Nothing Like a Dame." Starr, in a tribute to the late Sonny Bono, has selected "I Got You, Babe" as his entry music. Both fighters will be tested for drugs before the fight to see if they have inhaled.

The bout will be held in Atlantic City. It was originally slated for Las Vegas, but the White House was concerned that Mills Lane might come out of retirement to referee the fight, and the president has had his fill of prosecutors. Arum sought to ease concerns about the site by telling reporters, "Larry Hazzard has assured me that the judges will be fair." To which George Foreman added, "If Bill Clinton thinks that Henry Hyde and Trent Lott are bad judges, wait till he sees Lawrence Layton and Calvin Claxton."

As for the undercard, Arum announced that he had planned to match Newt Gingrich and Robert Livingston against one another, but that both of them had pulled out. Thus, the featured undercard bout will pit Monica Lewinsky against Linda Tripp. "With Christy Martin's recent loss," the promoter told reporters, "this is the bout in women's boxing that everyone wants to see. We considered using Monica as a round-card girl," Arum added. "But that might have been perceived as exploitative. And besides, her ass is too big."

At the close of the press conference, Arum told reporters that, if Clinton wins, he'd like to match him against Butterbean in November.

A BEAUTIFUL SICKNESS

Boxing is known for famous couples. Thus, in celebration of Valentine's Day 1999, I ruminated on some of the greetings that might have been exchanged over the years in the boxing community.

Fistic Valentines

JOE LOUIS AND MAX SCHMELING

Louis and Schmeling met in the ring twice. Joe felt their relationship was "lovelier the second time around" when he had both feet planted firmly on the ground. Meanwhile, Max was partial to their first encounter, in which the Brown Bomber fell in twelve. One can imagine Schmeling penning the following lines:

Joe, my old friend, people forget
But I still remember the first time we met
I won fair and square on that warm summer night
To your great chagrin and my great delight
Then storm clouds gathered; the ugliness grew;
And in our second fight, the right man won, too

SUGAR RAY ROBINSON AND JAKE LAMOTTA

From the police blotter:

February 14, 1951, Chicago

Witnesses Jimmy Cannon and Dan Parker were at the scene of an event that is fast becoming known as the "St. Valentine's Day Massacre." According to Mr. Cannon, Mr. Robinson (who Mr. LaMotta calls "Sugar") brutally beat Mr. LaMotta before thirty million witnesses for the better part of an hour. Mr. Parker confirms the above, adding that Mr. LaMotta was "beaten to a bloody pulp." This is the sixth time that these two have been involved in a public altercation.

TEDDY ATLAS AND MAX KELLERMAN

From *TV Guide:*

One of television's most popular sitcoms is an update of that old radio classic, *The Bickersons.* Every Friday night, Teddy berates Max for saying something stupid. Then Max kvetches and moans about one thing or another, and this goes on for two-and-a-half hours. What a couple!

DON KING AND BOB ARUM

Bob Arum would love to find someone to play Delilah to Don King's Samson. Then he could break King's power by cutting off the Great One's hair. One can imagine all manner of trickeration as Mia St. John or some other Arum operative pursues King, whispering sweet nothings in Don's ear. Meanwhile, let a simple Valentine's Day message from Arum to King suffice:

Hello Samson
This is handsome
Trust me

SUGAR RAY LEONARD AND ROBERTO DURAN

From page one of *The Inquirer:*

"It's the most amazing thing I've ever seen," said one veteran observer. "Roberto and Ray were dancing. And suddenly, right in the middle of the dance, Roberto said *'No mas'* and walked away, leaving Ray alone in the center of the floor. All sorts of rumors are flying. No one knows what happened. Two words; that's all he said: *'No mas.'* It's so unlike Roberto."

MUHAMMAD ALI AND JOE FRAZIER

Since Joe has a band, he'll sing his Valentine's Day greeting to Ali:

I love you a bushel and a peck
A bushel and a peck, and I'd like to break your neck

I'd like to break your neck, and I'd like to smash your nose
I'd like to smash your nose, and exchange some heavy blows
Me and you

Happy Valentine's Day, everyone.

Sooner or later, most writers try their hand at theater.

The Odd Couple
A Play in One Act

OFF–STAGE NARRATOR: Boxing's Fight of the Millennium wasn't Jack Johnson against Jim Jeffries in 1910. Nor was it Joe Louis versus Max Schmeling in 1938, or any of the Ali–Frazier bouts. As important as these fights might have been, they don't measure up to the war between "The Odd Couple."

SECOND OFF–STAGE VOICE: That's it! Hauser is crazy. He's lost his marbles. How can anyone say that Felix Trinidad versus Oscar De La Hoya was the Fight of the Millennium.

OFF–STAGE NARRATOR: No! Not that Odd Couple. I'm talking about Don King and Bob Arum.

[*The curtain rises to reveal two men in a sparsely furnished hotel room.* **BOB ARUM** *is pacing angrily.* **DON KING** *is sitting on the edge of the bed.*]

ARUM: I can't believe it.

KING: Believe it, Bob.

ARUM: I don't want to.

KING: You got no choice.

ARUM: I was willing to co-promote. And I was willing to put the fight in this God-forsaken country. Money is money. But no way was I willing to wind up sharing a hotel room with you.

KING: I'm no happier about it than you are.

ARUM: This is the worst thing that's ever happened to me. Sixty-seven years old, and I'm sharing my room with a convicted felon.

KING: It's not your room. It's our room.

ARUM: A convicted felon with a hair weave. Why can't you comb that thing to the side like Howard Cosell or Marv Albert?

KING: Viva, Puerto Rico!

[**ARUM** *gags, and* **KING** *begins singing softly to the tune of "Mickey Mouse."*]

KING: Who's the biggest fraud around . . . I know you will agree . . . B-O-B T-H-E S-N-A-K-E

[ARUM *kicks the bed, and* KING *laughs.*]

KING: Ah, yes. I love to sing. And I love this country we're in. Where are we, anyway?

ARUM: How should I know. Some third-world dictatorship that's putting up ten million dollars for a mud-wrestling match between Elizabeth Dole and Hillary Clinton.

[KING *continues singing.*]

KING: Who went to South Africa . . . Before its tribes were free . . . B-O-B T-H-E S-N-A-K-E

ARUM [*shouting*]: A criminal! That's what you are.

KING: And you, Bob, are an evil man. In your wicked sinister diabolical mind, you conjure up all manner of majestic trickeration. When Nelson Mandela was languishing in prison, you made millions of dollars promoting in South Africa.

ARUM: So did you.

KING: At least I had the decency to try to hide it.

ARUM: Viva, Jack Newfield.

KING: Now you're getting into the spirit of things. I love it when we go head to head like this. And I love you, Bob, because I always love the sinner if not the sin.

ARUM: You've got the gall to talk to me about sin?

KING: Absolutely. Because I am a God-fearing man, who believes in the Ten Commandments as handed down to Moses on Mount Sinai and recorded in Chapter Twenty of the Book of Exodus. "Thou shalt not bear false witness against thy neighbor." You, on the other hand, are known for the mantra, "Today, I'm telling the truth; yesterday, I was lying." I never said anything like that.

ARUM: That's because you never tell the truth. You're the original Lyin' King.

KING: And you, sir, are the ultimate promoter of garbage. Muhammad Ali against Antonio Inoki; Evel Knievel and the Snake River Canyon; Mia St. John, Butterbean . . .

ARUM [*interrupting*]: Wait a minute! We're not finished yet with the Bible. "Thou shalt not covet anything that is thy neighbor's."

KING: So?

ARUM: What about Floyd Mayweather Jr.?

KING: And thus it is written in the good book. I must go where the wild goose flies.

ARUM: And Mike Tyson?

KING: Thus it is written in the good book. I must definitely go where the wild goose flies.

ARUM: And there are other Commandments. What about—

[*The telephone rings, and* ARUM *picks it up. The voice of an* OFF-STAGE OPERATOR *is heard.*]

OPERATOR: I have a person-to-person telephone call for Mr. Don King from Oscar De La Hoya.

KING: Viva, Mexico! Viva, Running Coyote! Only in America!

There are very few quality women boxers today. Keisha Snow may, or may not, be one of them.

Ms. Heavyweight Explosion

Once a month for the past six months, Cedric Kushner has been promoting Heavyweight Explosion fight cards at the Hammerstein Center in Manhattan. Some of the bouts have been less than scintillating, but the atmosphere is entertaining and an appealing public persona is in the making. More to the point, New York boxing fans have seen a woman who gets in the ring, does her thing, and after each victory, accepts the cheers of her adoring followers like a triumphant queen.

Keisha Snow is thirty-one years old. She was born and raised in Brooklyn with six brothers and seven sisters who range in age from ten to thirty-three. "My father's got a lot of children and my mother's got a lot of children," she explains, "but we're all family."

Snow graduated from Jamestown Community College with a degree in human services and currently works as a sales representative for Radio Shack at the Starrett City store in Brooklyn. She also trains two hours a day, five days a week, in pursuit of her dream to become a quality professional fighter. She's very sweet with a good sense of humor. "And I'm a real sensitive person," she adds. "I don't like to see people mistreated. I try to be the sunshine in everybody's rainy day. I'm a people person; so when people enjoy being with me, I love it. People come up to me a lot now to talk about boxing, and it makes me feel good."

And, oh yes. Keisha Snow is five-feet-seven-inches tall and weighs 228 pounds.

"My father got me into boxing," Keisha explains. "He was a weight lifter, always at the gym. And I'm a daddy's girl; so what daddy did, I did. Then, in 1996, I started boxing. I love it; it's exciting for me. Every time I get in the ring, I find stuff inside me that I didn't know was there. You walk up those stairs and stand across the ring from your opponent. And you know that, in the end, there can only be one. The first time I got hit good, I asked myself, 'Why am I doing this?' And like I told you, I'm a people person, but in boxing, you also have to hit your opponent. So I just say to myself, 'It's nothing personal; this is business. It could be her, and it could be me.'"

Snow was 4-0 with 2 knockouts as an amateur. Her professional record is 5-0 with 2 KOs on the ledger. Her self-chosen nickname is "Ms. Awesome."

So what does the future hold for Keisha Snow? Her biggest problem at the moment is that she can't get fights. And that, of course, leads to comparisons with some of her more famous fistic siblings

"I get heated when see Laila Ali and Jacqui Frazier," Snow acknowledges. "Here I am, striving. I've been doing this for years. I'll fight anyone they put in front of me. And someone throws Jacqui $25,000 for a fight against no one after she's been training for a couple of weeks. But Jacqui and Laila were blessed. They're doing their thing, so I can't complain. Maybe I should just tell people that I'm Sonny Liston's illegitimate daughter."

How good is Keisha Snow? Jackie Tonawanda, who blazed a trail for women boxers in the 1970s, says, "Right now, she's the best out there." But Michael Katz (an astute observer of ring talent) holds to a contrary view. "She doesn't look like a fighter," Katz said after Keisha's last bout. "All she looks like is a fat lady who throws punches. Lucia Rijker gives her eighty pounds and beats her."

Objectively speaking, that's probably right. Clearly, pound-for-pound, Keisha Snow is far from the best in the world. But she's got a lot of pounds. "Try to beat me," she says. "Let's all get together to see who's best. That's what boxing is supposed to be about. Everyone knows that I'm here."

Meanwhile, Keisha Snow has her dreams: "Sometimes, I dream about what it would be like if there was women's boxing in the Olympics," she says. "With the men, they'd never let professional fighters in. But with the women, who knows? And if I get to the Olympics, I can see myself on the platform with someone putting a gold medal around my neck. I'll never be a household name. I'll never be as famous as Ali or Tyson. But I love boxing, and I'm gonna ride boxing till I can't ride it no more. Whatever else might come my way, I made a promise to myself to be the best that I can be. I want to be the best in the world at what I do."

Hugh McIlvanney (the awesomely talented British boxing scribe) wrote recently that Laila Ali and Jacqui Frazier were "shamelessly plundering" their respective fathers' good names. Having attended Jacqui Frazier's pro debut, I find it hard to disagree with him.

"Sister Smoke" Turns Pro

On Sunday February 6, 2000, in Scranton, Pennsylvania, boxing and professional wrestling moved closer to one another. Actually, professional wrestling didn't move. But boxing did. Jacqueline Frazier-Lyde (better known to the world as Joe Frazier's daughter) made her ring debut at age thirty-eight.

The opponent was nineteen-year-old Teela Reese, who sported a professional record of no wins and one knockout loss with no amateur experience of any kind. Jacqui's husband Peter was worried the night before the fight. "I know she's going to get hit," he acknowledged. "And you can't imagine how I feel about that."

Not to worry. It wasn't a boxing match. It was a mediocre toughwoman contest. Whatever Jacqui had learned in the gym, she forgot in the ring. Her punches lacked snap and her only defense was her offense. Meanwhile, Reese had no idea how to fight. Her offense was non-existent, and her idea of defense was to turn her back whenever Sister Smoke threw a punch. Mercifully for the sweet science, referee Gary Rosatto stopped bout at 1 minute 23 seconds of the first round. The stoppage was premature because no real damage was being done, but no one cared. In truth, the event should have been ruled "no contest." As Steve Dunleavy of the *New York Post* wrote afterward, "It belonged in a comedy routine."

Reese put the matter in perspective when she declared, "Her punches didn't hurt me. They were slaps, really. I've been hit harder in lots of street fights, and my other professional fight was much badder because I got knocked down and my jaw hurt afterward."

Did Reese think her fight against Jacqui had been stopped too soon?

"Yes, but it doesn't bother me, because I didn't want the hole in my tongue to close."

The hole in her tongue?

"I paid fifty dollars for a tongue stud," Reese explained. "And the guy who put it in told me the hole would close if I took it out before March. The commission people made me take it out this afternoon, but they said I could put it back as soon as the fight was over."

What this is all supposed to be leading to, of course, is Ali-Frazier IV. Or as the Frazier camp calls it, "Frazier-Ali IV."

As most boxing fans remember, Muhammad Ali's youngest daughter, Laila, turned pro last October with a thirty-one-second knockout of an overweight waitress named April Fowler. After the bout, Bernard Fernandez of the *Philadelphia Daily News* telephoned Jacqui for a quote, and Jacqui offered, "I could kick Laila's butt." Later, that escalated to, "I'll whip her. Then I'll pick her up, kiss her, take her to dinner; and if she wants a rematch, I'll dust her off and do it again."

After a while, Jacqui versus Laila began to seem inevitable.

What will it prove? In fistic terms, nothing. Still, there's a lot of emotion involved in what's building now.

Laila Ali, it seems, is fighting for glory and perhaps in some convoluted way to win her father's attention and approval. Obviously, she's also motivated by money, but apparently not to the same extent as Jacqui. There's a lot of talk in the Frazier-Lyde camp about "the fifteenth round" (flashing back to Ali-Frazier III in Manila). But whether that sentiment is sincere or merely an effective marketing tool is subject to speculation.

Either way, Jacqui's deal with boxing guru Don Elbaum is paying her a total of $75,000 for her first three professional fights. To put that number in perspective, when Larry Holmes made his professional debut in Scranton in 1973, he took home $63 for the night. After Cassius Clay won a gold medal at the 1960 Olympics, the purses for his first *ten* professional bouts totaled $22,679. Jacqui and Laila have already been offered $250,000 each against a percentage of the gross for a four-round fight, and those dollars will increase as their confrontation looms closer. "When I talk with Jacqui and Peter," says Elbaum, "the discussions always focus on money. That's their ultimate goal in this."

Joe Frazier's sentiments are another matter. According to Peter, when Jacqui first broached the idea of fighting, Joe's response was, "Stay away from it." Yet Smokin' Joe is now being inexorably drawn into Ali-Frazier

IV. More and more, he sees himself in his daughter when she's in the gym hitting the heavy bag. Once again, he's readying for war. And that's sad, because Joe Frazier already carries enough emotional scars from his battles with Ali. The potential hurt to him in this is enormous. And if Jacqui and Laila fight, most likely Laila will win

Jacqui Frazier doesn't know how to box. And one doesn't learn how to box by going to a gym and throwing punches for a few months. It takes years to develop a quality fighter. Laila Ali is seventeen years younger than Jacqui. At this point in her life, her physical abilities are superior to Jacqui's. And working in the gym for over a year, Laila has developed some skills; not a lot, but a lot more than Jacqui.

Looking ahead to Ali-Frazier IV, Jacqui is relying on "the Frazier spirit" to see her through. Muhammad Ali, the theory goes, was a better athlete than Joe Frazier, but Joe made their bouts competitive with his blazing spirit and indomitable will. Jacqui believes that, against Laila, she can do the same. But if boxing were that easy, there'd be a lot of strong-willed thirty-eight-year-olds making their pro debuts. The truth is that Ali-Frazier IV shapes up like Foreman-Frazier combined with Ali versus Japanese wrestler Antonio Inoki.

Meanwhile, it should be noted that, if this is the pinnacle of woman's boxing, then women's boxing is on flat terrain. Ali-Frazier IV will be a continuation of the Margaret MacGregor/Mia St. John circus, nothing more. It ain't what Susan B. Anthony had in mind.

Marilyn Cole Lownes and I collaborated on this text for a photo essay on Gleason's Gym.

Works in Progress

"Street fighters are nothing," Billy Conn once said. "Fighting a tough guy who doesn't know how to box is like fighting a girl."

Once upon a time, there were dozens of gyms in New York City where young fighters learned their trade. Now the number has dwindled to a few Police Athletic League facilities and six professional gyms, the most famous of which is Gleason's.

Gleason's has been in existence since 1937. Over the years, more than one hundred world champions have trained there. In its first incarnation, the gym was located in the South Bronx. In 1974, it moved to Manhattan. Since 1986, it has been situated on the second floor of a shabby industrial building in the shadow of the Brooklyn Bridge.

> • Walking up the stairs to the gym, one can't help but think of the thousands of young men who climbed these same stairs before. Many felt trepidation upon opening the door. All of them carried hopes and dreams.

> • The rough-hewn look of the gym reflects the hard realities of boxing. Exposed pipes run parallel to the ceiling. The walls are painted battleship-gray, matching the pockmarked concrete floor. Cheap mirrors reflect distorted amusement-park images of fighters who shadow-box before them.

> • The sounds of a boxing factory fill the air: gloves thudding into heavy bags; the rhythm of jump-ropes snapping against the floor; the whappity-wap of taped hands impacting on speed bags; the grunting that accompanies the emission of air with each punch thrown. At regular intervals, a buzzer sounds, simulating three-minute rounds and the one-minute rest period in between.

• Muscular young men take on the look of vulnerable children as they seek approval from trainers who are the closest thing to a father that many of them will ever have.

• There are no shortcuts to becoming a quality professional fighter. The intricacies of boxing take years to learn.

• Practice . . . Practice . . . And more practice . . . A fighter gets to a certain level and it's the small things that make him better. Meanwhile, mistakes in the ring have to be corrected. If not, they become bad habits; and bad habits are death for a fighter. They're like running a stop sign. One day, there's a car.

Shortly before Lennox Lewis fought David Tua, I explored the "sweet side" of the heavyweight champion in conversations with Lennox and his mother.

Lennox's Mum

Lennox Lewis's father was never an active presence in his life. The formative influence on the man who is now heavyweight champion of the world was his mother, although Violet Blake is hardly a public figure. "Mum doesn't talk to the media much," Lennox acknowledges. "She's afraid of saying the wrong thing. But there is no wrong thing. She's my mum."

It's a loving relationship. Here's what Lennox Lewis and Violet Blake said recently about one another.

Lennox Lewis: I lived with my mum in England until I was nine. Then we took a trip to Canada, where my mum had friends. And after a while, she sent me back to England to live with my aunt. The separation was hard for me. I spent a lot of time at boarding school. There were two boarding schools, actually. I was always running away from the first one. I liked the second, but the government stopped paying for it and I needed someplace else to go. Mum's situation in Canada had gotten better by then. She'd found a job and saved some money and had a place to stay. So when I was twelve, I went back to Canada to live with my mum. And from then on, it was just her and me.

Violet Blake: When Lennox came to Canada, I met him at the airport and I told him, "I'm not gonna ever leave you no more." He was a good boy. The only problem I ever had with him was, the other children would tease him about his accent and sometimes he got into fights over it. But mostly, Lennox was a quiet child. The way you see him now is the way he always was. Very quiet most of the time. And he thinks a lot.

Lennox Lewis: When I was young, if I said I was going out, my mum would ask, "Where are you going? Who are you going with? Be careful. How are you getting home?" And she'd always wait up until I got home. She'd breed worry into me before I went out, and that always made me more careful. Then I started boxing, and my mum didn't mind. After school every day, first there was basketball and then boxing. I wouldn't get home until eight o'clock at night. But mum knew where I was. She knew I was safe and doing something positive, and I wasn't home bugging her. And mum still doesn't mind my boxing. Every mother worries about her son getting hurt, but my mum knows I can defend myself.

Violet Blake: When Lennox is fighting, I worry about him, and I worry about his opponent too. But I tell myself, "It's in God's hands." I say, "God, you gave me this child, and now I give him back to you to watch over him tonight."

Lennox Lewis: My mum and I pray together in my hotel room before every fight. And when we pray, she prays for me and my opponent, that neither one of us gets hurt. Then she goes to the fight. She gets there early, because she likes to watch all the matches. It gets her ready for mine. And when I'm in the ring, she doesn't look away or cover her face with her hands. She focuses fully on the fight.

Violet Blake: I wouldn't change anything about Lennox. He's happy, which is all I ask for him, and he puts a lot of joy in my heart. I wake up every morning and thank God for Lennox. He's a wonderful son.

Lennox Lewis: It was always very important to me that I not disappoint my mother. I never had a police record. I never got a girl pregnant. Although now, I think my mum wishes I'd get married and get a girl pregnant so she could baby-sit. But you know, you can be married and have a bad life, and my life is good now. What it comes down to is, my mum wants me to be happy, and I want her to be happy. Sometimes mum calls me her baby. When your mum says "my baby," it's different from when your girl says it. When your mum says it, it's a much deeper feeling. It has more meaning. And I guess I'll always be her baby. It seems like, every year on my birthday, mum gives me underwear and socks. And it seems like, every year, I need them. And when mum's birthday is coming, I ask her what she wants. She'll never want for anything, I promise you that. But all she ever asks for is something like a winter coat.

Violet Blake: Lennox cares for me so well. He's so good that way, and it means I have more to give to other people.

Lennox Lewis: My mum is a warm, caring, loving, positive person, who has feelings and trusts them. And my respect for my mum has continued to grow as I've matured and come to understand what she's gone through. People ask me, "What place do you consider home?" And I tell them, "My mother's womb." If they ask where I'm from, I tell them, "I come from Violet."

Author's Note: As soon as Lewis-Tua was complete, I reported Violet Blake's thoughts on Mike Tyson. This is what she had to say about the man who was threatening her son:

I don't really take notice of Mike Tyson. I hear what he's been saying, but I can't judge him. I don't know anything about Mike Tyson except that he needs help. He's somebody's child, and I know he could be a better person than he is. When Lennox fights, I always pray with him before the fight in his hotel room. I pray for Lennox and I pray for his opponent. I pray that neither one of them gets hurt. And if Lennox fights Mike Tyson, I'll pray for both of them. But I have to say, I wish some of the people around Tyson would take care of him and not just use him.

Satire has a long and important tradition in western culture. It's used by people without power to criticize capricious rulers and unjust governing bodies. That was the spirit behind "Rating the Heavyweights," which dealt with the fact that the World Boxing Council rated John Ruiz as the number-one challenger for the heavyweight crown. WBC president Jose Sulaiman was not amused. Responding to this article and several others I'd penned, Senor Sulaiman sent me three letters. Among other things, he wrote, "Tom, I am very sorry for the respect and high esteem that I have always had for you. You do not deserve it."

Rating the Heavyweights

Last month, World Boxing Council president Jose Sulaiman issued a statement with regard to proposed federal and state legislation regarding professional boxing. "The WBC Board of Governors," Sulaiman declared, "has voted unanimously to move forward in support of all the changes that are feasible and productive. We have already offered to the U.S. Senate Committee our absolute respect and support."

However, Sulaiman drew the line at inquiries regarding the manner in which the WBC rates fighters, asserting, "We have the same confidence and faith in our ratings committee, and absolutely reject accusations of any wrongdoing on their part. We believe that the integrity and work of our ratings committee is impeccable. It is a great source of pride to the WBC, and we stand strongly in their corner."

In the wake of Sulaiman's firm reasoned even-handed statement, some malcontents continue to complain about the WBC ratings. If I understand the situation correctly, they can't take a joke and hold some kind of grudge over the situation that developed when the WBC designated Ricky Frazier as the mandatory challenger for Roy Jones's 175-pound title. Also, several spoilsport commentators object to the fact that the WBC ranks John Ruiz as the number-one challenger for Lennox Lewis's heavyweight crown. And on a broader scale, some humorless critics complain about the fact that Jade Scott, Robert Hawkins, Ross Puritty, and Danny Williams enjoy top-ten heavyweight rankings, courtesy of various world-sanctioning organizations.

But let's be fair about this. And I'm talking now directly to Jose Sulaiman. If John Ruiz deserves to be the number-one-ranked challenger in the world, doesn't Peter McNeeley deserve to be ranked second? After all, look at their records against common opponents.

Both Ruiz and McNeeley fought Miguel Rosa and knocked him out in the second round. Ruiz and McNeeley also both fought Phil Prince. Ruiz knocked Prince out in round one. But McNeeley did him one better by knocking Prince out in the first round twice. Nitpicking critics might discount these victories by noting that Prince has a record of 1 win and 9 losses. But Ruiz and McNeeley have also beaten some guys with multiple victories under their belt.

Doug Davis has nine wins, which means he's pretty tough. Ruiz knocked Davis out in six rounds, while McNeeley won a six-round decision over Old Double-D. That gives a slight early edge to Ruiz over McNeeley in terms of comparative matchups. But both men also fought Juan Quintana (a seasoned pugilist with seven victories. And while each man decisioned Quintana, McNeeley had the strength of character to go back for more. And the second time around, McNeeley knocked out Quintana in the second round. John Jackson is another common opponent and a proven winner with four victories to his credit. Ruiz and McNeeley each fought Jackson twice. And while Ruiz won two six-round decisions over Jackson, McNeeley decisioned Jackson once and knocked him out in round five of their rematch.

Taken together, Doug Davis, Juan Quintana, and John Jackson have twenty—count 'em, twenty—victories among them. A few curmudgeons might make a big deal out of the fact that Davis, Quintana, and Jackson also have 134 losses. But, hey, is a cumulative record of 20 wins, 134 losses, and 4 draws really so bad? I mean, these three guys can punch a little. They have nine knockouts in 158 bouts.

But back to common opponents. More of them. Both Ruiz and McNeeley knocked out Jose Rohena in round one. And McNeeley one-upped Ruiz by knocking Rohena out a second time. Rohena, by the way, was also a winner. He had a victory over the aforementioned Phil Prince to go with his eleven losses. In fact, the only common opponent faced by John Ruiz and Peter McNeeley who is without a victory is Lorenzo Poole. Poole, to be honest, has had some trouble breaking into the win column. At last look, his record was 0 wins and 12 losses, with ten of his losses coming in the first round. But Poole did make it into the second round twice, and I'm certain that someday he'll get as far as round three. Incidentally, one of the two times that Lorenzo Poole made it into the second round was against Peter McNeeley, which is why I'm suggesting that the WBC rate John Ruiz number one and Peter McNeeley number two instead of the other way around.

In sum, while most of today's ranked heavyweights have been padding their records against soft touches, Peter McNeeley has fought eleven bouts against the same tough world-class opposition that John Ruiz has fought. And McNeeley has won all eleven of those bouts.

I know there are critics out there—members of the so-called "boxing intelligentsia"—who will point to McNeeley's recent first-round knockout loss to Butterbean as evidence that he's unworthy of the WBC's number-two ranking. But let's be fair about this. Against Butterbean, McNeeley was only seventy days removed from serious drug and alcohol problems. On several occasions during the bout, Butterbean moved his head to avoid punches, which he'd never done before. And McNeeley was fighting before a hostile crowd. Plus, Butterbean came into the ring at 311 pounds, and McNeeley weighed a mere 212. Remember, I'm saying that Peter McNeeley should be the second-ranked heavyweight in the world, not the second-ranked superheavyweight.

Anyway, John Ruiz got stiffed by David Tua in 19 seconds, and it didn't keep him out of the WBC's number-one slot. Henry Akinwande was disqualified for cowardice against Lennox Lewis, and he's the WBA's number-one challenger.

And so, I speak now directly to Jose Sulaiman. Jose, you are a man of integrity. And I know that you care deeply about the sport of boxing. For the good of boxing, I urge you to hold an immediate urgent meeting of the WBC board of governors to implement a number-two ranking for Peter McNeeley. And if Lennox Lewis persists in his plan to fight Evander Holyfield this November, I ask that the WBC strip Lewis of his title and order a championship bout between these two evenly matched worthy contenders—John Ruiz and Peter McNeeley.

The Once-in-a-Lifetime Boxing Fundraising Auction

Dear Boxing Fan,

Boxing has long been regarded as "the red light district of professional sports." But now the pugilistic community has come together and pooled its resources for a once-in-a-lifetime fundraising event. As is often the case with the sweet science, no one is quite sure where the money is going. But rest assured, it will wind up in the coffers of a worthy cause. All of the donors are fine upstanding individuals and organizations who have consented to participate in this one-time auction. The items to be sold are:

(1) *A lock of Don King's hair*—There's a lot more gray than there used to be, and it's thinner now. But let's face it. Compared to Big Don, Dennis Rodman is a rank amateur when it comes to hair. Don assures us that the hair will be free of lice. And if Don says so, you know it's true

(2) *A job with the New York State Athletic Commission*—The nice thing about this auction item is that the commission has lots of positions that require very little work; so for a small investment, you can keep your day job and get two salaries instead of one.

(3) *Election to the International Boxing Hall of Fame at Canastota*—As you all know, it's possible to be elected to the hall with the votes of just three electors. Now we've arranged for induction to be even easier.

(4) *An autographed copy of* The Lou Duva Guide to Nutrition and Good Health—In this informative book, Lou reveals his secrets for good health, along with special tips from Cedric Kushner and Garing Lane.

(5) *A date with Ike Ibeabuche*—Ike is a great guy. And as David Tua and Chris Byrd will tell you, Ike never stops coming.

(6) *A top-ten heavyweight ranking from the WBC*—In the past, top-ten rankings from the major sanctioning bodies have been reserved for fight-

ers like Jerry Ballard, Adilson Rodrigues, Jade Scott, Willi Fischer, Kim Weber, Pele Reid, Fabio Moli, and Jorge Dascola. Now your name can be up among these heavyweight greats.

(7) *Lose weight with Arturo Gatti*—Arturo has a special plan that will enable you to lose up to twenty pounds in two days. You'll gain it all back on day three. But, hey, no weight-loss plan is perfect.

(8) *Media advice from Scott Trent*—As a public information officer for the State of New York, Scott has done a great job of shaping the image of the New York State Athletic Commission. One can only begin to imagine what he can do for you.

(9) *Spend the High Holy Days with Bob Arum*—Bob is known for his piety and high moral standards. Let him be your guide for a fascinating religious and cultural experience.

(10) *A mandatory challenger slot from the WBA*—Why should Rito Ruvalcaba, Mamadou Thiam, Leo Gamez, Jose Bonilla, Joma Gamboa, and their brethren be the only ones who are ranked number one by the WBA? This is a chance for you to get a title shot.

(11) *A decision for the fighter of your choice in New Jersey*—Larry Hazzard has shown time and time again that he's a man who puts himself on the line for causes he believes in.

(12) And a Special Bonus Item: *Do drugs with Michael Dokes*—Michael knows what's available and where to get it. If "Dynamite" is unavailable for this special opportunity due to incarceration or abstinence, it shouldn't be hard to find a champion alternative.

Please come to the auction with lots of cash. Personal checks will not be accepted.

Fistic Musings

Michael Katz made a name for himself long ago as one of America's finest boxing writers. But in 1997, he made a name for Oscar De La Hoya. Katz felt that the "Golden Boy" wasn't fighting quality opponents. Ergo, he rechristened him "Chicken De La Hoya." Unfortunately for Oscar, the name took hold, although some observers later shortened the appellation to "the Chicken." Now De La Hoya is fighting the likes of Ike Quartey and Felix Trinidad, and it seems unfair to list him among boxing's poultry champions. However, a worthy big-name successor is in clear view.

Naseem Hamed is currently making gobs of money fighting the likes of Wilfredo Vazquez and Paul Ingle. But in doing so, he has ducked the most credible challengers in the featherweight division and nixed all talk of looking up or down four pounds to fight Floyd Mayweather or Erik Morales. Also, with the complicity of the WBO, Hamed has ducked Juan Marquez (the number-one-rated mandatory challenger) for two years. Indeed, it now appears as though Hamed will give up his title and challenge for the WBC featherweight crown rather than fight Marquez.

The "Chicken" may be gone, but boxing's poultry division lives on. Henceforth, "the Prince" should be known as "the Duck."

No ring battle of late has been more ferocious than the war now being waged between the rival United States Senate campaigns of New York City mayor Rudolph Giuliani and First Lady Hillary Clinton. Giuliani alleges that Hillary is a carpetbagger who doesn't know the geography of New York. If Hillary were real clever, she'd respond that at least she knows Yankee Stadium belongs in the Bronx; not in midtown Manhattan, where the mayor is trying to build a one-billion-dollar stadium complex. Regardless, residents of the Bronx are understandably angry at the mayor, and he could soothe their feelings with a simple gesture.

Why not put Madison Square Garden in the Bronx?

After all, the Garden has moved three times before, and there's a rich tradition of boxing in the Bronx. Jake LaMotta was known as the "Bronx Bull" long before he raged in Hollywood. Joe Louis defended his title seven times in the Bronx, including his historic first-round knockout of Max Schmeling. Sugar Ray Robinson wilted in the heat against Joey Maxim in the Bronx. Gene Tunney, Ezzard Charles, Rocky Marciano, Floyd Patterson, and Muhammad Ali, each defended his heavyweight championship in the Bronx.

Madison Square Garden in the Bronx. Silly, you say? No sillier than the idea of moving Yankee Stadium to Manhattan.

And while we're at it, here are a few thoughts from some of boxing's finest:

Larry Holmes (explaining his participation in this past June's "Legends" boxing event): "I've got a lot of common sense. I just don't use it."

Billy Costello (explaining his participation in the same "Legends" event): "I'm not fighting because I need to fight. I'm fighting because I need the money."

Donald Turner (on whether he objects to his fighters having sex while in training for a bout): "Sex is fine. It's the chase that kills them."

I collaborated with Marilyn Cole Lownes a second time on a trip to Las Vegas for a "styles" piece on Lennox Lewis versus David Tua.

The Epitome of Style

Last month, the heavyweight championship of the world was contested by an Englishman of Jamaican parentage who grew up in Canada and a Samoan who grew up in New Zealand. That's a far cry from years past when boxing's most coveted prize seemed as American as apple pie. But as Bob Dylan once wrote, "The times, they are a-changin'."

Boxing styles are changing too.

In the old days, heavyweight championship fights were contested at venues like Yankee Stadium and Madison Square Garden. Now, as often as not, they take place at Las Vegas sites like Mandalay Bay—an eleven-acre "tropical rain forest and South Pacific water environment" featuring a huge swimming pool with an air machine capable of producing six-foot waves that roll onto an artificial beach.

In the old days, the audience for fights was virtually all men, and virtually all of them wore suits, ties, and proper hats. Now the crowd is mixed, and fashions run the gamut from men in fur coats to women wearing next to nothing at all.

In the old days, the apparel fighters wore into the ring was fairly simple. Black trucks for one fighter and white for the other, accessorized by black gloves. The robes were terrycloth, although a champion might opt for satin. Then color television came along, and the gloves turned red for better viewing. Muhammad Ali stretched the envelope further with tassels and a beaded robe given to him by Elvis Presley. After that, Hector Camacho wore a leopard-skin loincloth into the ring, and things got out of hand.

It all culminated on November 11, 2000, with Lennox Lewis versus David Tua, a contrast in styles if ever there was one.

The six-foot-five-inch Lewis looks like a graceful Michelangelo sculpture. He's carefully groomed with no tattoos and a clean wholesome look. He's also almost always impeccably dressed, the most stylish champion since Ali. Patrick Drayton estimates that he has designed fifty suits for the champion, which are then cut and stitched by the famed Saville Row tailor, Fallen & Harvey.

By contrast, the five-foot-ten-inch Tua looks like a sumo-wrestler with a punch. He is, shall we say, a more casual dresser than Lewis. Or phrased differently, David Tua makes Lou Duva look like the Duke of Windsor.

And then there was the matter of the fighters' hair.

Once upon a time, Lewis's hanging dreadlocks would have been a source of controversy. By his own reckoning, they haven't been cut in eight years. By contrast, Tua's hair rises upward toward the heavens like the coiffure of a well-known boxing promoter. "I'm not trying to look like Don King," Tua explained recently. "I just thought I'd try something new. People expect that of me. I'm Tuaman."

Thus, it came to pass that, during a week in which the American presidency hung in the balance, the dominant story in Las Vegas was David Tua's hair. The Lewis camp expressed concern that (1) Tua might load his hair with chemicals that would get into Lennox's eyes and impair his vision and (2) a hard gel applied on fight night would turn the challenger's hair into dozens of spikes, any one of which could become the equivalent of a thumb in the eye.

Larry Merchant put his hand in Tua's hair the day before the fight and pronounced it "natural," but Lewis remained unconvinced. "You never know what compounds a man might put in his hair at the last minute," the champion reasoned. Then Marc Ratner (chairman of the Nevada State Athletic Commission) promised a close examination of Tua's hair in the dressing room immediately before the bout, and that calmed things down a bit.

Meanwhile, what did referee Joe Cortez think about the controversy swirling around Tua's hair?

"I wish he'd give me some," the balding referee said.

When the hour of reckoning finally arrived, the crowd was in its sartorial glory. Among the more noticeable feminine fashions on display were sequined zebra-striped trousers, bronze leather suits, and mink coats draped over silk in a manner reminiscent of Rat-Pack–era glamour.

Considerable attention was also paid to a particularly striking beauty showing ample cleavage in a magenta satin dress, matching jacket, and rhinestone sandals with an ankle strap and four-inch heels. None of the women had hair more bouffant than Tua.

Lewis entered the ring as a knight in white satin with red lettering on his trunks. Tua wore black trunks with white trim. As the fight wore on, the challenger's hair was never a factor. But Lewis's jab did make it a bad hair day for Tua.

Years ago, in The Black Lights, I wrote, "If catastrophe hit the world and men could prevail only by living in the jungle, Don King would be a survivor." That came to mind when I spoofed today's most popular made-for-television reality show.

Survivor

Houseofboxing.com has scored an incredible coup. We've learned the results of *Survivor 2,* which was taped last month and will debut on CBS on January 28, 2001, immediately following the Super Bowl.

Unlike the original Survivor competition, there were no teams in *Survivor 2.* The group was confined to a twenty-acre section of the Australian outback. Under the rules, venturing outside this twenty-acre "tribal territory" meant instant disqualification. At the end of each day, the remaining participants met in a tribal council to vote one of their brethren out of the camp. The final survivor received one million dollars. The participants, in alphabetical order, were

Bob Arum
Teddy Atlas
Jimmy Binns
Michael Buffer
Voom Voom DeVore
Lou Duva
Shelly Finkel
Andrew Golota
Roy Jones Jr.
Michael Katz
Max Kellerman
Don King
Cedric Kushner
Mills Lane
Jose Sulaiman
Mike Tyson

Day One: Voom Voom DeVore is the first to go. A large-breasted round-card girl from Las Vegas, she takes one look at the other participants and pleads, "Get me out of here."

Day Two: The competitors spend most of the day building shelters, gathering firewood, and hunting for food. Alliances form among promoters (King, Arum, Kushner); lawyers (Arum, Lane, Binns); and fighters (Jones, Tyson, Golota). Michael Buffer is eliminated from the group when Andrew Golota mistakes him for a department store mannequin and throws him onto the fire.

Day Three: Jimmy Binns suggests to Teddy Atlas that Atlas rid himself of Max Kellerman (his ESPN2 nemesis) by voting to kick Max out of the group. Atlas contemplates the suggestion and acknowledges, "I get on Max sometimes, but he's not a bad guy. There's a lot of really bad people here, so why not throw them out first?" Hours later, Binns (the only member of the tribe wearing a gray pinstripe suit) is removed from the competition.

Day Four: Cedric Kushner is granted immunity for the day when he wins a buffalo-chicken-wing eating contest. Don King urges Jose Sulaiman to strip Cedric of his immunity, and Kushner appeals to the tribe for fair play. Whereupon Mills Lane pulls a gun and announces, "I'm the law in this tribe; the rules are the rules; and I'm gonna enforce 'em. Anybody messes with me, they're gonna regret it." Sulaiman is voted out of the group.

Day Five: Don King invites Bob Arum, Shelly Finkel, Michael Katz, Max Kellerman, and Cedric Kushner to his shelter for a Friday night gathering. When they arrive, King is wearing a yarmulke, a mezuzah, a Star of David, and a "Joe Lieberman for Vice President" button. "I want to talk with you gentlemen about an alliance," King tells them. Later that night, Andrew Golota is voted out of the competition.

Day Six: Lou Duva goes nude and is immediately removed from the tribal camp.

Day Seven: Food is scarce, tempers are short, and Shelly Finkel is voted out of the tribe, with the deciding vote cast by Bob Arum. After the vote, Finkel shouts at Arum, "How could you do this to me? Yesterday, you swore we had an alliance." Arum responds, "Today I'm telling the truth. Yesterday I was lying."

Day Eight: Arum and Mike Tyson get into an altercation when Iron Mike eats a pet snake that Arum captured and was planning to put under Don King's blanket. Arum's remains are removed from the camp.

Day Nine: The day is marked by a torrential downpour and the realization that Tyson has run out of Zoloft. Iron Mike is quickly voted out of the tribe. King breaks the news, telling him, "Mike, I love you like a son. However . . ."

Day Ten: Max Kellerman lectures the group on the best way to train a fighter, at which point Teddy Atlas joins with the others to remove Max from the competition. "I know there's one really bad person who needs a haircut who's still here," says Atlas. "But I can't take Max any longer."

Day Eleven: Michael Katz, who has maintained a low profile from the beginning, is voted out of the tribe. "That's not the person who needs a haircut that I had in mind," says Atlas.

Day Twelve: Cedric Kushner, Mills Lane, Roy Jones Jr., and Atlas are gathering firewood when they hear a loud shriek from a ravine at the edge of the encampment. They rush to the edge, look down, and see Don King's lifeless form two hundred feet below them. "I hate to see a fellow promoter fall two hundred feet to his death," Kushner says with a smile. "This is a terrible tragedy."

Day Thirteen: The Final Four embark upon a new round of challenges. Kushner loses to Roy Jones Jr. in the marathon run. Teddy Atlas and Mills Lane battle to a draw in a "philosophy of morality" debate. The finalists are so focused on the competition that they fail to notice Don King sneaking back into camp. King, it seems, never fell into the ravine. Rather, he wrapped his clothes around a passing kangaroo, threw the unfortunate marsupial to its death, let out a scream, and hid in the high brush to escape detection. King grabs Mills Lane's gun, starts shooting, and the Final Four run for cover with Big Don in close pursuit. The safest haven is a cluster of boulders overlooking the tribal territory. Running for their lives, the four finalists reach sanctuary, whereupon King announces that each of the four is disqualified for venturing outside the twenty-acre survivor playing field.

"The rules are the rules," King tells a worldwide television audience as he accepts his check for one million dollars. "These men didn't follow the rules. Therefore, they were disqualified and, as the only honest morality-loving, rules-following individual left in the competition, I am the survivor."

Don King . . . Sole survivor . . . Did you doubt it for a second?

Given his conduct in and out of the ring, Mike Tyson is fertile soil for satire.

Tyson–Golota: The Whole Story

It's over now, the biggest-grossing fight in boxing history. Finding a site for the bout was more difficult than first imagined. The Nevada State Athletic Commission refused to grant Tyson a license, and there were similar problems with the Michigan Department of Consumer and Industry Services. The British Home Secretary announced that Iron Mike was no longer welcome in England; and the Polish Ministry of Sports said "nyet" to the contest. There was momentary hope when the New York State Athletic Commission agreed to the bout on the condition that the fighters donate five percent of their respective purses to the New York State Republican Party, but then Madison Square Garden declined to bid on the venture. Finally, Tyson–Golota landed in Atlantic City under the sponsorship of Donald Trump. Now Houseofboxing.com revisits the highlights of Mike Tyson versus Andrew Golota.

September 12, 2000: At a kick-off press conference, America Presents announces that it will promote the bout. At the same time, Tyson–Golota is formally titled in accord the results of internet voting. "The balloting was quite close," Dan Goossen tells the assembled media. 'Anything Goes,' 'Disgusting,' 'Protect Yourself at All Times,' 'Gory Glory,' and 'Yuk!' all received considerable support. But the top vote-getter was 'Psycho.'" At the close of the press conference, Tyson throws Donald Trump through a plate glass window.

September 19, 2000: A fight-promotion poster shows a grinning New Jersey Governor Christie Todd Whitman frisking Mike Tyson for weapons and drugs while two New Jersey state troopers look on. Meanwhile, Showtime reports that pay-per-view orders are running ahead of any fight ever at such an early a date.

October 2, 2000: Tyson visits a children's petting zoo in New Jersey and bites the head off a baby duck. "Mike has been under a lot of pressure lately," explains Shelly Finkel. Meanwhile, Larry Hazzard (chairman of the New Jersey Board of Athletic Control) tells reporters, "There's nothing to worry about. Both fighters will be muzzled during the fight."

October 6, 2000: Showtime announces that Howard Stern will team with Steve Albert and Bobby Czyz as a guest commentator for the bout.

October 9, 2000: Tyson stops taking his Zoloft in preparation for the fight. Later in the day, witnesses report that Iron Mike has driven his motorcycle down the middle of the Boardwalk in Atlantic City, run over seventeen tourists, and snatched the purse of an eighty-five-year-old woman who had just won thirty-seven dollars at the slot machines. Shelly Finkel tells reporters, "Mike is upset because he feels that the media focuses on the negative aspects of his life and overlooks the positive." Challenged to name one positive aspect of Tyson's life, Finkel responds, "Mike has done so many positive things, I can't begin to name all of them."

October 13, 2000: Showtime announces that two exotic dancers named Busty Dusty and Wendy Whoppers have been recruited as round-card girls for the fight.

October 16, 2000: At the final pre-fight press conference, Tyson tells Golota, "I'm going to push your nose bone into your brain, punch your testicles into your stomach, rip out your kidneys, cut open your chest, masturbate on your heart, and eat your children. Then my pigeons will peck out your eyeballs." Shortly thereafter, Shelly Finkel explains to reporters, "Mike was upset because last night he was watching television and saw a documentary about a poor baby seal that was clubbed to death for its fur in Alaska."

October 17, 2000: Shaken by Tyson's savagery, Andrew Golota falls into a deep depression and starts taking Zoloft. Meanwhile, Larry Hazzard announces that, in addition to the regular ringside physicians, the State of New Jersey will provide a psychiatrist for each corner.

October 18, 2000: Tyson is photographed with George W. Bush and his mother, Barbara, who are campaigning in New Jersey. Later in the day, Barbara Bush files sexual molestation charges against Tyson, claiming that Iron Mike fondled her breasts and whispered, "I want to suck your pussy." Shelly Finkel tells reporters, "Mike is very upset by these unfounded allegations, which he feels are nothing but an attempt to set him up for a civil lawsuit. If Barbara Bush wants to get rich, she should buy a lottery ticket."

October 19, 2000: Larry Hazzard acknowledges that he's having difficulty finding a referee for the fight, and assures prospective candidates, "There will be no danger to the referee. Security personnel armed with stun-guns will be stationed in each corner in case either fighter gets out of control during the bout."

October 20, 2000: Mike Tyson versus Andrew Gotota lives up to its billing. Neither fighter can bite because of the muzzles, but the bout is replete with, head butts, low blows, punches after the bell, arm twisting, and knees to the groin. Midway through round five, Tyson leaves the ring and charges into the press section to slug Wally Matthews and Michael Katz. After a quick conference with Larry Hazzard, the referee orders that two points be deducted from Iron Mike's score. Hazzard will later explain, "There was no disqualification because Mike got back into the ring within the time allotted under New Jersey rules for a fighter who has been knocked from the ring." At the end of round nine, Tyson is bleeding badly from both eyes, his nose is broken, and he's helpless against the ropes. At this point, Golota tells the referee, "I think I quit now." At the post-fight press conference, Tyson tells the assembled media, "I'm the baddest man on the planet. Tell Lennox Lewis that I'm going to eat his children, beat up his mother, and split his head open like a baby seal."

After Mike Tyson fought Andrew Golota, his camp tried briefly and unsuccessfully to put a more positive spin on Iron Mike's image. Tongue in cheek, I responded.

Gentleman Mike Tyson

Mike Tyson's advisor, Shelly Finkel, has just received a comprehensive report from a public relations agency hired to rehabilitate Iron Mike's image. Houseofboxing.com has acquired a copy of the report (which is highly confidential) and is pleased to share it with our readers:

MEMORANDUM FOR SHELLY FINKEL
FROM PR ASSOCIATES
OCTOBER 23, 2000

As you know, Mike Tyson versus Lennox Lewis is starting to have an inevitable feel to it.

As you are also aware, the folks at Showtime were enormously impressed by the fact that, in six minutes of ring action last Friday night, Mike threw only four elbows and head-butted Andrew Golota only twice. Steve Albert waxed eloquent for a national television audience about how Mike "never did anything in a misconduct way," and added, "I was impressed by his deference to the referee." Bobby Czyz, who was so busy talking about himself that he didn't hear Golota tell Al Certo to "stop the fight" after *round one* was equally impressed, noting, "Mike, to his credit, didn't respond to any of the things that annoyed him." And, Shelly, you put it best when you told Showtime's Jim Gray, "The thing I was most happy about was, every time the ref said 'break,' Mike went out of his way to break clean."

Shelly, we have a wonderful opportunity in the aftermath of the Golota fight to reshape Mike's image for Tyson-Lewis.

The American public has a short memory. The fact that Mike has been convicted of rape, bitten off part of Evander Holyfield's ear, announced to the world that his male organ isn't functioning properly, says he wants to kill people, and last week addressed reporters as "white boy" and "nigger" is old news.

Meanwhile, Lennox Lewis has been outspoken in calling Mike "an imbecile . . . a misfit . . . a disturbed person . . . a madman . . . and a moron."

The American people don't like ugly. Let's blast Lennox for going negative. And then, let's implement the following nine-step program:

(1) Bring Barney to the introductory press conference announcing Tyson-Lewis. He can replace the guy in Mike's entourage who wears camouflage fatigues, shouts at people, and goes by the name of "Crocodile." Mike can lead everyone at the press conference in singing the Barney theme song ("I love you; you love me; we're a happy family."). Then he can remove his cap and show everyone a tattoo of Barney on his head. The beauty of this is, if Mike ever feels silly walking around with a Barney tattoo on his head, he can grow his hair long to cover it up.

(2) It's important that Mike evince a more enlightened and respectful attitude toward women. I want you to leak a story to *USA Today,* saying Mike loves the way Joyce Carol Oates writes and has requested that she serve as a round-card girl for Tyson-Lewis.

(3) To further emphasize Mike's sensitive side, let's arrange for him to have tea with some old people and read poetry to them. I recommend "Ode to a Nightingale" by John Keats. And, Shelly, make sure the tea cups are china, not plastic. Some lace doilies would also be nice.

(4) "Iron Mike" has a forbidding ring to it. Midway through the promotion, let's announce that Mike has decided to change his nickname to "Happy Mike."

(5) See if you can track down one of the old ladies that Mike mugged when he was twelve years old and arrange for a touching photo-op reunion.

(6) While we're on the subject of reunions, lets do our best to effectuate a reconciliation between Mike and Greg Garrison, who prosecuted Mike for raping Desiree Washington. Garrison, you'll recall, is the man who recently opined, "The last thing that's going to quit working on Mike Tyson is his dick; so if his dick isn't working anymore, he's in really bad shape."

(7) Ask Kellogg's if they're willing to market a Mike Tyson cereal, something along the lines of ear-shaped bites promoted by the slogan, "If you can't beat 'em, eat 'em." It will give Mike a jollier image and could make some money for all of us. After all, it worked for George Foreman with cheeseburgers and that "lean mean grilling machine."

(8) Start airing a televised community service message from Mike Tyson to the youth of America. Shelly, you have a background in music, so you understand the power of song. Mike should rap the following lyrics:

> I love white people
> They're so cool
> Boys and girls,
> Stay in school

(9) On fight night, have Mike enter the ring to more soothing music than in the past. Mozart's Symphony #39 in E-flat Major would be a good choice.

Once the bell rings, you'll have done everything possible to help Mike reshape his image. From that point on, he'll be on his own.

Don King has mastered the politics of boxing. And Don King is a resident of Florida. Ergo . . .

How George W. Bush Won Florida

In the early morning hours of Wednesday, November 8, the outcome of the 2000 presidential election was very much in doubt. Everything hinged on the State of Florida. Then George W. Bush received a telephone call from Don King. For the next ten weeks, details of their conversation were shrouded in secrecy. However, as Inauguration Day approaches, Houseofboxing.com has obtained a transcript of their talk and we proudly present it to our readers:

Don King: Hey!!!! How's my main man?

George Bush: Who is this?

Don King: This, Mr. President-Elect-Great-and-Wise-Leader, is your humble and obedient servant, Don King.

George Bush [*with his hand over the mouthpiece*]:   Laura, it's another nut. I told you and the kids to screen my calls.

Don King: Are you there, my compassionate-and-conservative sovereign?

George Bush: Yeah, I'm here. What did you say your name was?

Don King: I, Sir, am your humble and obedient servant, Don King.

George Bush: Don, I'm kinda busy at the moment. Do you think you could call back after I get this election thing sorted out?

Don King: That, my exalted-magnanimous-visionary hero, is why I am calling.

George Bush: I appreciate that, Don. I love the support of the American people. But I've got a problem right now, because more of them supported Al Gore than supported me.

Don King: Which might pose a dilemma in a backward third-world nation, but not in a great country like the United States of America.

You see, like you, I love this country and its people, which is why I want you to lead us.

George Bush: That's very nice

Don King: It's more than nice. It's splendiferous, because I can make it happen just like I make things happen in boxing.

George Bush: Don, politics is different from boxing.

Don King: George, you don't understand. Boxing is politics, and politics is trickeration, and I am a master of trickeration. Do you remember the first fight between Evander Holyfield and Lennox Lewis?

George Bush: Yeah, Evander was barely hanging on at the end.

Don King: That, my bold-and-gallant majesty, is correct. But in boxing, as in politics, with the proper strategy, hanging on is enough. You see, in that fight, we had a very nice woman judge named Eugenia Williams who counted all of the punches Evander landed but didn't count all of the punches Lennox landed. And therefore, when all of the statistical tabulations were complete, Evander was ahead on her scorecard. Now suppose someone in Florida wanted to vote for Al Gore and punched his ballot but that little piece of paper you call a chad didn't get knocked out. Punching a ballot is the same as punching an opponent. If that chad is hanging on, just like Evander hung on, the judges can count the vote or not count the vote as they see fit.

George Bush: Don, I'm starting to like the way you think. Keep talking.

Don King: Certainly, my brave-courageous-respected standard-bearer. Now the key to any championship fight is the judges. The best thing to do in your case would be to get everything before a federal judge named Lawrence McKenna, who holds court in the Southern District of New York. I've had several wonderful experiences with him. The way I see it, Florida is in the south and south sounds like southern, so we might be able to swing it.

George Bush: We could do that. Or if that doesn't work, my daddy appointed some of the judges on the United States Supreme Court. They might help.

Don King: Wonderful.

George Bush: And my brother Jeb is the governor of Florida. He'll get his people out to make sure that whoever counts the ballots doesn't see all the punches, uh, votes.

Don King: You're a fast learner, o' distinguished-scholarly-reformer-who-gets-results.

George Bush: Right. Now one thing, and I hope you'll forgive me for asking: Is there any catch to this?

Don King: Catch?

George Bush: Yeah, like, you know, I appreciate your support, but will you want something in return once this is over.

Don King: George; I'm deeply wounded by the suggestion that I'm offering my services on your behalf for self-gain. I'm speaking with you now because I believe in the same things that you believe in. Al Gore wants to raise the minimum wage to $6.25 an hour. You say $6.25 an hour would be bad for the economy, and I agree with you. We have a comparable problem now in boxing, where some fighters expect to be paid thousands of dollars for an hour's work. A man who punches people or loads boxes onto trucks all day long doesn't deserve more than $5.15 an hour. Al Gore wants to teach evolution in our public schools. You say that evolution is only a theory, and I agree with you. In fact, just the other day, I was praying with Evander Holyfield and telling him how much I believe in creationism. Al Gore is in favor of affirmative action for downtrodden minorities. You say that affirmative action works best when it lets stupid rich white people into Harvard and Yale because their daddies went there. And George, once again, you and I are in accord. Downtrodden minorities don't have to go to college. They can punch people or load boxes onto trucks for minimum wage.

George Bush: Don, you sound like my kind of guy. How would you a job in a Bush administration?

Don King: I appreciate the offer, my noble-glorious chief executive. But the truth is, I'm happy doing what I'm doing now. All I ask is that you appoint a high-quality individual as attorney general of the United States to make certain that the Justice Department doesn't unfairly attack me in the future.

George Bush: Consider it done. And Don, anything else you need, just give me a call. In fact, once Laura and I get settled at the White House, I hope you'll come visit and spend the night with us in the Lincoln Bedroom.

Don King: That, glorious sir, would be an honor. And if I may say, it's the kind of honor that could happen only in America.

Over the years, George Foreman has become one of boxing's best "feel good" stories.

Two Conversations with George Foreman

What's George Foreman really like? I don't pretend to have a definitive answer. But I'd like to share some thoughts regarding two days that I spent with him a dozen years apart.

The first day occurred in December 1988. I'd begun working with Muhammad Ali on a book entitled *Muhammad Ali: His Life and Times,* and was in Las Vegas for the taping of a documentary entitled *Champions Forever.* The producers had brought Ali, Foreman, Joe Frazier, Larry Holmes, and Ken Norton together to reminisce, and it was an opportunity for me to talk with them.

Foreman's "second ring career" had begun by then, and he'd amassed thirteen comeback wins against opposition like Tom Trimm, Guido Trane, and Ladislao Mijangos. The common denominator among his opponents was that they were short, fat, and out-of-shape. George said he was fighting them because they were "the Mike Tyson type." Tyson, of course, was the undisputed heavyweight champion of the world back then. Many considered him more powerful than Godzilla, and he was expected to reign well into the next millennium. Meanwhile, George had shed the surly image of his youth, and seemed to have a more promising future as a preacher than as a fighter.

George and I talked about Ali for several hours that day, and the generosity of his spirit shone through. He talked about falling in love with Ali as an adolescent, the evolution of his own career, and the night Ali knocked him out to regain the heavyweight championship in Zaire. "After the fight, I was bitter," George confessed. "I had all sorts of excuses. The ring ropes were loose. The referee counted too fast. I was drugged.

I should have just said the best man won, but I'd never lost before so I didn't know how to lose. I fought that fight over in my head a thousand times. Then, finally, I realized I'd lost to a great champion, probably the greatest of all time. Muhammad won fair and square, and now I'm proud just to be part of the Ali legend."

But what impressed me even more about George that day was something that happened after the documentary taping was done. I have a friend named Neil Ragin, who was about to celebrate his forty-eighth birthday. Neil was, and still is, a huge boxing fan and a great admirer of George Foreman. He's five-foot-ten and, to his great dismay, had pushed past two hundred pounds. As a birthday present for Neil, George taped a second interview with me. I asked who he wanted to fight next, and George responded as follows.

"Being that I want to fight Mike Tyson for the heavyweight championship of the world, I'd like a tune-up with Neil Ragin. They've got similar styles. All I need is to get Neil in the ring, and I'll show the world that George Foreman can beat the Mike Tyson type."

Did George think he'd have trouble with Neil Ragin's speed?

"No trouble at all, because I'll cut the ring off and work on his body a lot earlier than I did with Muhammad. I went head-hunting with Muhammad. But with Neil Ragin, I'll start off on his body and stick with the body attack."

What about Ragin's power?

"No problem. He'll try to hit me with those Joe Frazier–Mike Tyson type of punches, but I'll stay low, work the body to drain him of his power, use the left jab as much as I can, and eventually get him with an uppercut. You tell Neil Ragin that I'm going to knock him out."

Neil loved it. So did I. Very few sports legends would have taken the time, or had the presence of mind, to perform a kindness like that.

Meanwhile, George's comeback continued. In 1990, he raised some eyebrows with a second-round knockout of Gerry Cooney. But Cooney had won only once in the previous five years, so the victory was discounted. There was a win over Alex Stewart and losses to Evander Holyfield and Tommy Morrison. Then came the night of November 5, 1994. George Foreman versus Michael Moorer—KO 10. And suddenly, at age forty-six, George was a beloved champion. The whole country fell in love with him.

George played his role well. "The question isn't at what age I want to retire," he told one interviewer. "It's at what income." Lucrative bouts against Axel Schulz, Crawford Grimsley, Lou Savarese, and Shannon Briggs followed. But more significantly, George was parlaying his celebrity status and cheeseburger-eating image into a financial bonanza via "George Foreman's lean mean grilling machine." When the company that held rights to the grill was sold, George's take, according to the *Wall Street Journal,* was the staggering sum of $105,000,000.

During those interim years, I saw George on a number of occasions. But we never spoke at length, and he remained something of an enigma to me. In that regard, my experience was similar to those of other people who have spent considerably more time with him than I have.

Larry Merchant, who has teamed with Foreman at HBO for over a decade, admits, "Personally, I can't say I know George well. I sense a toughness to him that's left over from the days when he was young, but there's no need for him to use it anymore and he disguises it well. As a general rule, he's fun to be around. But I can't say that I socialize with George. Nobody I know does."

"George's persona when I've been with him is pretty much the way he is in public," Merchant continues. "As far as his work for HBO is concerned, he's a professional. He does his homework. He shows up for every production meeting and briefing session. He does little kindnesses for people and some pretty big ones too. I've heard people say—and it's true—that George has put a wall around himself through which nobody is allowed. One reason for that might be, he's become such a huge public figure that he has to do it in order to maintain his sanity. And I'm sure there are other reasons as well. But all in all, I think he's a good guy. If he's fooling me, it's an awfully good act."

Jim Lampley (Foreman's other broadcasting partner) fills out the profile a bit more. "George is unique," says Lampley. "I don't know anyone like him. It's not difficult to offend him if you're insensitive to who he is, because his principles are so rigid and powerfully felt. I remember, once after a fight, I brought a couple of beers into the limousine that was taking us back to the hotel. George didn't say a word to me about it but, next fight, he had his own limousine. Drinking and his view of Christianity simply don't mix. But if you respect George and his principles, you'll receive complete loyalty in return."

"Little things are important to George," Lampley continues. "I've never seen him really angry, but he can be easily hurt. He's very self-protective. He knows that, in life and particularly in boxing, people will use you if they can, and he guards himself carefully against that. In some respects, he's tight with money, but there are times when I've seen him be unbelievably generous. And more than anything else, except for his religion, George is adamant about maintaining his privacy. He has a powerful sense of privacy. He'll never give it up."

All of which brings me to November 2000. I was in Las Vegas to cover Lennox Lewis versus David Tua for Houseofboxing.com. On November 10 (the day before the fight), I attended an HBO briefing session with Lewis and Emanuel Steward. When the session was done, I asked George if I could talk with him.

The subject was God. More specifically, why people believe in God and the differing beliefs that people have. I'm in the process of writing a book on the subject. Over the past year, I've done a lot of research, some of it scholarly, some less formal. One of the things I've done is talk at length with people who have a firm belief in God. George agreed to share his thoughts with me.

We live in an age when many believers of all faiths assert that their way is the only road to heaven. George has a contrary view. I won't write at length here about what he said. That's for another forum. But as we approach the first Christmas of the new millennium, I'd like to pass along a few of words of wisdom from George Foreman:

> • Someone who has no faith in God should be embraced, not with doctrine, but with love.

> • A preacher can preach without a tongue and without a Bible by simply doing good works.

> • Good is good, whether or not one believes in Jesus. To be good is to be saved.

• If I treat everybody nice, that's religion.

So that's George Foreman. He's a legendary fighter, a shrewd businessman, and an intensely private person. He's deeply spiritual and, in the words of Jim Lampley, "a Christian in the best sense of the word." He's a good messenger for this holiday season and every other day of the year.

A Christmas Eve Visit from George Foreman

T'was the night before Christmas, and all through the home
Big George was eating at the start of this poem.
A holiday banquet; burgers with cheese
Pizza and chocolate, tacos and peas.
Then it was time to take out the trash
And up on the roof, George heard a loud crash
Followed by moaning and groaning: "Oh, my!
I've broken my leg," he heard Santa Claus cry.
George carried Santa Claus down from the roof.
"Oh, what a blunder! Oh, what a goof!
Oh, what a mess," Santa Claus wailed.
Then Santa's shiny red rosy cheeks paled.
"Can't travel," said Santa. "My leg hurts real bad.
Children all over are gonna be sad.
No presents this Christmas, that's how it will be.
It's the worst thing that ever has happened to me."
"Oh, this is awful; it's tragic," George cried.
"This will bring teardrops to children worldwide
Isn't there anything that I can do
To help in this moment of crisis for you?"
Then George sat with Santa Claus right by the fire
And stared at the flames as they rose ever higher.
He furrowed his brow ever deeper in thought
And clenched his fists like he once did when he fought.
"I've got it," George said. "I know what I'll do.
I'm big and I'm strong and I'm built just like you.
I can handle a sleigh; I'm still kind of cute,
And I can fit into that Santa Claus suit."
So Santa Claus took off his holiday wear
And gave it to George, who took it with care.
Then George put it on; it fit him just right.
Said George, "I'll deliver those presents tonight."

A BEAUTIFUL SICKNESS

"Fantastic!" cried Santa. "But before you deliver
There are rules to be followed if you're the gift giver.
Now and then someone will make a request.
I've got a long list of which presents are best.
As a substitute Santa, please take my advice."
George took the list and read it through twice:
Mike Tyson wants to learn how to behave.
Bob Arum wants to give Mike Katz a shave.
Mike Katz, in turn, wants to give Arum tsouris.
Butterbean wants a defense that's less porous.
Andrew Golota wants true peace and quiet.
The Duvas want to put Lou on a diet.
Lucia wants Christy; MacGregor wants guys.
Julio writes. "Please, not Willy Wise."
Lou DiBella wants to escape from the greed
Of Pretty Boy Floyd and dream David Reid.
Mark Johnson would like to become better known.
Roger Levitt wants someone to float him a loan.
Rich Giachetti wants love and respect.
The Goossens want to see Main Events wrecked.
And here's a request that came in by fax;
Teddy Atlas would like a gun to shoot Max.
Don Elbaum would like to pick up a quick buck.
Frans Botha would like a change in his luck.
Jay Larkin wants a much bigger budget.
If Holyfield fights, he wants Jean to judge it.
Here's one that seems an improbable dream:
Erik Morales wants Prince Naseem.
Roy Jones would like a monster to fight.
The U.S. Attorney wants to indict.
Bill Cayton wants joy for his lovely wife, Doris.
Showtime wants to forget Orlin Norris.
John Ruiz wants to continue to rate.
Cedric would like a real heavyweight.
Oscar wants Felix early next year.
Budweiser wants to sell fight fans more beer.
Arturo Gatti wants skin that is thicker.
Michael Grant wants to have hands that are quicker.
Art Dore has asked for a cute Playboy bunny.
Sulaiman, Lee, and Mendoza want money.
And here's an attempt to bribe Santa's chief elf:
Don King wants all of the toys for himself.

"This list is confusing," George said with a sigh.
"I'll never remember what goes to which guy;
So I'm gonna give out the best gift ever seen
Everyone's getting a grilling machine."
And that night, Big George did just what he said.
With grilling machines piled high on his sled
He went round the world in the spirit of joy
Giving grilling machines to each girl and boy.
It made him feel good, and the part he liked best
Was wherever he went, to the East or the West
To the North or the South, lower or higher
People left cookies and milk by the fire.
George thought the snacks were a wonderful treat
He ate every one, a remarkable feat;
And I heard Big George say when he came home that night,
"My stomach is stuffed, and my pants are too tight."